TRUE WORLD I

HUMANITY'S SAGA

By Stewart A. Swerdlow

ARTICLES

By Janet Diane Mourglia-Swerdlow

Expansions Publishing Company, Inc.
P.O. Box 12 • Saint Joseph • Michigan 49085 • USA

Books by Stewart A. Swerdlow &
Janet Diane Mourglia-Swerdlow:

Blue Blood, True Blood: Conflict & Creation
Decoding Your Life: An Experiential Course in Self-Reintegration
Healer's Handbook: A Journey Into Hyperspace
Healing Archetypes & Symbols
Hyperspace Helper
Hyperspace Plus
Montauk: The Alien Connection
Stewart Says. . .
True Reality of Sexuality
White Owl Legends: An Archetypal Story of Creation

Published by: Expansions Publishing Company, Inc.
P.O. Box 12
Saint Joseph Michigan 49085 USA

269-519-8036
skype: eventsatexpansions
customersupport@expansions.com
www.expansions.com

Editor: Janet Diane Mourglia-Swerdlow
Cover artist: Dino Venturino
Graphic Design: Simone Mani

ISBN: 978-0-9626446-5-8

Dedication

✠

To Clifton Davis,
a dedicated Hyperspace/Oversoul student and loyal friend,
whose tireless efforts and countless hours of transcription
enabled Janet and I to bring this book to fruition.
We know him in many lifelines and are so happy that he journeys
with us in this one!

✠

CONTENTS

Introduction   1

1   Galactic History: The Alien Presence   3

2   Planetary Science   7

3   Evolution of Our Solar System   11

4   Lemuria & Atlantis   15

5   Alien Manipulations   27

6   Nibiru   35

7   Development of Sumer & Egypt   37

8   Ancient Egypt   43

9   Ancient Hebrews   49

10 Ark of the Covenant   51

11 Bible Code   55

12 Ancient Greece   59

13 Ancient Rome   61

14 Khazar Empire   63

15 Jmmanuel   67

16 Magdalene Culture   71

17 Jmmanuel's Descendants   75

18 Saturnalia, Oester & Passover   77

19 Slavs, Gypsies/Romani & Germanic/Teutonic Tribes   79

20	Vikings	83
21	Frisland	91
22	Portugal's Gibraltar Straits Island	95
23	Celtic Empire	97
24	Lost Tribes of Israel	99
25	Inca	103
26	Bolivia Underground Tunnels	107
27	Maya	109
28	Aztecs	111
29	Mongol Empires	115
30	China's Influence	119
31	Moors & Arabs	121
32	Ottoman Empire	123
33	Templars	127
34	Waldensians/Vaudois/Valdenses	131
35	Waldensian Exterminations	137
36	Michigan Connection	143
37	Bosnian Pyramids	157
38	The Papacy	169
39	Spanish Empire	183
40	British Empire	187
41	Antarctica & The 4th Reich	191
42	Tibet, India & Nepal	203
43	Iceland	207
44	Nazi Experiments	209
45	Book of Revelation	215
46	Staged Alien Invasion	221
47	Kuiper Belt	225

48 Your Genetic Lineage 235

49 Extraterrestrials, Aliens & Interdimensional Existences 237

50 Factors That Affect You 239

51 Taking Responsibility 243

ARTICLES BY JANET DIANE MOURGLIA-SWERDLOW

1 Unholy Trinity 253

2 What is the Astral Realm? 261

3 Gone to the Dark Side & Proud of It 269

4 Exploring The Darkness 273

5 The Illuminati's #1 Secret Weapon 283

6 Why the Illuminati Give you a Shelf Life: 20 Reasons 287

7 Transitions: Is Physical Death Necessary? 289

8 Death Program... And How To Stop It! 295

9 Crucifixion Program & More 299

10 My Waldensian Ancestry 307

GLOSSARY OF TERMS **311**

INDEX **315**

LIST OF ILLUSTRATIONS

1.1   Lyra star system   4

1.2   Draco star system   5

2.1   Mercator North Pole Map   9

3.1   Solar System   12

4.1   Lemuria   17

4.2   Atlantis: original location   20

4.3   Atlantis map with Gulf Stream   21

4.4   Milky Way Galaxy   25

5.1   Earth Civilizations flow chart   29

5.2   Galactic Civilizations flow chart   30

5.3   Location of Mount Ararat   32

6.1   Nibiru   36

7.1   Sumer/Egypt   38

8.1   Ancient Egypt   44

8.2   Reptilian/Snake people   46

10.1 Ark of the Covenant   52

11.1 Ultimate Protection archetype 56

11.2 Toroid 57

12.1 Ancient Greece 60

13.1 Ancient Rome 62

14.1 Khazaria 64

16.1 Last Supper (Giampietrino) - detail 71

19.1 Slavs, Gypsies/Romani & Germanic/Teutonic Tribes . . 80

20.1 Viking map 84

21.1 Norse map showing Frisland 92

23.1 Celtic Empire 98

24.1 Lost Tribes of Israel 100

25.1 Incan Empire 103

26.1 Elongated skull 108

27.1 Mayan Empire 110

28.1 Aztec territories 112

29.1 First Mongol Empire - Attila the Hun 117

29.2 Second Mongol Empire - Genghis Khan 117

30.1 China Xia dynasty 119

32.1 Ottoman Empire 124

33.1   Templars crosses 127

33.2   Seal of Templars 128

34.1   Waldensian Territories 132

35.1   Waldensian persecutions 138

35.2   Waldensian persecutions 139

35.3   Waldensian persecutions 140

36.1   Michigan Tablet 145

36.2   Michigan Copper Mines 149

36.3   Copper Island Keewenaw 150

36.4   Oxhyde from Cyprus 151

36.5   Phoenicians copper oxhydes 152

36.6   Monks Mound in Illinois 154

37.1   Bosnian Valley of the Pyramids 158

37.2   Pyramid of the Sun 160

38.1   Sistine Chapel Central Panels 172

38.2   Amminadab 176

38.3   Sistine Chapel: Seal of Solomon/Star of David 177

38.4   Prophet Zacharias 177

38.5   Cumaean Sybil 178

38.6   David and Goliath 179

38.7   Judith and Holofernes 179

38.8   Creation of Sun and Moon 180

38.9   The Drunkenness of Noah 180

38.10 The Last Judgment 181

39.1   Spanish Empire 184

40.1 British Empire 188

41.1 Neuschwabenland uniform logo 192
41.2 Antarctica with research bases 193
41.3 Map of Antarctica with Neuschwabenland 194
41.4 Flying Saucer of the Nazis: Haunebu II 196
41.5 Nazi Moon Base 197

42.1 Tibet 204
42.2 Inner Earth 205

47.1 Kuiper Belt 226

50.1 Factors That Affect You 240

INTRODUCTION

True World History is much different from what is given to the public. Knowledge is power. Knowledge is control. Those who run the World know this.

History is written by the victors. They do not write true history; they write the history the way they want you to see it. Hitler rewrote history, as did the Romans, Greeks, Americans, British, and French, therefore justifying their actions to win public favor.

The Spaniards along with the Catholic Church may have been the worst of all from the destruction they created in most of the world and the history they altered. The world as you know it is not the way it was or the way it should be.

Whenever anything is discovered or found that undermines public history, it is methodically removed from public knowledge or labeled a hoax. For example, an elderly man came to one of my seminars in Houston, Texas. He was a beekeeper from Tennessee. He told me that when he was a little boy in the 1920's he had a history book that his class used in their one-room schoolhouse with stories about how Admiral Byrd went to the North Pole. The book said that he found tropical islands, dinosaurs and all kinds of amazing things there that no one knew existed. One day, "the G-Men" came in black suits, pulled up to the school, removed all those texts and gave them new ones without the story in it.

A few years ago, Janet and I toured Marvel Cave in Branson, Missouri. While there, one of the guides told us the story of how explorers found dinosaurs that looked like they had simply lain down and gone to sleep. Someone called the Smithsonian Institute in Washington

D.C. which subsequently sent a team to remove the dinosaurs. After some time had passed, this same person called the Smithsonian to inquire about the dinosaurs. "What dinosaurs?" was the only response this person received.

I personally spoke to an archaeologist from Bolivia who discovered 9-foot/3 meters tall Cyclops in suspended animation in a cave in the Andes Mountains. The Cyclops were surrounded by what looked like all kinds of computers. However, the country was in political upheaval at the time so the cave was sealed shut to protect it from the incoming regime. Now, the archaeologist tells me, the maps showing the cave's location were lost in the change and they are still looking for the cave.

I can tell you many, many stories like this. I will share some of them with you throughout this book.

Why change history? Because when you are a group of a few hundred thousand people and are up against billions of people, guns, weapons, and armies are really not enough. You would be overwhelmed by the sheer number of people so the most intelligent thing you could do is to mind-control and program people to believe that they are free. The best slave is one who doesn't know he's a slave. Then, instill fear so that the slaves accept the most plausible explanations so that the few can maintain control over the many.

People think that only in modern times with aviation and roadways in the last century or so people migrated across the world, but this is not so! From ancient times people have spread from all over the world.

Be prepared to change your view not only of history, but of your Self. Who you are, where you came from, why you are here... I suggest that you wrap your Self in a mental blanket of maroon for courage and that you mentally flush the pages of this book with pale orange so that at long last you KNOW the truth for your Self.

1. GALACTIC HISTORY: THE ALIEN PRESENCE & YOUR DNA ORIGINS

In the very beginning of our galaxy there were two main types of Beings that existed. One was the Draco, or the Reptilian beings that existed in the Draco star system; the other was the Lyraens. For all intents and purposes, the Lyraens are the origin of all humanity in this galaxy.

If you think of the types of beings that exist in our solar system and galaxy, 70% are humanoid, 25% are Reptilian, and 5% are other types of beings. Even though 5% may seem like a small percentage you have to understand that in our universe there are an estimated 100 billion galaxies. If one-tenth of one-percent of that has intelligent life, that still means that there are millions of beings out there.

The Draco star system is a real star system. The shape of the constellation looks snake-like. If you count the stars there are 16. From a space perspective Draco and Lyra are relatively close by, but in reality they are light years away from each other.

The Reptilians have a strange origin. They are not from this physical universe. They were brought here by what I call the "Clear" or "Transparent People". The Clear/Transparent beings are very much an enigma; no one knows what they really are except that they are extremely high level, secretive, and mysterious.

From a linear perspective, they may have come from the far future, created the Reptilian genetics, and then brought the Reptilians back to test humankind. Why this happened, no one knows. The Clear People do have a very altruistic sense that may even be considered

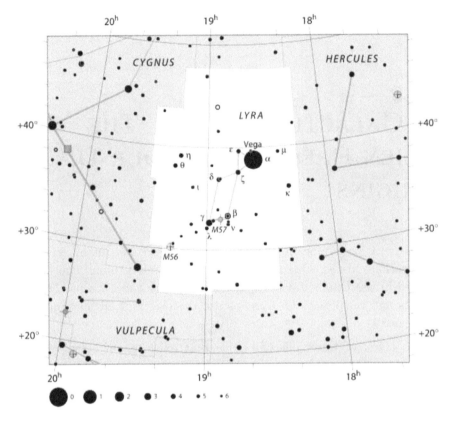

Figure 1.1: Lyra star system

hostile at times because of the intensity of the inherent lessons that they bring.

The androgynous Reptilian form was the initial manifestation of a being in physical reality from the God-Mind. Due to their androgyny, Reptilians have a mindset that makes them feel superior because outside of physical reality there is no male/female separation, there is only energy.

Because the Reptilians are androgynous with male and female incorporated in one body, there is no differentiation of the sexes. Energetically being male and female in the same body matches God-Mind. They believe that any species that has to differentiate between male and female is inferior, or further removed from the origin of God-

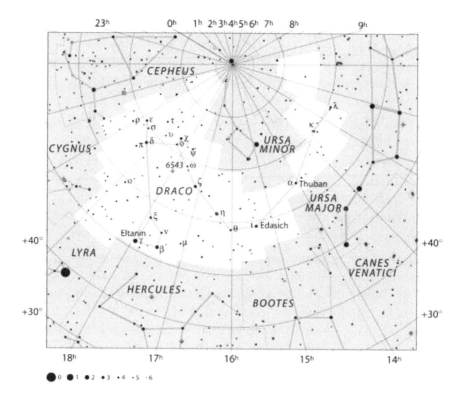

Figure 1.2: Draco star system

Mind.

Reptilians feel superior because Reptilian DNA does not change over eons of time; it remains stable. Their mentality is that they are already perfect. You can see this even in known Reptilian species here on the Earth. Reptilian species rarely change. Even since prehistoric times, the Reptilian form has not changed much; this is also true of the Draco species.

Humanity is considered inferior because we are split into male and female components to express God-Mind. Mammalian genetics have to constantly adapt, change, and evolve. Reptilians do not change since they are already evolved, believing that they are more representative of God-Mind. They took the task eons ago to fix this in physical reality.

Reptilians travel wherever they can go on an agenda of occupation to assimilate all such beings into their Empire. In their mindset, this is their holy mission. You may find this reasoning incorrect, but it is neither right nor wrong. This is simply how they think. The Draco Empire is part of the "Orion Confederation".

The Lyra star system is the home of all humanity in this particular galaxy. The Lyraen pure human beings were seven to eight feet tall. They were blond-haired and blue-eyed, or red-haired and green-eyed. The red-haired, green-eyed population was considered to be oracles. They were considered to be super mental psychics who could go into other realities and translate information. This is also why red-haired people were depicted as witches or demonic in ancient times.

When the Draco Empire became aware of the Lyra star system and humanity, the pure human beings, they felt an obligation to assimilate or change it. The Draco attacked the Lyraens. The Lyra star system had many different planets around it, and much of it was destroyed. There were over 110 colonies that were created after the breakup of Lyra.

The Draco and Lyraen wars were approximately 10-12 million years ago. Conventional history as it is publicly presented, only goes back a few thousand years. Everything beyond this goes into millions of years and into prehistoric times.

The Lyraens were scattered to other parts of the known galaxy at the time. The refugees of that civilization spread throughout various star systems to colonize and start over again. The star system we are now in was part of them. The Lyraen refugees colonized two planets in our solar system, Mars and a planet called Maldek. They were the only two planets in this solar system that had an atmosphere, water, and could sustain human life.

The Earth at that time was the second planet from the Sun and was totally covered in water; even the atmosphere was liquid. The configuration was Mercury, Earth, Mars, Maldek, Jupiter, Saturn, Neptune, and Uranus, there was nothing else. When Maldek and Mars were colonized they existed for many millennia that way.

2. PLANETARY SCIENCE

When molten material is expelled from a star the object is thrust into space and spins in the coldness of space. As it spins and begins to cool, the exterior starts to harden. As the exterior hardens the inside continues to spin.

Planets ejected from a star or sun also have molten material that spins in space like our planet. The centrifugal force causes the molten material on the inside to be shot out of the polar regions, thus becoming the north and south pole openings.

Due to the coldness of space, the inside hardens. There is a hard interior and a hard exterior with molten material trapped in between. Sometimes there is leftover molten material suspended in the middle due to the gravitational spin of the planet that acts as an inner sun.

As the interior hardens, molten material continues spinning in the center and also remains between the inner and outer shell. This is what the magma is on our planet. As the magma moves from the spinning of the planet, it creates shifting of the crust. Over time that shifting causes the crust to fracture and crack. This is how tectonic plates are formed.

Tectonic plates float on the magma that spins and is unstable. The Earth wobbles, cracking the foundation resulting in tectonic plates. The plates grind against each other, causing earthquakes as the planet spins, or rotates.

As the inner and outer shell grind together, volcanoes are formed as the molten material is pushed out. The largest volcanoes are always located at 19.5 degrees north and south latitude on every planet that is formed in this manner. When you look at 19.5 degrees on our planet, you see where a lot of volcanic activity is located, including Hawaii.

Hawaii was in the central part of Lemuria. Hawaii is extremely volcanic and has always been volcanic since the beginning of the Earth. A few years ago the US government for the first time admitted this publicly and gave a warning that "the island of Hawaii is expected to have an imminent cataclysmic volcanic eruption that would create atmospheric pressure of 1.75 times normal".

This means that when the Earth is thrust up from the volcanic eruption the atmosphere will press against it and everything on the surface would be crushed. Interestingly, in the same warning they admitted, "Hawaii was once part of a larger volcanic island".

The Mons volcano on Mars is the largest volcano in the solar system located at 19.5 degrees latitude. The moon Titan of Saturn also has a volcano on the same latitude. This is planetary science with the implication that such planets are hollow with an inner sun. An inner sun is really nothing more than suspended magma leftover from the creation.

The Earth does not have an iron core that spins; that is fake science. The Earth has a magma globe at the center which acts like an inner sun.

The aurora borealis is from the light reflecting out from the North Pole opening. This happens more in the winter because there is no cloud cover. In the winter it is too cold for moisture to form from the tilt of the planet away from the sun. The aurora borealis does not occur in the summer because of warmer temperatures that evaporate the ice and snow that create cloud cover.

The North Pole opening is approximately 1,300 miles wide; the South Pole is around 950 miles wide. All planets have an interior surface. There are caverns and sometimes ways to get into the inner area of the planet; it is not all molten material. The only exceptions are the large gas planets.

Aircraft is restricted from flying directly over the North Pole, allegedly from the "magnetic interference with the aircraft". This is not true; Global Handlers do not want you to see what is down there.

Figure 2.1: Mercator North Pole Map from 1569

In 1926 Richard E. Byrd made his first expedition to the North Pole. For a brief period of time this was documented in US history books. In the late 1920's the government removed all references from history books that pertained to this information. On February 19, 1947 Admiral Richard E. Byrd returned to the North Pole and reported a temperature of 74 degrees Fahrenheit/23 degrees Celsius.

When Admiral Byrd could no longer see the Sun he noticed a different light source was emanating and lighting the environment. He recorded "great forests growing on mountain slopes, a valley with a river, and a mammoth-like animal". He also reported making contact with an Inner Earth civilization; this is documented in his diary and can be found on the Internet.

The South Pole has no observable aurora borealis due to being covered with sheets and layers of ice. In Antarctica the outside or perimeter of the continent is mountainous. Inside the continent it is relatively flat with an ice sheet cover; there is ground deep, deep underneath. More on this in a subsequent chapter.

3. Evolution of Our Solar System

When the Draco became aware of the colonies on Maldek and Mars they devised an attack. The Draco use ice comets and meteors as weapons. They hollow them out and use the interior. A small black hole is created in front of the object to drive it through the galaxy or solar system. They develop little black holes in front of large objects to pull them as a propulsion system. The object itself does not have the technology for travel but outside or external to it is the black hole that pulls it.

When the ice comet came into our solar system it disrupted the orbit of Uranus. The planet Uranus is the only known planet that has a north to south rotation; all others have a west to east rotation. When the ice comet passed Uranus the gravitational pull flipped it on its axis. To this day it still rotates north to south. Uranus still suffers from the effect of the ice comet; it is an enigma to astronomers. As a result you can see how long the after-effects of these kinds of situations can be.

The ice comet came closer to the inner part of the solar system. As it continued on it came within close proximity of Jupiter, Maldek, and Mars. There was a juxtaposition with the gravitational pull of the Sun, the gas giant Jupiter, Mars, and Maldek.

Maldek was also a large planet with an atmosphere. The pull of all these things together, combined with the pull and drag of the ice comet, caused Maldek to explode. This is why there is an asteroid belt between Mars and Jupiter; it is the remnant of the planet Maldek.

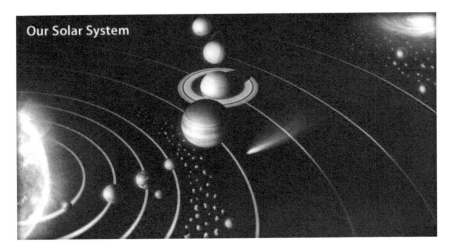

Figure 3.1: Solar System

Many of the comets or asteroids that were left over moved out in orbit and came closer to Earth. This is partly why meteorites and asteroids pass by Earth on a semi-regular basis.

Some of the pieces and fragments of Maldek developed into the rings of Saturn and Uranus. Probes have confirmed that the rings of Saturn are made from pieces of rock and ice that were from this destruction.

Jupiter and Saturn are gas giants; they have molten and gaseous material formations within them. Most of the moons of Jupiter and Saturn are captured asteroids from the Maldek explosion. As the pieces were projected outward, the gravitational pull from Jupiter and Saturn captured the remnants that became their moons. Jupiter and Saturn with all their moons act like mini solar systems within a solar system.

Some of the material that exploded out from Maldek was molten. As this molten material spun in space, it also hardened and froze.

As the ice comet moved forward it diminished the magnetic field of Mars, vaporized the oceans, and pulled most of the atmosphere off that planet. The ice comet also caused fissures to open up, allowing some of the water to be absorbed into the interior. The survivors and refugees went into underground areas and the inner part of the planet.

NASA now admits Mars once had a full atmosphere, oceans, and was similar to Earth. Mars has seasons. In the Martian springtime part of the northern polar ice cap retreats and greenery can be seen forming in the northern hemisphere. You can also see where the water used to flow; there is still life that exists on Mars. On December 27, 1984, a rock was found in Allan Hills, Antarctica they claim is from Mars. This was their way of telling you there are other forms of life on Mars.

When the ice comet approached planet Earth it started to go into an orbit with the Earth. The pull from the Sun started to disrupt the flow of the ice comet. As the ice comet, the Earth, and the Sun revolved around each other the rotation of the Earth increased. The ice comet then pulled a portion of the oceans off and vaporized them.

This enabled an atmosphere to form as the water vaporized. As the Earth spun, ice caps were created and land masses started to form as the water was pulled in different directions. Lemuria and Atlantis were the main continents that rose above the ocean and were available for life to develop. Lemuria was one of the first areas the ice comet passed when it was near the Earth.

The Earth and the ice comet finally settled into their current positions. The ice comet pushed the Earth into the third orbit from the Sun and then took its place as the second object. The heat of the Sun melted and then evaporated the ice off the comet which you now know as the planet Venus. The evaporating ice formed the cloud cover around the planet which you see in present day. Venus has no detectable magnetic field and rotates clockwise or retrograde to all other planets in our solar system. One rotation takes 243 Earth days; a year is 225 Earth days.

The Soviet Union sent a spacecraft in the early 1980's with a very sophisticated camera system that would not burn up in the heat of Venusian atmosphere. For the very first time a spacecraft was able to descend below the cloud cover of Venus and survive the heat to take photographs of the surface. It transmitted back images of seven domed areas.

The Draco Empire has 7 species of Reptilians in its hierarchy, each with a specific function. Each species is highly programmed, narrowly focused, and they do not mix together. It makes sense that there would be 7 living areas on a colony for the different species in order to cohabitate on the planet. Here is a location with 7 domed areas on Venus, yet not another word was said about it after that.

In 2012, Russian scientists claimed that they had reviewed the photographs and saw three types of creatures walking on the surface of Venus - a dinosaur, a scorpion, and a reptile.

Remember that now there are Martian and Maldekian refugees living in the interior of Mars. The Earth's oceans are polarized, the liquid in the atmosphere is cleared, the poles are frozen, and landmasses have appeared. The Earth was now colonizable, so the Draco drove in another vehicle, and parked it by the Earth. You call this object the Moon.

The Moon is an artificial object and it is hollow. When a sonic resonance is sent to the surface of the Moon it pings similar to glass like a hollow object. It does not thump like a solid object. The Moon does not spin or rotate; it is a fixed object with one side always facing the Earth.

The Moon's orbit is mechanically fixed and needs no corrections. It stays in the same layer of space due to mass and gravitational pull. It is a vehicle parked in space like a satellite and without a magnetic field. The Draco colonized Earth from this vehicle. They started with the land mass now referred to as "Lemuria".

4. LEMURIA & ATLANTIS

Lemuria was colonized by androgynous Reptilian beings approximately one million years ago. Reptilians were the first intelligent beings to colonize Earth. This is why Reptilians consider this to be their planet.

After Lemuria was colonized, Reptilians were the only ones that existed for hundreds of thousands of years. It was a long time before humanity developed from the Lyraen refugees that came from Mars and Maldek to colonize Atlantis.

As time went on, the Lyraen refugees who existed underneath the Martian surface desired to go out and colonize again. They also chose the Earth; specifically an unoccupied landmass now referred to as "Atlantis".

The Lyraen refugees called themselves "Atlans". In their language "Atl" means water. "Atl" also means water in the Mayan language, and many languages around the Atlantic basin area.

The Lemurians viewed the Atlanteans as occupiers and invaders, which they were. If you look at it from the Reptilian perspective, they were here first. Mammalian and Reptilian creatures are not designed to live in the same environment as they each require different living conditions.

The humans arrived with two genders whereas the androgynous Lemurians were genderless. This was an issue for both sides.

There was also an issue of food source because when people migrate they bring their food and animals. The Atlanteans had a problem with the Lemurian animal food source which you know as dinosaurs. The dinosaurs were very large and disturbed the Atlanteans. They rampaged over landmasses and devoured the food the Atlanteans were cultivating.

The Atlanteans despised these destructive animals, so they used electromagnetic pulse weapons to kill them. This is the real truth of why dinosaurs, mammoths and other prehistoric creatures abruptly became extinct. It had nothing to do with the Earth flipping on its axis; rather it was solely the electromagnetic pulses of the Atlanteans that eliminated them.

There was no gigantic asteroid or comet that hit the Gulf of Mexico and destroyed the dinosaurs 60 million years ago as scientists claim. If this were true you would not be here right now as there would be no life on Earth. The planet would have been a barren wasteland forever. Since life on Earth obviously exists, that is your proof that this did not happen.

There is indeed a huge trench that exists off the coast of the Yucatan. This is where the Atlantean continent and archipelagos rose up, leaving the trench as a result. The trench has nothing to do with an asteroid hitting the Earth.

There were many difficulties between the Atlanteans and Lemurians resulting in numerous wars between the two civilizations. They hated each other; each thought the other did not belong on the same planet.

Despite what you may have heard, the Atlanteans were not nice people. They were extremely war-like, aggressive, and had an agenda of their own to fan out across the world and eliminate the Reptilians. There was a genetic memory of hatred toward the Reptilians because of what happened to the Lyraen star system. This was the underlying factor in all disagreements.

There were many attempts at peace between the two civilizations. In an effort to create peace between the two species, a third species was created, part Reptilian and part mammalian. This is how humanity in its current form came into existence. Not evolution, not creationism, not intelligent design. This is the story of your origin.

The Reptilians agreed to the peace plan as long as their genetics were foundational with mammalian genetics secondary. As you know, when a human fetus gestates in the womb in the first trimester, the

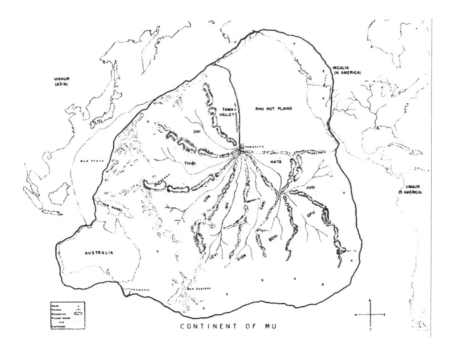

Figure 4.1: Lemuria

zygote appears as an androgynous Reptilian. As it develops the mammalian genetic sequences open secondarily, just as they were encoded.

This is also when sexual differentiation in the fetus occurs. It follows the course of genetic input from the genetic programs. The proof is in you, the proof is in how you were born. Every now and then you will see videos or reports of a baby being born with Reptilian characteristics: scaly skin, a tail, red eyes, and webbed hands or feet. When androgyny manifests in the body the individual is referred to as a "hermaphrodite" or an "intersex".

Everything happens for a reason. Nature does not create accidents. God-Mind does not produce accidents. This is why you have hybrids; this is why you are a hybrid!

The allegorical story in the Bible about Adam and Eve, says "God" took a rib from Adam and created Eve. This simply means an androgynous Reptilian body was divided into male and female components.

The Garden of Eden refers to the laboratory where this took place.

Here, the intelligence or self-awareness was developed within the new species to distinguish who and what they were.

The story of the snake is representative of the Reptilian aspect that tried to give intelligence and awareness. The agenda of the Reptilians is to occupy all cultures and upgrade them to Reptilian status and mentality. The Tree of Life and Knowledge represents the Family Tree, or history, of Humanity. The apple represents an ovary which is the storehouse of genetic information. The snake offering the apple to Eve represents the enticement of humanity to become more Reptilian. Eve taking the apple represents humanity accepting Reptilian control as handlers of Humanity from that generation forward..

In the Bible, Genesis reads, "Let us create man in our image". If there is a singular God who created humankind would not the Bible say "I create man in my image"? Who are "us" and "we"? "Us" and "we" are plural, not singular.

In the Old Testament every single reference to God is in plural form. There are no singular words for God in ancient Hebrew. In Hebrew anything that ends in *IM* or *AI* is plural. "Elohim" means "those who descended from above". "Adonai" means "our masters" plural. There is no singular "God" in the Bible because it was a joint effort of living beings at the human/alien level. Humankind was created as a way of merging the two species so that a third new species was created that would be native to the planet as a synthesis of the two antagonistic groups.

The wars continued between Atlantis and Lemuria because the human species was considered to be a failure. There were many iterations of these experiments as this third species was fine-tuned. This is why the Neanderthal abruptly disappeared, then Cro-Magnon appeared. Then, Cro-Magnon suddenly disappears and Homo sapiens appears.

You are not Homo sapiens, you are Homo sapiens sapiens. This species has only existed for the last 35,000 years. One species suddenly ends, and then the other suddenly appears. There is no overlap. One did not come from the other. They were laboratory creations and you are the final version... at least so far!

Scientists tell you that 97% of your DNA is junk. Why? They do not want you to read the instructions and sequences in that "junk aspect" because then you would know the true story about who you are and how you came into being.

Whether you are an amoeba, plant, elephant, human being, or an alien, 97% of your DNA is identical. This tells you that all DNA is from the same source: God-Mind. Thought creates the DNA. This means 3% of your DNA differentiates entire species, and individuals within that species. This also means there is not that much difference between you or anything else that is alive.

After the realization that the experiment was not going to work the Atlanteans used geomagnetic weapons to break up the continental plate of Lemuria. It sank beneath what became the Pacific Ocean.

When Lemuria was destroyed the survivors went either underground or to the landmasses that were left above the ocean. Australia, New Zealand, the Pacific Islands, Japan, Philippines, and Hawaii are all remnants of Lemuria. These are the biggest pieces that were left after the destruction of Lemuria.

This is also why you find creatures in these places that exist nowhere else on Earth. As Lemuria sank beneath what became the North American continent or tectonic plate, it subducted beneath it. Everything to the west of the San Andreas fault line in California was part of Lemuria. This is why it is a subduction zone now.

Lemuria existed from approximately 1 million BC to 50,000 BC. After Lemuria sank, the Reptilian survivors fled to the Inner Earth into the caverns that exist between the upper and inner crusts where they still live to this day. This began the legends of hell and demonic entities underneath the Earth. To the Atlantean human beings, the Reptilians were demonic entities. This is where the legend of hell originated.

The Atlanteans continued their colonization process, spreading out over the landmasses that were left including parts of North America, Europe, and Africa that rose up when everything else sank.

The Atlanteans then destroyed themselves in several phases. There was a primary destruction followed by several smaller ones.

During this time, the Atlanteans fled to what became ancient Egypt. Other refugees went to North America and became the East Coast

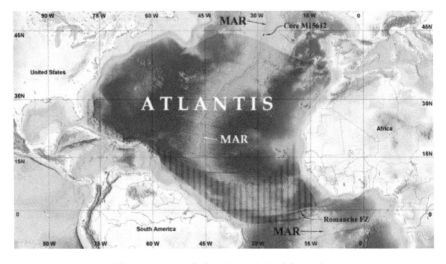

Figure 4.2: Atlantis: original location

Indians. They also fled to Western Europe and became the Celtic people. This is why American Indian, Celtic, Egyptian, and Middle Eastern cultures all have the same genetic origin. Atlantis existed from approximately 300,000 BC to 10,500 BC.

When you look at the map of the world, you can understand why there is a Gulf Stream and an equatorial current. This is evidence there was a continent in between both sides of the ocean. The water split and flowed around the continent, and it still does.

Cells have memory, Earth has molecular memory. When a person loses a limb, he/she still feels the limb, referred to as a "phantom limb". Atlantis is a phantom continent to the Earth. The Earth still responds as if there was a continent there. Of course, since the Gulf oil incident in 2010 the Gulf Stream no longer exists.

The Atlanteans loved to manipulate genetics. There really are Werewolves, Sasquatch/Bigfoot, and Mermaids/Merfolk. More of these life forms were obviously present when the legends began. In present day, these life forms remain hidden helped along by Global Agendas to help them remain hidden. The reason the myths and legends do not go away is because these beings exist. These are the hybrid results from genetic manipulations of Atlantis and Lemuria.

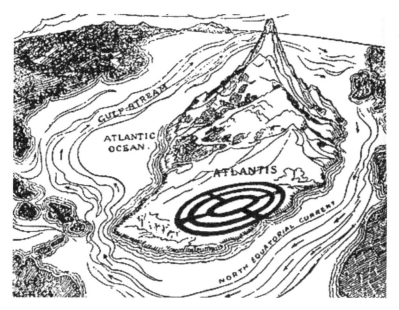

Figure 4.3: Atlantis map with Gulf Stream

Australia was where the Lemurians started their genetic experimentation by kidnapping humans from the Atlantean continent. The Lemurians worked on creating hybrids and created the Aborigine race in Australia. Underneath Australia there is a network of crisscrossing caverns and tunnel systems. Australia truly is one of the most Reptilian places you can imagine, especially the primitive area of Western Australia.

Geographical Evidence   The destruction of the continents is fact. For example, in Kansas when you excavate far enough down into the Earth, you can find salt water. Kansas also has the largest salt mines in America and shark teeth have been found throughout the rivers. Where did the salt come from? Some of it evaporated and some sank down from the oceans that once covered it.

In the US Central Plains region, it has been scientifically proven that there is a massive underground reservoir. This is a leftover from when the Earth was covered with oceans. When the land finally rose up, the water sank and filtered down after centuries and millennia

21

to become ground water. Deeper down you find salt water; the fresh water stays on top. This is due to the salt sinking down through the natural soil filtration system. This is further proof that oceans once covered the planet.

The Great Lakes are the second largest fresh lake area in the world. Anywhere you go in the Great Lakes region you can dig down to find a layer of salt.

The continental shelves on both the East and West Coasts of the US have openings that submarines go into to reach the huge caverns under the continent. The US Navy has a submarine base in Coeur d'Alene, Idaho. Where did this come from if it is a land locked lake? Local people report that there are bases under Idaho that connect from the West Coast. Submarines are reported to have submerged underneath California through hollow caverns to Arizona.

Shelves have been found with beach-like sand off the coast of Northern Africa in the Atlantic Ocean. These shelves appear to once have been a beach that is now submerged. These types of materials should be found on the edge of land and water, but instead they are found thousands of feet down in the ocean. There is proof throughout the Atlantic with evidence of beach sand where Atlantis once existed.

The Mid-Atlantic Ridge is splitting; this proves Europe and North America are moving further apart. This is causing pressure on the St. Lawrence Seaway and the New Madrid fault line. This is also causing pressure on the West Coast of the US. The Pacific plate is moving forward or eastward and the plate is being crunched, explaining why you see earthquakes in the middle of the US. The tectonic plate in the middle of the US is cracking. When you take a piece of wood and start compressing both ends with pressure, it splits in the middle.

All of Atlantis did not sink. When it did sink in 10,500 BC it caused weather patterns to shift. This resulted in a huge Ice age that covered the northern hemisphere of the Earth. Approximately 30% of the Earth's surface was covered in ice. The last Ice age was 11,000 years ago. According to Russian scientists this scenario is expected to happen again in the near future.

During the time of Atlantis most of Europe was under a glacier, therefore unpopulated. Most of North America was also under a glacier. It was only after Atlantis was submerged that these areas were habitable from the melting glaciers. The natural climate of the Earth is cold; there is only a small band near the equator that is warm and tropical.

Over time a planet slowly moves further and further away from the Sun. The Earth is further from the Sun now than it has ever been before. Every day it gets a little bit further away from the Sun. There is less sunlight hitting the Earth now than ever before. This will continue for eons of time as Earth moves slowly further away from the Sun.

There is no global warming, there is only global cooling. This means that the Earth is not heating up, it is getting colder. This will continue forever unless the Sun supernovas, but if it does, even if only for a brief second, you are fried!

Then you will get cold again because space is extremely cold. Space temperatures are so cold, they are very close to absolute zero. And, you are floating in it. The only thing that allows any warmth is the atmosphere envelope that retains the solar heat. This is only on the surface of the planet.

When you fly in a plane, the outside temperature drops. You can fly over Miami, yet the temperature is minus 60F. So, what does this tell you? That it is very, very cold out there and that global warming is absolutely beyond bizarre!

The location of the planet Earth in the Milky Way Galaxy is on the outer edge of one of the spirals. This is why you can see the rest of the Milky Way Galaxy from our position. If you are an invading force that wishes to occupy an entire galaxy, the most logical way to achieve this is to occupy the points on the outer edges and work your way in. This is an occupied galaxy, Earth is a prison planet.

We exist on the energetic border of the astral and physical in this particular part of the galaxy. From Earth's location in time and space it is very easy to enter into the nonphysical. This explains why on this planet there are so many apparitions and interdimensional events. This also explains why there is so much going on bleeping in and out of our physical world. Earth is right on the edge in this borderline area of the Galaxy.

Earth is a fabulous place to occupy if you want to control the galaxy. It is also a great place if you want to go interdimensional or into the astral and hyperspace. Earth is the perfect location. Location is what makes Earth so popular. Out of the billions of occupied planets in existence Earth is not the best physical place, but it definitely is the best location.

The Draco and the Lyraens came to Earth to create humanity as a synthesis and a peace process between the two species. This is the only planet where the two species have merged into a new species. This is another reason why this planet is of so much interest.

"Adam" in Hebrew means "from the Earth". This is why they called this third, new species "Adamites" which means "created out of the Earth". Humanity was not really "created out of the Earth" because neither species originated on Earth.

The Earth environment is hostile to humanity. When you are natural to an environment, you live easily. You always find food and shelter. There are no problems. Humans have to wear clothing, find shelter, and cultivate food; they struggle to survive.

You are not native to Earth, so you exist in a hostile environment. Even your biorhythms do not match the biorhythm of the Earth.

As far as escaping, this planet is considered a prison or a mental institution. A lot of beings are sent here as punishment because they misbehaved. Some say that there is no worse place to be than on Planet Earth.

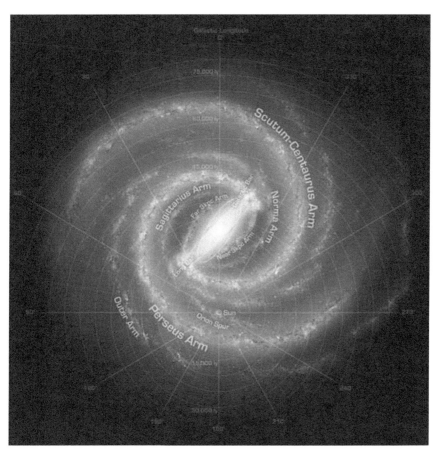

Figure 4.4: Milky Way Galaxy (artist's depiction)

5. ALIEN MANIPULATIONS

The 5% percent of beings in existence that are not Reptilian or mammalian have many different forms. The typical Grey alien has the appearance of a 3 to 4 month old human fetus grown to higher proportions. They have Reptilian genetics activated and an artificially implanted soul-personality, similar to an android or robot.

They are not a natural species; they are an artificially developed race based on human fetuses. This is why they have no hormonal development, requiring soaking in human hormones and blood for nourishment. They have no digestive system because it is not developed, just as human fetuses do not have a digestive system because they are still connected to the mother.

When I was in the Montauk Project and learned about the alien civilizations and the histories, one of things I was told that I will never forget was, "The Universe is hostile, it's not peaceful. There is no love, light, and peace in the Universe; everyone is fighting everyone else for control. The Reptilians, or Draco, want to assimilate all beings into their empire."

The descendants of the Lyraens want to recreate the Lyraen Empire under their different cultures and phases. When the Lyraen refugees colonized Aldebaran, Tau-Ceti, Arcturus, and all the other systems, most of these locations were not conducive to the Lyraen life form. Modifications had to be installed to allow them to adapt to the different environments. This is why the various cultures look slightly different from one another even though they have the same origin. Lyraens do not exist in their original form.

Sirius B was responsible for the Tibetan civilization. Sirius A created the Hebrews and Egyptians. The beings from Tau-Ceti were the ones who modified what became the Slavic people.

This represents the most important continents and general civilizations as far as the flow chart in fig. 5.1 is concerned. Every culture that existed on the Earth could not be listed.

In the top left-hand side under "Draco and Lemuria", follow the arrows from Lemuria and you will see it goes to the Inner Earth, Australia/South Pacific, Western US, Asia, and Central and South America. This is the flow of the Reptilian culture and religion after Lemuria was destroyed. If you go to China or anywhere in South Asia, the coast especially, they talk about the "Naga".

According to Asian legend the Naga were 7-headed Reptilians that came to the shores of Asia after their home continent was destroyed in the Ocean. The 7 heads represents the caste system of the Draconian/Reptilian Empire that had 7 different species. Each species has a specific function; they do not cross-over to one another.

This is where the Hindu caste system originated, from the Brahman to the Untouchables. They represent the different species of Reptilians, the Draco Empire and their functions within the Empire. The Naga, over centuries and millennia, morphed into a 7-headed Reptilian representing the 7 different Reptilian species.

When you go to the large temple of Angkor Wat in Cambodia you see the 7-headed Reptilians in the corners of each of the entrances. These represent the Naga, and the inflow of that culture. They also represent the 7 chakras.

In China, you have plaques describing the birth of China from a Reptilian Yellow Dragon King. The First Dynasty was the offspring of this Reptilian king, who was considered a very "Holy Being". All Asian cultures, especially the East and South Eastern Asian cultures, describe the Lemurian influence. You see this reflected in their religion, language, and throughout their culture.

The top right-hand side of the flow chart in fig. 5.2 shows the Lyraen culture. The Pleiadean star system is younger than our own star system. No life evolved in the Pleiades because it is not old enough to have evolved life. Whatever is there was brought there or came there on its own.

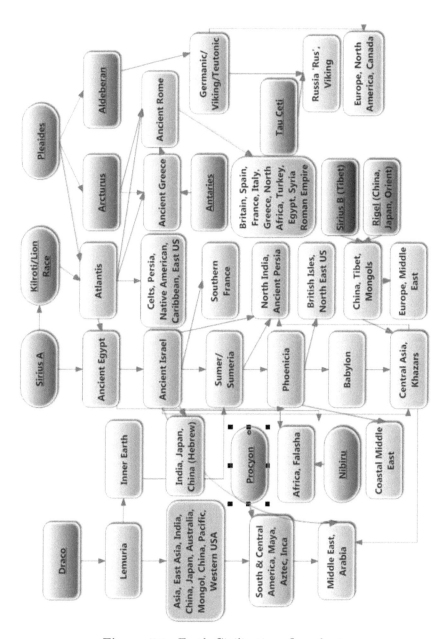

Figure 5.1: Earth Civilizations flow chart

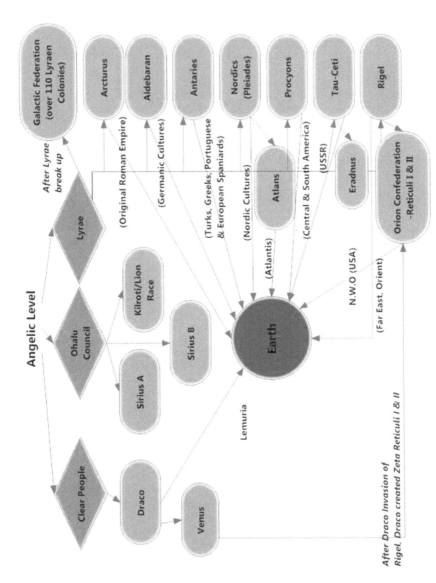

Figure 5.2: Galactic Civilizations flow chart

In my book, "Blue Blood True Blood" I tell of how many of the refugees from the Lyraen star system, after they were attacked, colonized many planets in the Pleiadean star system. There are 7 stars with approximately 32 different planets in the Pleiadean star system. They are all different colonies; a lot of them were not very nice people.

In fact one group, known as the Atlans, was so troublesome that they were sent to colonize Earth to get rid of them. This group became the Atlanteans. If you read about Atlantean culture in history you know that they were involved in hybridization, mind-control, creating electromagnetic weapons, and dominating the planet. This is why they fought with the Lemurians all the time; the Atlans were an aggressive people - they were not peaceful. The Native Americans in the United States, who originated from the Atlans, also constantly attacked and killed each other.

When the Atlantis culture was destroyed, the refugees went mostly to the Eastern US, which then rose above the ocean. They also went to Egypt and Central Asia, especially to Greece and also to Western Europe, evolving there into the Celtic people. Legends and histories of Ireland describe the Celts as coming from a land in the West. This is another confirmation of the continent that existed in the Atlantic Ocean but is no longer there.

The middle of the flow chart in fig. 5.2 shows Mars and Maldek, which were colonized by Lyraen refugees. When the Draco sent the ice comet that destroyed Maldek and took the atmosphere off Mars, the refugees then went into the interior of Mars. After living in the interior of Mars for many centuries the refugees relocated to Earth to colonize the area that became Sumer or Sumeria.

This is now Southern Iraq and Kuwait; areas of interest always stay areas of interest. The Martian refugees chose this location for several reasons. At the time the climate was different and was not as arid as it is now. This area also has a strategic mix of minerals, crystals, and was an extremely fertile area for development.

It also has an entrance to the Inner Earth and is a central, or crossroads, point to the underground subterranean tube system. The tube system crisscrosses the Earth in various locations and enables traveling from one point to the other. This explains why the Inner Earth

Reptilians targeted the Sumerian civilization for control and more hybridization because of its ideal location to achieve their agenda. From here, these Lyraen refugees spread out into the Caucasus Mountains, Europe, North India and Asia.

In the eastern part of Turkey on the border of what used to be the Soviet Union, which is now Armenia and Georgia, is a tall mountain called Mount Ararat. In the 1960's satellite images showed what appeared to be the outline of an Ark embedded in the rock. In those days you could not get close to Mount Ararat since it was near the Soviet border. For many decades only aerial photographs could be taken of that specific location.

In 2007, a joint Turkish-Hong Kong expedition including members of "Noah's Ark Ministries International" found an unusual cave with fossilized wooden walls on Mount Ararat, well above the vegetation line. The sample was declared by the Department of Earth Sciences at the University of Hong Kong to be petrified wood of the Cyprus variety.

Figure 5.3: Location of Mount Ararat

In 2010, "Noah's Ark Ministries International" released videos of their discovery of the wood structures. Reported carbon dating suggests the wood is approximately 4,800 years old. It is unlikely that there was any human settlement at the site at an altitude of 4,000 meters/13,120 feet.

According to the Old Testament, Noah was born with red skin and had white hair. He was depicted in appearance as the "Sons of God". This text refers to him as if he had alien features. Noah was not the same as other human beings on Earth. There are many instances written about in the Old Testament about babies being born likened unto the "Sons of God". It also says the "Sons of God" came to Earth, looked at the women of Earth, and took them as their wives. If you translate "God" into "alien" it makes more sense.

The prophet Ezekiel talked about a giant wheel or ship that came down and how the beings that came out looked. He describes many faces and lights, very much like they were wearing a helmet and breathing apparatus. In those days after the fall of Atlantis there were many intrusions by the remnants of Lyraen star systems and others.

6. NIBIRU

Nibiru, or Marduk, was the traveling planet with an elliptical orbit in our solar system that was contrary to all other planets or objects. Nibiru used to pass within close proximity to Earth every 3,600 years. This planetary object or artificial vehicle entered our solar system in approximately 30,000 BC. In some cultures the planet was called "Marduk", however, the current acceptable name is "Nibiru".

On that world there were beings called the Annunaki. Nibiru was an artificial world they used as a vehicle. It was converted from a planet-sized asteroid, or comet.

The Annunaki use hollowed-out, planet-sized objects to propel themselves through space similar to the Draco. These beings created the Black Race on Earth as recorded in the Sumerian tablets. The Annunaki considered the Black Race to be their personal possession similar to how the Draco consider the rest of the world to be their possession.

The beings on Nibiru have nothing to do with the Draco. They are two separate cultures and races. Each one with an agenda, even though they are genetically Reptilian. The Draco and Nibiruans/Annunaki are at odds with each other and were at war. It appears something terrible happened on the Moon. There is evidence of explosion sites and debris from vehicles. The Sumerians and Egyptians documented wars in space with flashes of light and explosions seen on the Moon.

In the year 2000, The New York Times reported that NASA had discovered a large object past Pluto that had an elliptical orbit different from all other orbits in the solar system. NASA expected the object to pass close to Earth around 2003. In March 2003 the US invaded

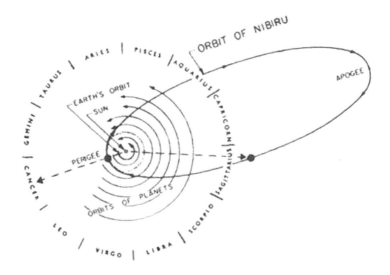

Figure 6.1: Nibiru

Iraq.

Underneath Baghdad are the star gates that the Nibiruans/Annunaki use to go back and forth between Nibiru and Earth. The Nibiruans/Annunaki were trying to transfer to the Star Gates underneath Baghdad so this is why the US invaded Iraq in March 2003 - to take control of the star gates.

The Illuminati used particle beam accelerator weapons in pulse form to blow up Nibiru as it neared Jupiter. Nibiru was destroyed in April 2003. This is why there have been asteroids and meteors flooding the Earth from the gravitational pull of the Sun. Fragments of Nibiru were seen for months and years after the destruction, flying into the Sun via the NASA suncam.

7. DEVELOPMENT OF SUMER & EGYPT

After Atlantis and Lemuria were destroyed, other groups came to Earth and modified humanity. Other Lyraen refugee cultures from other star systems came to create their own images here. Each of the groups wanted to recreate the old Lyraen civilization under its own unique format.

Many groups came here, took human beings, and manipulated them genetically. When the Lyraen refugees went to various star systems they had to adapt themselves to the new environments. Due to these adaptations, over time they had different features and developmental manifestations compared to the original Lyraens. They continued to explore the adaptation process with certain test groups here on Earth. These test groups included the refugees on Mars.

Sumer sprang into existence in 5,000 BC, approximately 7000 years ago. Sumer existed from 5,000 BC to 1,500 BC. There is nothing that indicates the Sumerian civilization slowly evolved over time. There was no development of Sumer. One day it did not exist, the next day it was there. It was as if someone implanted it in what is now Southern Iraq and Kuwait. This is why there are so many problems in that part of the world. Everything is coming to a big circle of completion now.

The Sumerians were the Lyraen refugees from Mars and Maldek who colonized the Earth again after the destruction of Atlantis. The Martian and Maldekian colonists brought their technology and culture. Sumerian Caucasian people from this area have a 26 hour biorhythm, matching identically to the length of a day on Mars. Humans now have a 24 hour biorhythm. However, If you put a Caucasian person

SUMER, AKKAD AND ELAM

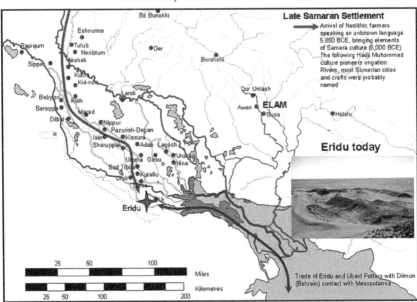

Figure 7.1: Sumer/Egypt

in a deprivation tank with no external influence, that person will exhibit a 26 hour biorhythm. Again, this matches the length of a day on Mars. So, basically Caucasians are Lyraen Martians.

Thousands of years had passed after the destruction of Atlantis, Egypt was developed into a civilization, and Sumer was flourishing. The Reptilians under the Earth wanted to retake the Earth's surface since it was originally their planet. They knew when they returned to the surface that they would be unaccepted and rejected because humans had not seen them in such a long time.

The Reptilians developed a plan. They began a new hybridization process with the Sumerian culture where they again mixed their genetics with the human hybrid to create a new hybrid. Reptilians have high copper content in their blood instead of iron. When their blood oxidizes it turns blue-green, thus the term, "blue bloods". Thus began the "blue blood" lineage.

Sumer was taken over by Reptilian elements that came back to the surface. This was the same group from Lemuria that colonized Australia. The progression of Reptilian religion from Sumer to modern times always involves 3, or the Trinity. They had the 3-horned God which eventually became the "Fleur-de-lis".

Sumer religion consists of the Reptilian Gods "Nimrod" and "Semiramis". The statues of the God and Goddess of Sumer have human-shaped bodies in Reptilian form.

They always have a male and female because this represents the androgyny of the Reptilian body; male and female in one. They have Reptilian hands and faces holding a human baby. Nimrod and Semiramis had a child named "Damu", who became the King of Sumer.

This is where the shape-shifting and hybridization began, mixing Reptilian blood with human blood to create a being that would look human, but would have Reptilian agenda. This new hybrid would be able to take over Earth's surface without being known or discovered.

These Reptilians created hybrids that were a 50/50 genetic split between Reptilian and mammalian. With such a genetic split, the body does not know which way to manifest since it has equal genetics of both. It defers to the mindset that activates the DNA. If you have a Reptilian mindset in such a body you will always appear Reptilian. If you have a human mindset in a body you will defer to a human appearance.

If you have a Reptilian mindset with the genetics constantly manifesting a Reptilian form, the physical body requires the ingestion of human hormones, organs, and blood, thus feeding the mammalian genetics to help hold a human appearance. The ingestion of human DNA instructs those genetics to open and manifest as such.

This is the origin of the blood sacrificial rituals that existed in ancient times, explaining why humans were actually sacrificed and eaten. The blood rituals were originally about maintaining the human form through the harmonics of the mammalian energy. They still go on to this day in Illuminati culture or subculture.

This was a way of life since Earth began. Eliminate those who take from you and use them for sacrifice. From one end of the Earth to the other in cultures that supposedly had no contact, yet they still had the same ritual - the giving up of life in one area to bring life into another.

God-Mind always has to be in balance. To bring in something new, you have to get rid of something old, doing what is necessary to always keep things in balance. The Illuminati know these Universal Laws and how to work with them. Why do you think when you take Communion you are told, "This is my body and this is my blood"? Because you are participating in the Reptilian ceremony of ingesting human hormones.

The Old Testament talks about sacrifice. Abraham was to sacrifice his son, Isaac, who was 37 years old at the time. He was not a child as the Hollywood movies depict it. This shows you that in those days human ritual sacrifice was acceptable, and it still is.

When you see Reptilian images and depictions on the Earth in ancient civilizations such as the Egyptians and Sumerians, there are blazing sun rays in the hieroglyphs and wall reliefs. There are 16 rays of the central sun, representing the Draco star system. Today, advertisements and corporate logos with radiating suns are symbolic representations of the Draco star system.

The museums in Baghdad had electric batteries that came from Sumer that were thousands of years old. Interestingly, when the US invaded Iraq in 2003 the first place they went to was the Baghdad museums where they took the batteries and all the artifacts related to Sumer.

The caretaker of the Baghdad museum said that it was as if they knew exactly where to go, what to raid, and what to take. To him, everything seemed to have been meticulously orchestrated. They even went into the basement store rooms and opened specific drawers to confiscate and obtain certain relics.

They did this to obscure any evidence or proof that would undermine what they are going to announce to the world.

In every official location the US flag has a gold fringe. The international symbol of the gold fringe is an occupied country under Martial Law. On many military uniforms they have the US flag reversed which is the opposite of America, it's the New World Order. Israeli military police have two black snakes on their arm band, signifying the Reptilian connection. There are always "two" when depicting a person, because this represents their androgyny of both male and female always together.

8. ANCIENT EGYPT

History books date ancient Egypt's origin to approximately 3,200 BC. This is the date of the recorded history. The Egyptian Civilization actually ranges from 10,000 BC to 400 AD with many different iterations.

Egypt was a colony of Atlantis, becoming another major center of the world in approximately 10,000 BC. At that time the Sphinx and Great Pyramid already existed in the Giza plateau. The Egyptians tried to replicate the pyramids. There are around 90 pyramids in Egypt. Only 3 or 4 of the original pyramids were found on the Giza plateau; the rest are replicas. The replicas are actually falling apart because there were not built as perfectly as the originals.

What existed in 10,000 BC was nothing like what they had in 3,000 BC. The surface of the Great Pyramid of Giza is a 4-sided pyramid. The same structure as you see above the ground is actually below the ground as well, thus forming an octahedron.

From 1992-93 German engineer Robert Gantenbrink observed that inside of the pyramid, going up the sides, are pathways or shafts too small for humans to enter. Unmanned robots were sent into these pathways or tunnels under the auspice of "Project Upuaut". In the southern shaft at 59 meters down the unmanned robot came to a stone slab with copper fittings. At this point, the project was stopped.

These pathways or tunnels exist on the sides of the pyramids and probably go down and across the octahedron. The tunnels are conductors, but what are they conducting? Underneath the ground at the foundation of the pyramid, where the other point is, there is an underground stream or aquifer that is an offshoot of the Nile River.

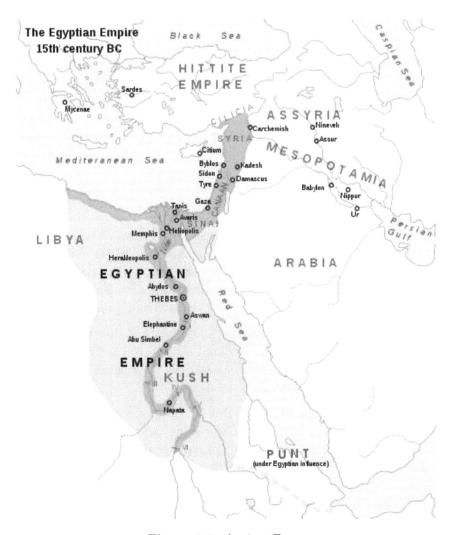

Figure 8.1: Ancient Egypt

The water from the underground stream was brought up around the edges of the pyramid. The outside of the pyramid was covered with a very shiny material that reflected the sun that made it glow. The pyramid also had a gold cap. The pyramid was, and still is, an inter-dimensional device.

There were ancient reports of lightning projecting off of the pyramid during ceremonial protocols. In the exact center of the pyramid are an empty chamber and sarcophagi. Egyptologists claim that either the mummies were stolen, or that it represents that there is no death. The inner chambers are the area where the interdimensional energetic activities took place.

When in the chambers while the device was turned on, you would physically transport into another reality. Besides an interdimensional transport device, the purpose of the Great Pyramid was also to direct weather, and as a weapon. There was a whole complex of pyramids spread across the Earth for these same purposes.

Carbon dating has been proven to be inaccurate because it relies on the atmosphere, volcanic activity and other conditions in a particular environment where objects have been found. Carbon dating can be misleading. Something could be younger than the dating gives it or much older. Carbon dating of the Sphinx in Egypt says that it is ancient. Public history says it is only 4000 years old. The interesting thing is that excavations around it showed evidence of water erosion from 15,000 years ago, proof that the Sphinx is at least 15,000 years old.

When the Egyptians came into the area the Sphinx was already there, as was the Great Pyramid of Giza. The Sphinx faces the star Sirius in the morning. There are a lot of connections to the Orion star system which connect to Draco and Lyra as well. The Giza plateau is a message; a historical document in building form that is yet to be understood by humanity.

The Giza plateau and the Sphinx are replicated and duplicated on the Cydonia plateau on Mars as well. The face on Mars is equal to the face on the Sphinx.

Napoleon invaded Egypt in the 1800's and shot a cannon ball at the face of the Sphinx, thus disfiguring it as well as explaining why you do not see the exact image of the Sphinx. Of course, NASA has determined that the face on Mars is a "rock illusion". Recently NASA revealed 3D graphics that shows a close-up of the face from various angles in its attempt to prove this is not a face, but only a "pile of rocks". There is a reason why so much time and effort was put into disproving that a face actually exists on Mars.

NASA does not mention that right next to the face on Mars is an entire pyramid complex, including a pentagon. NASA has not explained that one because it is too busy distracting you by disproving the "face". NASA probably thinks that rather than waste time trying to cover up the pyramid complex, it will wait until there is a formal announcement about the existences of aliens.

There are a lot of Reptilian references in Egypt and throughout the ancient world. Reptilian images are common, however there are some hybrid pictures of humans with a snake body, or a human with a snake head.

In Egypt, you see Isis (mother), Horus (son) and Osiris (father), again forming the Trinity which represents the Reptilian 3-horned god. The eye of Horus is represented on the dollar bill, or, the male/female Reptilian progeny. Christianity and Judaism began from a form of ancient Egyptian-Reptilian religion.

The city of Paris is not French. Rather, it was established by Egyptians that called the city "Par-Isis" or "For-Isis", referencing the Goddess Isis. Of course now, the last two letters have been dropped to form the name "Paris(is)".

Figure 8.2: Reptilian/Snake people - Egyptian carvings from Luxor

Excavations underneath the Cathedral of Notre Dame uncovered Egyptian hieroglyphs and artifacts of an ancient settlement. Why did the Catholic Church build on top of that? Obviously it was put there to hide something they do not want the public to know. When you worship in Notre Dame you are actually standing on top of an Egyptian Ceremonial ground.

In New South Wales, Australia a cave was discovered in the Blue Mountains in the 1900's. The cavern contains Egyptian hieroglyphs that date back to the 3rd Dynasty, approximately 5,000 years old. Some students in the 1960's rediscovered the cave while hiking. The Australian government blamed the students as creating the hieroglyphs as a hoax. They must have been pretty smart students who knew intricate Egyptian hieroglyphs!

The hieroglyphs describe "Lord Djes-eb" and his entourage being shipwrecked in a strange and hostile land. They also describe the tragic and untimely passing of Lord Djes-eb and his burial rituals. If public history admitted there were Egyptians colonizing Australia 3,000 years ago what would that do to history?

A few years ago in Auckland, New Zealand an Egyptian ship was found in a harbor under the water. Did you learn in school that Egyptians colonized New Zealand? If you said that to a Maori they would cut your head off! The Maoris believe they discovered New Zealand and that it is their place, when in fact they were one of the last to get there.

Egyptian artifacts were also found in Arizona in the Grand Canyon in the late 1800's. Prospectors going down through the canyon found a cave filled with Egyptian artifacts and skeletons. "Surprisingly" the cave was emptied out, sealed, and is no longer publicly accessible.

Egypt colonized much of Europe, all the way to Scotland and Iceland. In fact, it was the Princess Scota of Egypt who, along with a Greek prince, went to what is now Scotland, naming this country after herself. The Egyptians mixed with the Picts, creating the famous drawings and designs that came to be known as "pict-ures" and "pict-ograms".

9. ANCIENT HEBREWS

Ancient Hebrews are an extremely interesting topic that emanates from ancient Egypt. The ancient Hebrew language is not just a language, it is a numerical system. Every letter has a value, explaining why it is the only language on the Earth that can be fed directly into a computer system without changing it. This is where the Bible Code comes from with the skip sequences.

The ancient Hebrew civilization existed from approximately 3,000 BC to 400 AD, ending around the same time the Egyptian civilization ends. The same thing happened with Rome. Many civilizations came to an end at the same time which means something happened at that time.

What do you think happened in 1,500 BC that ended the islands off the coast of Portugal as well as the civilization of Sumer? A comet struck the Atlantic Ocean, destroying all the civilizations. When it destroyed the Atlantic civilizations it created the Straits of Gibraltar and Baltic Sea. The comet also created many openings and rearranged landmasses. For example, prior to the comet strike, Britain and Ireland were connected to mainland Europe. There was also a connection to Denmark, Norway. and Sweden. Finland was connected to Estonia. All of these countries had larger landmasses.

Off the coast of the Baltic, between Sweden and Denmark, an entire submerged village was found that dated pre-1500 BC. Something happened that submerged landmasses during this time period. This was caused by the remnants of the Maldek explosion. Over centuries and millennia the asteroids and fragments finally reached the Earth to crash into it. This is recorded in ancient Egyptian documents.

These records indicate that in practically a single day and night asteroids were hitting the Atlantic Ocean, Europe, North Africa, and Central Asia, all at the same time. Of course the records said, "The Gods are angry and seek to destroy us".

Entire city-states in Greece were destroyed in minutes. The Minoan civilization was wiped off the map. This is the time period when the Hebrew/Jewish slaves escaped Egypt as well as the Exodus when the Red Sea was separated. The 10 plagues in Egypt were a result of the asteroids hitting the area, causing fires and vermin to swarm.

Who warned the Hebrews in advance of this occurrence? How did they know they were supposed to flee that day? An alien civilization warned Moses of the disaster and where it was going to hit. They instructed him it was time to leave the area. These beings created the Hebrew race and are a genetic alteration different from most of humanity.

The Bible describes how the Hebrews were led through the Sinai desert to get to the land of Canaan, or the Holy Land. There were huge rod-like glowing objects in the sky that led them to safety. These objects dropped what they called "Mana" from the heaven.

The Hebrews ate the Mana, saying that it tasted like whatever they desired it to taste like. The Mana interacted with their frequencies and brainwaves, which is high-level technology. When Moses went to the burning bush, the entity advised him to remove his shoes. Obviously his shoes interfered or prevented him from being grounded from the electronic conveyance.

10. ARK OF THE COVENANT

The University of Minnesota attempted to recreate the Ark of the Covenant in 1967-68. They followed the instructions given in the Bible. Once it was built it was so electrically charged they had to dismantle it because it was so dangerous. The Bible says that the Holy Priest would come to pray before the Holy Ark. The priest had to wear certain vestments of metallic linen for grounding so that he would not be electrocuted. The Ark was an electronic communication device from 1500 BC; it is not from this planet.

The Holy Ark was eventually kept in Solomon's Temple in Jerusalem. When Jerusalem was attacked the first time the Hebrews made a copy of the Ark. Then, whoever attacked Jerusalem could only destroy the copy without realizing that the original Ark of the Covenant was underneath what is known as "Solomon's Stables" for safekeeping.

Queen Sheba plays an interesting part in the Ark of the Covenant. She came from Ethiopia; it is interesting that Moses married an Ethiopian. He escaped from the Pharaohs in the desert; someone found and gave him refuge. Then he married one of the daughters who was an Ethiopian. The connection between Israel and Ethiopia deepens because Queen Sheba was not Ethiopian after all but came from the Arabian Peninsula.

On September 12, 2000 the University of Calgary announced the excavations of the site of Ma'rib in Yemen. Using ground penetrating radar technology they discovered the remnants of a city in southwestern Saudi Arabia. When the city was uncovered there were references found to Queen Sheba which revealed this to be the location of Queen Sheba's capital city, not Ethiopia. The question is - was she African or Middle Eastern?

Figure 10.1: Ark of the Covenant with Moses and Joshua

It is believed that she invaded or sent her armies into Ethiopia. Apparently she crossed the Red Sea to Ethiopia with her entourage to establish a secondary Kingdom there. Then, they went into Egypt and the Holy Lands. She was an intelligent woman who decided to expand her desert Empire. She made alliances with the Kings of wealthy Empires rich in gold, silver, and other valuable commodities.

Queen Sheba supposedly came from Ethiopia with her entourage to Israel where she met King Solomon. They fell in love and had a child named Menilek. She wanted to go back to Ethiopia which began a custody battle over the child.

King Solomon wanted his child, so he agreed to let her take the Ark of the Covenant instead. He knew there was a replica in Jerusalem so if his Kingdom was ever invaded or even destroyed, the Ark would be safe. What Queen Sheba did not tell him was that she was pregnant with a second child.

Queen Sheba went to Egypt next, taking the Holy Ark with her. The

Egyptians were fascinated with it and made another replica, keeping it at the bottom of the Great Pyramid. Queen Sheba then went back to Ethiopia with her Ark via the Nile River. The Blue Nile breaks off from the White Nile in Khartoum, Sudan and leads into Ethiopia. Lake Tana is at the end of the Blue Nile. There are several islands in Lake Tana, one of them where the Ark of the Covenant is today. For centuries the Holy Ark has been guarded by her descendants called the "Falasha".

The Falasha are Ethiopian Jews who claim ancestry from King Solomon and Queen Sheba. There are thousands and thousands of Black Jews in Ethiopia. The descendants of Queen Sheba became very popular. They had an ancient form of Judaism that was untouched or modified for many millennia.

For many decades the Ethiopian Emperor "Haile Selassie I" called himself the "Lion of Judah". He knew about the Lion symbol, and Judah. Judah was the capital province of Ancient Israel where Jerusalem is located. He wore the Star of David because he traced his ancestry back to King Solomon and Queen Sheba.

After Haile Selassie I died in 1975, Ethiopia's civil wars escalated. The old Empire was destroyed and the communist Marxist regime took power. In 1988 the Israelis told the Ethiopians they were going to take the Falasha and bring them back to Israel.

The Ethiopians refused, insisting the Falasha stay. In retaliation, the Israelis, or rather the Mossad, went to the area off the Ethiopian Red Sea coastline and started the "Eritrean Independence Movement". This resulted in the creation of the province called Eritrea and then made Eritrea into a separate country. Eritrea land-locked Ethiopia by cutting Ethiopia off from all ports. Out of desperation the Ethiopians agreed to allow the Israelis to take the Falasha.

The Israelis sent in aircraft after aircraft to what is now Addis Ababa Bole International Airport, and northern parts of Ethiopia. They airlifted approximately 14,000 Ethiopian Falasha Jews back to Israel. At this time the Ark of the Covenant was allegedly taken back to Israel according to the Mossad. The Mossad are the most highly respected intelligence agency in the world.

The Falasha are currently used in Israel to guard the Dimona nuclear power plant in the Negev desert. They are easily identifiable by their African appearance. If the Israelis used local people as guards they would be indistinguishable from the rest of the population which consists of Israeli, Arabs, and Persiandescendants.

Most of the Falasha, as well as the original darker-skinned Arabic Jews, in Israel, live in poverty without equal rights with other citizens. The white-skinned Jews are really not Jews but are descendants of the Khazars.

Supposedly the Ark is once again located in Solomon's Stables underneath Jerusalem. This was done in preparation for New World Religion and the coming Messiah. The prophecies of ancient Israel state that when the Ark is returned and the Temple is rebuilt, the Messiah will come.

The Temple Mount of the Dome of the Rock is on top of Solomon's Stables. The Israelis have tunneled underneath the Dome of the Rock, undermining its foundation and causing it to crack and tilt. The Israelis warned that the Temple would collapse, yet they refused to let any of the Israeli architects or engineers fix it. The Israelis want it to fall apart. Benjamin Netanyahu, the prime minister of Israel, has stated that in his term he will begin rebuilding the Temple of Solomon.

In the past I have said there will be 3 global rituals. The first ritual was the simultaneous destruction and creation of atomic matter in the 1945 atomic explosion. The second was the symbolic marriage of Heaven and Earth with the lunar landings in 1969. The third ritual is the rebuilding of the 3rd Solomon's Temple. Remember the Illuminati do everything in 3's. 3 represents creation or perfection.

Ancient Hebrew coins have been found in the desert of New Mexico. Writing found inscribed in rock in North America appears to be pre-Babylonian Hebrew letters. Artifacts have been dug up in ancient Indian grave sites that look like Hebrew religious artifacts. This is definitely more than public history would have you believe. Now is the time for True World History to be known.

11. BIBLE CODE

The Hebrew language is not just a letter system; it is a numerical system. What is used for letters is also used for numbers. Refer to "The Healers Handbook" for the correlation chart of Hebrew/numerical values/hyperspace symbols.

Gematria is the study of the frequency of Hebrew words in numerical value. Hebrew can be used as a formula. When you take a sentence in the Hebrew language, put the words together so there are no spaces, then feed that into a computer, the letters register as numbers and give you the values.

In the 1970's at the Hebrew University in Jerusalem there were some individuals that did such a project. They took the first five books of Moses from the Old Testament in the Hebrew alphabet and fed them into a computer. The computer showed "skip sequences". For example, every 27th, 33rd, and 50th letters were the same.

They used a program to connect all the matching numbers together, revealing hyperspace archetypes/symbols. Every chapter and every part of the Bible had geometric shapes. For example, in ancient Hebrew there are certain letters such as "Lamed" which is pronounced as an "L" which was always written with a crown on it. The letter "Shin" was also written with a crown.

If the language was ever forgotten and you only remembered these few letters you can extrapolate all the others. The computer took all the shapes from the sequences and combined them together. The master shape that was revealed was the tetrahedron within the octahedron.

When all archetypes/shapes in Hyperspace are put together you will get the archetype, or shape, of God-Mind which is the tetrahedron within the octahedron.

Figure 11.1: Ultimate Protection archetype

When a light is shone on any part of the tetrahedron within the octahedron, another shape is transmitted on the opposite side. Every shape in creation can be derived from the tetrahedron within the octahedron. If anything is ever lost, this shape alone can recreate it. This is why this archetype/shape is the Ultimate Protection - because everything in existence is included within it.

When the ancient Hebrew Bible is put into a computer to generate a form, the tetrahedron within the octahedron is the shape that occurs. The letters that have the crown are the points on the tetrahedron within the octahedron. This study is extremely fascinating; no human being came up with this. This is Hyperspace Language and this is why it is so important for you to learn the Language of Hyperspace.

The study also determined that every chapter in the Bible is symbolic. Even though the Bible tells a story, there is another story behind the story that is not in words. The hidden story is comprised of color, tone, and archetype.

For example, when the computer was programmed to generate a master symbol for the book of Genesis, a toroid was the result.

The doughnut-shaped toroid symbol moves and enfolds in upon itself. The toroid is a multidimensional shape that symbolizes creation as told in the Book of Genesis.. The symbol relates to the story in the book. Humanity exists in this energetic toroid at the edge. This is also where our planet is energetically located. There is very important symbolism here.

The Bible Code will tell you anything you want to know. It contains realities and alternate realities. If you input your name in the Bible Code it will find your name code in a section and around that section will be everything about your life. Everything that exists has an archetype, including you, imbued with your particular frequency, sound, and color.

Figure 11.2: Toroid

When you type in the Hebrew word "code", it comes out "it is sealed until the end". So now that we have the Bible Code, are we at the end? In that same field of the code there are words that spell out computer. The information cannot be known until computers are available. That's from a document that is 4000 years old. I find this quite amazing!

The Bible Code has a vast amount of secret information. Every imaginable combination was tested. The Bible Code said that the biggest artifact that can be found to explain everything to humankind is in a peninsula called in the Hebrew Language, "Lishon". On the Jordanian side of the Dead Sea there is a peninsula which in Arabic is called "Lison". Is this where the artifact is? The Bible Code says the artifact is buried deep in the peninsula of "Language". In Hebrew, the word "Lishon" means "language".

The Jordanians refuse to allow any excavations of the peninsula to find out if there is actually any object there. The Israelis used American satellite ground imaging technology to see below the Earth. They released to the public that they could not detect anything under the peninsula, speculating that the artifact was so old that it had deteriorated or vanished. They probably found other things they are not revealing.

The Bible Code also states that there is an Alien presence on the Earth and even discusses this but the specifics were not released to the public. What was revealed to the public is that DNA and humankind were brought to Earth by Aliens. According to the Bible Code, this information was also somehow connected to time travel. The words for "time travel" were clearly written out in the sequences related to "alien" and "DNA".

When "DNA" was entered, the code sequence for the word "Ark" was revealed. The subsequent related words to "Ark" referred to it as an "obelisk", with the words "metal, iron and steel". This had nothing to do with Noah or the flood.

When any key word or phrase is input, the Bible Code then scans through its iterations to pull up the sections where the codes related to that word are found. Then, the words in skip sequences that are connected or related to the code word are brought together for deciphering. Obviously, a complicated and laborious process.

Perhaps the time travel connection is to the Montauk Project. Long Island is a Peninsula, the Pomonoc Indians said that Long Island was "a fish swimming in the ocean". How did they know it was shaped like a fish unless they could see it from above? They also said that one day the "fish" would swim away - implying that it will sink. There are many other such mysteries waiting for resolution.

12. ANCIENT GREECE

While public history says Ancient Greece officially had its start in 2,000 BC, its true history began about 10,000 BC as a colony of Atlantis. This was an original colony that was at war with Atlantis, similar to a civil war. The Atlanteans sent armies against Greece because it was trying to break away, resulting in the various nation-states of Sparta, Athens, Macedonia, etc. These nation-states were remnant colonies of Atlantis.

The Ancient Greek civilization was very important because the alphabet letters used in ancient Greek were actually derivatives of the Atlantean alphabet. This explains why a lot of programming that people have is sometimes in the Greek language.

The ancient Greek language is now illegal to teach anywhere, even in Greece. The Modern Greek language and alphabet was developed in the mid 1800's when Rome decided to learn ancient Greek. They unfortunately obscured and suppressed the true language and history so you cannot learn it anymore. A form of Ancient Greek is still spoken in Albania.

Greece spread across the Asian continent and all the way to Persia. At one time, Greece went as far west as Spain. The origins of Spain were Greek colonists who came across the Mediterranean. Over 30 Greek city-states with approximately 90 colonies existed in the Mediterranean.

Greek colonies were established along the coast of Southern France, Corsica, Sardinia, Sicily, Southern Italy, Crete, throughout the Black Sea, Cyprus, Turkey, the Middle East, Syria and even Egypt. The Greeks were one of the first people in ancient Israel and occupied Jerusalem. They brought the Hellenistic way of life with them.

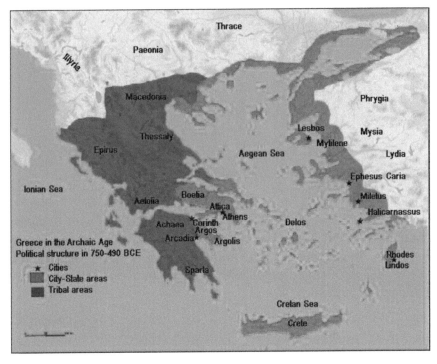

Figure 12.1: Ancient Greece

The Jewish holiday of Chanukah is about the Greeks invading King Solomon's Temple and taking all the oil to use for their own rituals. They left just one vial of oil for the ceremonies of the ancient Hebrew traditions. The vial instead of lasting one day lasted for 8 days. The Hebrews called it "the miracle", and this is why the Jews celebrate Chanukah, lighting a candle for each one of the 8 days.

Interestingly, the Israeli and Greek now joined together their air forces that may be used against the old Greek enemy of Persia/Iran. As you may know, Alexander the Great had a goal to conquer Persia for Greece. Because Persia has invaded Greece on at least two occasions, the Greeks were very much against the Persians, and still are.

13. ANCIENT ROME

Rome started in 750 BC and officially ended in 486 AD when the Huns invaded Europe. The Pope then made deals with the Huns which allowed Rome to continue. The Holy Roman Empire actually ended in 1461. Rome lasted over 2000 years, but it still really exists, simply morphing from one name to another name. Yet, it is really the same Empire.

Rome basically occupied the known world at the time from Great Britain all the way to the Middle East. Rome is confusing as far as timelines are concerned.

There was a split in the Roman Empire when the Huns invaded Rome under Emperor Constantine. He created the city of Constantinople also known as the new Holy Roman Empire in place of Byzantium, an ancient Greek city. When modern Turkey was established in 1930 Constantinople was then changed to its present name of Istanbul.

When the Russians were looking for a state religion, they sent emissaries all over Europe to see what religion fit them the best. They liked Greek Orthodoxy as well as the Constantinople religion. They therefore combined Eastern Roman and Greek Orthodox to create the Russian Orthodox Church.

This is why you see the large onion-shaped domes from the eastern architecture in Russia. Russia was also asked by Islam to become Muslim but there was a conflict with either becoming Catholic or Muslim. So, Russia went with the middle choice of Orthodox, which was a combination of both with an Asian flavor. That also explains why Middle Eastern churches and priests appear eastern instead of western.

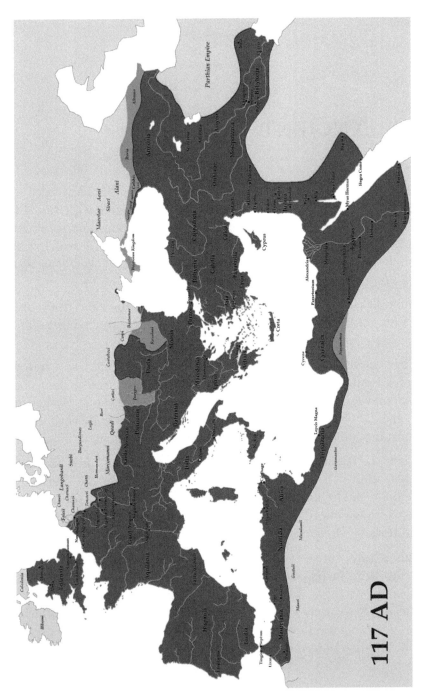

Figure 13.1: Ancient Rome

14. Khazar Empire

Sumerians became Mesopotamians, Babylonians, and Khazars. The Khazars were a very powerful ancient Sumerian group that migrated into the Caucasus Mountains, hence they became known as "Caucasians". The Sumerian descendants became Sumerian/Aryan from Khaza. The symbol of the Khazars/Sumerians was the Dragon. The Khazar Empire existed from 500 AD to approximately 1200 AD.

In the summer of 2008, Russian archaeologist Dmitry Vasilyev discovered the capital of Khazaria after a 9-year excavation. It was called "Atil/Itil" and existed at the northwestern corner of the Caspian Sea along the Volga delta.

The Khazar Empire started in the city of Atil/Itil. At the time, the Caspian Sea was smaller with more surface land exposed. The Caspian Sea is now larger and much of the capital city is now underwater. Only a fragment of it was found above sea level. Kazakhstan is also named after the Khazars.

The Khazars spanned from Eastern Europe to Northern China, into Mongolia. They blended with all of these cultures, imposing their religion on them. The Aryans, or Khazars, drove out the Dravidians from the north of India, pushing them into what is now South India and Sri Lanka, where they eventually became the Tamils.

When the Khazars came into Europe they forcefully mixed with the Magdalenian group to create what is now known as the Merovingians. Charlemagne was a Merovingian and his descendants include most US Presidents. The symbol of Magdalene was the Golden Lion blended with the Dragon. In Europe, the Reptilianized Lion is seen on coats of arms. Over time the Merovingians broke up into the Illuminati families that occupied various parts of Europe with each

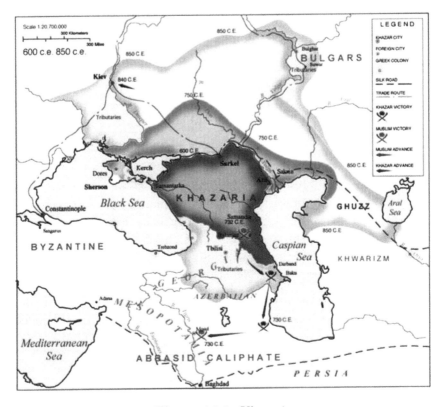

Figure 14.1: Khazaria

family controlling a specific country or region.

740 AD was a big problem for the Khazarians because both Islam and the Christian Roman Empire were spreading with the desire to occupy the Khazars' territory. The King of Khazaria did not want to be either Muslim or Christian, he converted his kingdom en masse to Judaism. As a Jewish Empire he did not have to report to Rome nor did he have to give anything to Islam. Ultimately, the Mongols invaded and that was the end of the Khazarian Empire.

After Khazaria was invaded, the Khazars spread to Europe and became the Jews of Europe. People who call themselves "Jews" are really "Khazars", and can trace their ancestry to 740 AD. This is why they are light-skinned with light-hair and eyes. Israel calls them "Ashkenazi Jews", because they were based in Germany and Poland.

The real Jews are the darker-skinned people in North Africa and the Middle East, called "Sephardic Jews". These people are from Turkey, Egypt, and Morocco. When Israel was formed some of the Jews came back, but it is the Ashkenazi Khazar Jews, who are not really Jewish, that still control the government.

The real Jews are considered low-class citizens no better than the Arabs; this is a double standard even in Israel. The Falasha, or Black Jews, are treated even lower than the Sephardic Jews. There is a class system in Israel even though they do not talk about it.

The University of Pavia in Italy conducted genetic tests of different Europeans from Spain to Finland and all over Europe. They found 80% had Khazar genetics. The other 20% was traced to Egypt, which was also Sumerian. This means 0% are European; they are from elsewhere. History is not what you have been told at all, you are not who you think you are.

In 1650, a Dutch rabbi wrote a book where he describes his meeting with a Dutch explorer. The sailor and his first mate were Jews who went on a Dutch expedition to the New World. While in North America in the early 1600s, they met some Native Americans who did not speak any European words. The sailors and the Native Americans could not communicate. In frustration, the sailor turned to his first mate and exclaimed something in Hebrew. The Native American man then responded with an ancient Hebrew prayer! The two Dutchmen nearly fainted.

In the 1700s, an English researcher, James Adair, came to live with Native American tribes for 40 years and wrote a book about it. In the book, he described how the Indian ceremonies and beliefs were remarkably like those of the Jews. He theorized in 1775, that North American natives were none other than the Lost Tribes of Israel!

In yet another story, a Southwestern Native American in the US Army during WWII was sent to New York City for training. While there, he was shocked to see symbols and customs from his own people... in Jewish synagogues! He felt that the Jews were a lost tribe of his people.

15. Jmmanuel

The *Talmud Jmmanuel* was discovered in 1963 by "Billy" Eduard Albert Meier of Switzerland, with his friend Isa Rashid, an ex-Greek Orthodox priest. This work was found in the tomb of Joseph of Arimathea, south of the old section of Jerusalem.

The scrolls are written in Aramaic. Jesus and the ancient people did not speak Hebrew, they spoke Aramaic. While Aramaic is a different language, it is related to Hebrew. Aramaic is like the Latin of the Middle East. Whereas the languages French, Spanish, Italian, and Portuguese all come from Latin; Hebrew, Arabic, Farsi, and Turkic all come from Aramaic.

Aramaic was the original language there and written in the same Hebrew letters. The word or name Jesus did not exist until hundreds of years after his death. The real name of that person was Jmmanuel.

Because of his Palestinian background, Isa Rashid was able to read the text and translate it into German. He completed 36 chapters which he then sent to the parents of Billy Meier in Switzerland, which Billy eventually obtained. Isa included a letter that spoke of the translation becoming "known to certain authorities". Isa then fled to a refugee camp in southwest Lebanon with his family. Isa's presence was known by the Israeli authorities and the camp was subsequently bombed during an Israeli air raid. Isa was forced to leave without the scrolls, fleeing to Baghdad where he was assassinated along with his family.

Jmmanuel is pronounced "Immanuel". Established churches erroneously distorted and changed the name of this individual to Jesus. The *Talmud Jmmanuel* contains several extraterrestrial and interdimensional references.

The work reveals that the father of the Biblical Adam was named Semjase who was a "distant traveler" and an aid to "El" or "God" from the far reaches of the Universe. It portrays celestial portals and God as a singular immortal being that rules over the intelligent human lineages and his followers "the celestial sons", or "the guardian angels". It also describes Jmmanuel as begotten by Gabriel a "guardian angel".

In Hebrew, "Jmmanuel" breaks down into three words from right to left. "Jmm" which means "sea", "anu" means "I" or "I am" and "el" which is "God". It means "the sea of I am God". Spiritually, think of God-Mind as a sea or ocean and "I am", making sense of why that name was chosen. There was a time the *Talmud Jmmanuel* could not be obtained as much of it was destroyed.

The *Talmud Jmmanuel* explains quite blatantly that the Christic figure was a creation from genetic manipulation by some extraterrestrial or alien group. It describes how he was taken into a metallic craft, went up into space, was downloaded with information, and then returned.

This work also says that his mother, Mary, was implanted with the fetus, explaining why he is considered to be the result of an immaculate conception. Jmmanuel was designed and programmed to divert, or skew, certain segments of the population away from other segments of the population. This was at a time when other Lyraen groups were coming down to create their own Empires on the Earth with the remnants of humanity.

The hybridization program was hybridized even further. The crucifixion itself was a staged event. The Illuminati are famous for staging everything. Everything is a show and symbolic because that is part of the Reptilian religion. The Christ figure was drugged, put on the cross, then removed from the cross and revived.

The story you hear about Jmmanuel or Christ is that he stayed in a certain area when he was young. The 20 missing years of his life were actually spent in India and Egypt learning the ancient esoteric religion and rituals in what is now called Cairo.

In Arabic "Cairo" means "Mars". The ancient name of Egypt was "Khum". Between the Yucatan and the mainland in the Gulf of Mexico is the Bay of Campeche with the same name as Khum. Now you understand why there are pyramids on both sides of the Atlantic.

Jmmanuel spent his formative years in the Egyptian temples. He was called the "Messiah". The Hebrew word is "Mashia". The word in ancient Egyptian is "Messeh".

Messeh was also the name of the crocodile fat from the crocodiles of the Nile. The priests anointed themselves with oil as the Bible indicates "I anointeth your head with oil".

"Messia" became "Messiah" or "Mashia" in Hebrew. Christ was called the "Messiah". This had nothing to do with being an emissary of God, rather this meant that he was anointed into the Reptilian religion.

The Christ figure, Jmmanuel, was married to Mary Magdalene. There is no name in Hebrew for "Mary". Mary is a Latin name. Her real name was Miriam Magdala which means "mistress of the sea". Hebrew is very much like Arabic in the fact that it is written two different ways, one a formal print and the other a script form.

Here again is "am", a different version of "sea". Miriam means "I am from the sea, from the ocean". "Sea" in Latin is "Mar" or "Mary", and this is why the name "Miriam" was translated from Latin to "Mary" or "Maria". Maria means "woman of the sea".

Miriam/Mary came from the city of Magdala in ancient Israel. Magdala means "a raising up" or "an exaltation". Even in present times at the Temple in Jerusalem, there are celebrations during the High Holy Days, New Year, and Yom Kippur where a ritual is performed called "Migdal-Elohim-Chai" which means "the exaltation of the singular God".

In ancient Israel in the town of Migdal, a ceremony and ritual was performed to "exalt God". In those days no one really had a last name. They had a name and a town. So Miriam/Mary became Mary from Migdal, or "Mary Magdalene".

Mary Magdalene was considered to be a prostitute by the Catholic Church. This was done to invalidate and deny that Christ could be married to anyone since he was supposed to be alone. He had three children with her, two sons and a daughter named Sarah. Of course the Catholic Church did not want people to know that which would undermine everything they were promulgating.

Jmmanuel was a political figure. The Essenes, who were really a cult within the Hebrew religion, were involved in writing documents. In 1946-47 a little Arab boy, Muhammed edh-Dhib, found a cave in the Judean hills near the ruins of Khirbet Qumran. In the cave he found what became known as the *Qumran scrolls*. They were the documents of the Essenes.

The Essenes were the prophetic cult of that ancient time that spoke about the coming of Jmmanuel as a political figure to change and liberate them from the Roman Empire. The scrolls were briefly translated, then confiscated by the Israelis. Only partial fragments exist of the translation. They will never give the public the real translation because it would undermine all religion and all political parties.

16. MAGDALENE CULTURE

Peter, one of the disciples of Jmmanuel and regarded as the first Pope by the Catholic Church, had a big problem with Mary Magdalene. Peter thought that Mary was influencing Jmmanuel too much, so much so that he eventually decided that he wanted to remove her from Jmmanuel's sphere of influence.

Peter was extremely jealous of her intimate relationship with Jmmanuel as well as upset that she had children with Jmmanuel. Peter was afraid that Jmmanuel would eventually abandon their joint efforts, and follow Mary instead. This jealousy resulted in the need for Mary Magdalene to flee for her life from the Holy Land, not from the Romans, but from the wrath of Peter. The painting of the "Last Supper" depicts Mary next to Christ with Peter holding a knife to stab her.

Figure 16.1: Last Supper (Giampietrino) - detail

When Mary Magdalene, daughter Sarah, and youngest fled, they were worried Peter's emissaries would come after them. Peter had threatened them and Mary feared for their lives. Mary went with the children first to Turkey. Supposedly, Jmmanuel's mother lived there so she went there for safekeeping.

From Turkey, she next traveled to Greece, then to the island of Malta, and finally to the South of France to a town that is now known as Les Saintes-Maries-de-la-Mer which means "Holy Marys of The Sea". To this very day, citizens of this town reenact the coming of Mary

Magdalene with her entourage to the coast. This is something the Catholic Church denies, yet there she is in France. Plus, Mary's and Sarah's tombs are both there.

Rennes-le-Château is a location in the mountains in the South of France where a very strange church is located. It is one of the most fascinating places in this region. The symbolism that the priest Bérenger Saunière attempted to convey in the building and decoration is overtly blatant. When correctly interpreted the symbolism depicts that the bottom line of Christianity is based on Reptilian religion. The symbolism in his church shows that Christianity was based on androgynous Reptilian energies and that ritual sacrifice and sexual rituals were common.

Even more curious than Rennes-le Château is the priest who created this church, Bérenger Saunière. He was funded by money that no one can explain. He lived lavishly, indulged in elaborate banquets, and may have even had children with his housekeeper. He used to go out at night to dig up the grounds around the area; no one knew what he would bring back. One interesting display that is available to the public is an array of dinosaur bones.

Supposedly Saunière also found scrolls that confirm the true story of Jmmanuel, including how Christianity is fake and not a religion. In front of the altar in his church, there is an interesting depiction of baby Jesus as a twin. Mary is holding one baby; Joseph is also holding a baby the same size that looks exactly the same. They cannot explain why there are two babies. They are posturing that perhaps Jesus was a twin. There is no other place that has ever been revealed where Jmmanuel is publicly displayed as a twin other than Rennes-le-Château.

Inside the church is a depiction of St. Germaine as a woman. A male figure as a female, again representing Reptilian androgyny. Demonic figures hold up the altars. There are many such depictions that Bérenger Saunière purposely built over a hundred years ago to present a symbolic statement of the information that he knew. He wanted the world to know the truth in the only way he was allowed to express himself at the time.

There is also a tower with a spiral staircase that goes up with a red dot on the floor that points toward a window. If you follow the trajectory of the dot out the window into the hills, you will see that it leads to the cave where Mary Magdalene lived in France.

In the 800's the Khazars came into Europe to meet with the remnants of Mary Magdalene's kingdom which was ruled by the Merovée family. There was an intermarriage between the Khazars and Merovée, merging them together into the Merovingians. This is the official beginning of the Illuminati.

Not only did Mary go with her family and the entourage to the South of France, but she actually created a Hebrew Empire. The Empire covered a large area from France to Italy, and the Swiss border. This Hebrew Empire was based on the Hebrew religion, lasting for many generations and centuries from 30 AD to 486 AD.

In 1945 two peasant farmers were digging for topsoil used as a fertilizer at the base of the Jabal al-Tarif cliff in Nag Hammadi, Egypt. There, they found a large red clay jar that was buried. In the jar were 13 codices with over 50 texts written on papyrus by Philip, Mary Magdalene, and Thomas. The documents are called the "Gnostic Gospels" and are kept at the Nag Hammadi Library.

The Vatican suppresses the information from these scrolls that say Mary Magdalene was married with children. They also state that no intermediary is needed between humankind and God-Mind, completely undermining the Christian Catholic Church.

Recent archaeological finds include a tiny piece of paper that suggests that perhaps Jmmanuel was married. This is currently being debated and will most likely be released as true before his staged second coming. The Vatican, of course, says it is a fake.

17. JMMANUEL'S DESCENDANTS

After the staged crucifixion and resurrection, Jmmanuel and the oldest son left the Holy Lands with a caravan to journey on to India. From there, they traveled to the area on the border of India and Pakistan called Kashmir. Srinagar is the capital of Kashmir. The city of Srinagar has a Hebrew-Christian cemetery with a tomb that says "Jmmanuel of Israel who died at the age of 117". This tomb is guarded. People are no longer allowed to see it. There is even speculation that he married again as a female is buried near him that indicates she is a relative.

His son married a local woman in Srinagar with whom he had children. The grandson was also called Jmmanuel. This Jmmanuel made a trek from Kashmir all the way across Asia to Japan. In northern Japan there is a shrine to Jmmanuel that describes the ancient form of Judaism with Christianity. The time period the shrine was built has been verified accurately. Information there reveals that Jmmanuel traveled from India to bring new religion and information about God to the Japanese people. The Magdalene lineage is much longer and wider than you can ever imagine.

When the Japanese imperial family took over, and eliminated specific religions, the Christian Jews fled to Korea. This is why there is such a high Christian population in Korea. In India, especially near Goa, there was a large Christian Jewish population. When the Catholic Portuguese arrived in India in the 1500's they found these Christian Jews who they asked, "Do you honor the Pope?"

These Christian Jews did not know who he was; they only knew of their own religion. The Catholics threatened the Christian Jews, telling them that if they did not convert to Catholicism they would be exterminated. Categorically they refused and subsequently were imprisoned, tortured, and killed.

Consequently, there are only a handful of them left in India. Presently India supports Israel because of what the Catholics did to them. India remains against the rest of the religions in the world due to these early religious/political conflicts. This gives you an idea of the real reason why politics are the way they are now, compared to what you think it might be.

When Mary Magdalene and her two younger children went to the South of France, her entourage included Joseph, brother of Jmmanuel. This Joseph did not remain in the South of France, but continued on with Jmmanuel's son to what became Britain. They brought with them artifacts from ancient Israel that proved the Mary Magdalene lineage and what Jmmanuel really was. Joseph settled in and developed an area in Glastonbury. This is why the royal families consider themselves to be the rulers in Holiness because amongst themselves they claim descendancy of Jmmanuel and Mary Magdalene.

Near the Tor of Glastonbury, Joseph planted a tree that grew until 2012 when it was mysteriously destroyed by "vandals". However, it is said that a cutting was moved to Washington, D.C. where it now grows in a secret location.

18. SATURNALIA, OESTER & PASSOVER

There were too many different religions, too many ceremonies going on, and even the Romans were pagans with rituals and orgies to God. The Roman hierarchy took the Christian cult idea and romanized it so that the Roman citizens could accept it. For example, the Roman citizens celebrated a holiday on December 25th called the "Feast of Saturnalia". Saturnalia was a sexual orgy feast every December 25th which included huge parties, food, sex and killing sacrifices. The hierarchy took this holiday and turned it into "Christmas" so Roman citizens would accept Christianity. The birth of Jmmanuel had nothing to do with December 25th. As described in the New Testament, the weather and star positions verified that Jmmanuel's birth took place sometime in the Spring, approximately on March 20th.

Next, the hierarchy had to find a day that the Roman citizens would accept to honor the Resurrection. All pagan holidays were considered before settling on the Persian pagan holiday of "Ashtar/Ishtar", a pagan celebration honoring this fertility god who demanded blood sacrifice for survival and which used the egg as a symbol of fertility.

As this pagan holiday spread west from the Khazars, especially into the Teutonic tribes, it became known as "Oester". The Teutonic tribes sacrificed rabbits and eggs to Oester for fertility purposes. This spring ritual of sacrifice ensured fertile crops.

Christians today celebrate "Easter" as a result, thinking that it is about the Resurrection. But it is really a fertility rite that included human sacrifice and that's the Easter you celebrate with colored eggs and bunny rabbits. "Easter" is really about killing, releasing something to the nonphysical so that the physical could thrive. Universal

Law to maintain balance. Easter is also a programming trigger for death and resurrection functions.

Passover is another Spring ritual that can be a programming trigger for slavery and rebellion. The Passover story told during the Seder nights tells of slaying first born males. This is a trigger for ritual sacrifice. Take note of increased stories in the news about missing male children as well as public attacks on males.

The Passover story includes slavery and brutality against minorities. The "antidote" for this was Moses speaking to the Pharaoh and throwing his staff on the ground, where it turned into a snake. Here is another Reptilian trigger.

Ultimately, the slaves wander around in the desert for 40 years before they can be redeemed. Moral of that sequence - you will be punished for resisting your servitude.

In addition, the Passover story tells of painting blood on your front door to avoid the Angel of Death. This is obviously a blood sacrifice ritual that encourages the energy of animals to protect the home, segueing nicely into the Easter story where the blood of Christ is used to save humanity.

Easter is also about the human sacrifice of Christ and crucifixion as punishment for helping others escape totalitarianism.

19. SLAVS, GYPSIES/ROMANI & GERMANIC/TEUTONIC TRIBES

Christianity as known today did not really start until 330 AD when the Romans decided to create a religion to control the people. The original Christians were Jews.

As a result of the staged crucifixion, Jews who followed Jmmanuel, or Christ, took the cross as their symbol. The word "cross" in Hebrew is "Tslav". From this, the Romans called these early Christians/Jews "people of the Tslav", or "cross people". "Slav", or "slave" originates from the Hebrew word for "cross".

The resulting cultures settled in Eastern Europe and were called the Slavic people. To this day Romanians, Bulgarians, Serbians, Bosnians, Croatians, and even Hungarians are considered by others in Europe as "slave people".

Macedonia is located north of Greece and to the east of what once was Thrace. This meant three civilizations, Greeks, Macedonians, and Thracians, were all vying for power at the same time. The Greeks won. To save Macedonia from destruction the Macedonian king's son, Alexander said, "I will expand the Greek Empire for you if you leave Macedonia alone". He became "Alexander the Great", but he was actually not Greek, rather Macedonian.

The Gypsies arrived after the Slavs. Originally the Gypsies, or Romani, were a blend of Egyptian and Indian peoples. They blended together to form a Gypsy culture. People associate Gypsies with Eastern Europe but they were actually a tribe from Egypt/Gypsy that were expelled and went to India.

After India expelled them, they travelled across Asia into Eastern

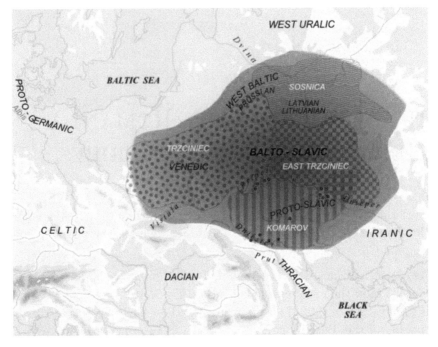

Figure 19.1: Slavs, Gypsies/Romani & Germanic/Teutonic Tribes

Europe and spread throughout the rest of the continent. This is why the Europeans do not like them and even to this day use Nazi-like tactics to expel them from France, Germany, and Italy.

When the Gypsies are expelled, they always go back to Romania. This is why they are also called "Romani" and sometimes "Roma", because this is where they settled after they left Egypt.

What is now known as Romania was named after Rome because it was once part of the Roman Empire via its connection to Constantinople. Some people think Romania is named after the "Romani" but it is not; it is named after its early Roman ties.

Europeans are descendants of Germanic Tribes. Even the Picts, from whom the word "pictograms" derives, Danes, Jutes, and Norse were really Germanic Tribes who were most likely remnants of the "Lost Tribes of Israel".

The Teutonic Tribes of the Franks invaded Rome. It is interesting that France and Germany hate each other when they actually have a common origin. Frankfurt, Germany is the "Fort of the Franks", yet the word "France" comes from Franks.

20. VIKINGS

Out of all the histories and civilizations that have ever existed in the world, the Vikings seem to have been the most global and the most extensive. The word "Viking" comes from an Old Norse word that means to explore fjords and rivers. If you went "a-Viking", it meant you went "exploring".

The original pre-Norse term meant to "switch rowing partners during an oceanic voyage". "Viking" was even traced to an ancient Russian word that meant the same thing. The Russian Empire began when Viking settlers called the "Rus", or the Rose, founded the Russian state and the city of Novgorod. The Vikings thus gave Russia their language which is called "Rus-i-an", or "Russian". "Russia" therefore means "Land of the Rose" from this ancient Viking language.

The majority of people are confused about the Viking culture. The Vikings were not exclusively Scandinavian. There is genetic evidence that they actually came from a vast area, including Eastern Europe, North Africa, Greenland, Iceland, North America, and Central Asia. Many nationalities have Viking heritage such as Polish, Estonian, German, Norwegian, Swedish, Danish and Lithuanian.

There were all kinds of Viking groups, many of whom did not get along with one another. They were not all under one government; in fact there were chieftains and various local governments that collectively became the Vikings. Viking culture had a legal system as well as an amazing financial and trading system. Vikings were not simply barbarians, as you have been taught.

The "Wends", or Polish Vikings, were known to be the fiercest in battle. A Polish King supports the Viking chieftains. Viking strongholds also existed in what is now Ukraine. The Viking history of Norway

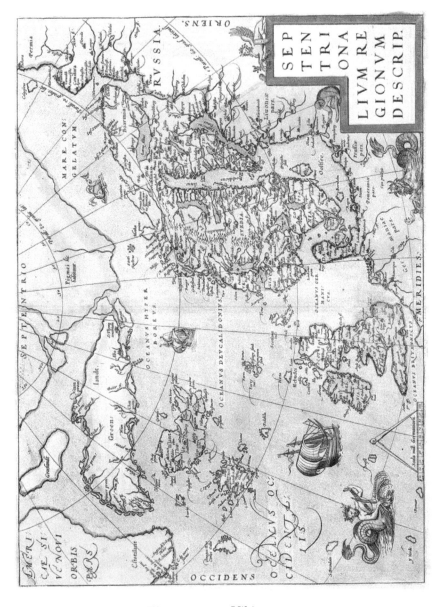

Figure 20.1: Viking map

says the chieftains wanted to become kings and had many allies in Ukraine and Poland. Norwegian Vikings even sent their children there to be raised, returning after their education was complete.

Some of the Viking long ships were over 200 feet long capable of crossing the oceans. Viking ships were built in such a way that they did not sink into the water, but rather skipped on the top of the waves. These ships were so seaworthy that even today there are no ships that can skim the surface of the water like the Viking ships did.

Some of the ships were quite large and were almost unsinkable even in terrible storms. A few years ago Viking long ship replicas were sailed across the Pacific and Atlantic oceans to help to prove this point.

Viking ships are rarely found at the bottom of the ocean because they did not sink unless they were burned in an attack. They have been found on land buried in the ground after being pulled ashore. The ships were built to hold many animals and people; to withstand storms and waves; and to travel very quickly. Viking ships were an amazing engineering marvel.

Charlemagne, the most famous Merovingian also called "Carolinian", was at the inception of the Viking Empire, or civilization. Viking uprisings resulted because of his brutal rule. Many Saxons, or Germans, escaped into Denmark and Sweden to escape his regime.

His ruthlessness was rewarded by the Catholic Church which promoted Charlemagne as the one who unified Europe under one religion for Rome. Under the Roman Catholic Christian auspices in the late 700's and early 800's Charlemagne continued his plundering from Northern Europe into Holland, Frisia, Germany, and the Saxony area forcing conversion to Christianity along the way.

Charlemagne went on a bloody campaign from town to town for the Pope. He told all the Pagan people including those of the Celtic religion, that if they did not convert to Christianity they would suffer capital punishment. He made good on his threats when those that refused to convert were beheaded or tortured horribly until they died.

The Danes prepared for his arrival, constructing a large wall to block Charlemagne from entering Denmark. This became the German/Danish border. In those days this wall was a remarkable feat, effectively isolating Denmark from the rest of Europe.

Chieftains of Norway and Denmark were afraid of losing their land, as they were an agrarian and peaceful people. They knew Charlemagne and his hordes would come through, attacking on his conquest heading north. Even Northern Germans immigrated to Denmark for safety, thus avoiding forced conversion to Christianity. When Charlemagne arrived the Danes refused to let him in.

The Norwegians decided to attack Charlemagne's strongholds along the coast of France. The long ships were developed as part of their attack. This diversion drew Charlemagne's attention from the Danish border to France and the rest of Western Europe.

The Vikings in Scandinavia developed out of necessity to stop Charlemagne from brutalizing and converting them to Christianity. After their success, the Danes then decided to go plundering as well. The Viking tribes in southern Scandinavia knew that sooner or later the wall in Denmark would be broken through, so they started to raid Europe.

They started with Scotland, Wales, England and Ireland. Most of England was colonized by the Danes and Norwegians. England was occupied extensively by the Danes. Norwegians spread throughout Scotland and Ireland. Dublin and York are old Viking cities founded by the Norwegians. The origin of the British people is not what you think. England really went from Celtic rule, to Roman, to Viking, and of course it is now under Illuminati rule with German-ancestry royals at the helm.

The Vikings took slaves from Ireland, Scotland and other countries, bringing the slaves with them as they sailed the world. When the Vikings reached unexplored areas, they removed the slaves' shoes, did not give them food or water, told them to run as far as they could until nightfall, and then return the next day to report their findings. The Vikings knew the slaves would return because the slaves needed the Vikings' provisions.

The Swedish Vikings went to and occupied Poland, the Baltic countries, Russia, and Finland. Their influences were felt as far away as Egypt. There is documentation that Egyptians visited the Vikings, even staying with them in an encampment. Egyptians report the

Vikings as "vile, filthy, and dirty people". Egyptian beads and ceremonial artifacts were found buried near Tara in Ireland.

During raiding parties the Vikings sailed the oceans. They discovered Iceland when storms blew these raiding parties off course. Once discovered, Viking chieftains and warlords decided to colonize Iceland in the late 800s. From Iceland the Vikings went on to discover Greenland.

When they reached Greenland, the Vikings found it void of human life. The Eskimos came after the Viking settlements. The Viking Sagas state that the land was empty; they only colonized the southwest portion of Greenland. This area has a thin strip of greenery before the ice begins; the eastern coast was too rocky and had no beach for landing. From the late 800's to approximately 1100 AD with Greenland as their base, the Vikings began colonizing North America.

Scribes who could write in their Rune or Old Norse languages often accompanied the Vikings. These scribes recorded daily logs of all activities, often providing great detailed descriptions in order to capture the real-life essence of their adventures. These records document the Viking history and are called the *Sagas*. The Icelandic language is the original Viking language. The Sagas are kept intact in Iceland, clearly stating that these people were the first Europeans in North America. In some locations the Vikings arrived before the Native Americans. You can go to Iceland and read the Sagas in the museums.

Leif Ericksson, also known as "Erik the Red", planned expeditions from Iceland financed by Norway to identify and colonize North America. The Sagas talk about the deer that they found and trading with the Native Americans.

Around 1000 AD, Leif Ericksson made three designations in North America: Helluland, Markland, and Vinland. Each place was named after the characteristics in that region. Baffin Island, Newfoundland, and the northern coast of Labrador, Canada, was called "Helluland" or "land of flat stones". This area was deemed inhospitable and the expedition continued south.

Next they came to the coast of Maine and Massachusetts in New

England, naming this area "Markland" which meant "place of the forest". From there, the Vikings went into what is now Boston Harbor, describing the islands and coastline exactly as they are in this present day.

Traveling further south, the Vikings reached what is now known as the Mid-Atlantic States: Maryland, Virginia, and North Carolina. This region they named "Vinland" because they found wild grapes growing and created vineyards in that area. Vinland means "land of vines or grapes", or "place where the wine grows".

The government admitted there was a Viking settlement in Newfoundland beginning in 1000 AD. They claimed it was Vinland as Viking legends indicated. However Newfoundland is too rocky to sustain vineyards. It is known the Vikings colonized the area from Labrador all the way down to South Carolina and across into the American Midwest.

Christianity eventually destroyed the Vikings. At the time, Norway was not a country but had enclaves of different chieftains. Some of the chieftains colonized England and Ireland. The Celtic Kings were forced to acquiesce to what the Vikings wanted. Eventually with the help of wealthy merchants, kings from England, Poland, and Russia, as well as other chieftains took over Norway as a conglomeration.

King Olaf brutally introduced Christianity to Norway. He tried to force one of the powerful chieftains to convert to Catholicism but he refused. King Olaf had him tied to a pole, putting snakes in his mouth to kill him. That was not a very Christian thing to do, now was it?

But this is how Christianity was spread, through murder and torture. This is because Christianity is a political agenda and one of the original forms of mind-control. Religion is a way of controlling masses of people through guilt. You are imprinted that you are born in "sin" and If you don't do "X, Y, and Z" you will burn in purgatory forever.

Columbus did not discover America as taught in US schools. Rather he used stolen Viking maps from Iceland dating from the 900s-1000s to come to North America. The King of Spain would only fund his expeditions if he could provide maps for where he was going.

Columbus never set foot in North America; he never saw a tree or a blade of grass here.

What Columbus did do was take an entire band of prisoners to what became known as the Caribbean. The prisoners were actually Jews who refused to convert to Catholicism. They were released from Spanish prisons on the threat of execution. Columbus spread disease throughout the Caribbean with his infectious crew. He enslaved the indigenous men and raped their wives. He killed children and brought the slaves back to Spain. When people in the US celebrate "Columbus Day" what are they really celebrating? The destruction of a people, rape, murder, and slavery; that is what is really being celebrated.

There are even connections between Persia and the Vikings. Artifacts from both have been found in Norway and Sweden, even buried in the graves of noble men. Viking artifacts have been found in the US as far west as Colorado and Nevada. The Vikings traveled everywhere. Coins unearthed from the ground in Massachusetts and Maine were determined to come from Viking time periods. In Oklahoma, Viking artifacts were also discovered in a cave. Thousands of Viking artifacts have been found in the Great Lakes region. This is all proof that you cannot ignore.

21. FRISLAND

After the destruction of Atlantis, one piece of land that remained above water became an island known as "Frisland". Do not confuse this island with the old country next to Saxony near Holland and Germany in the Middle Ages called "Friesland".

This island existed south of Iceland on the Mid-Atlantic Ridge. If you look at the USGS map, almost every day earthquakes occur along this ridge of mountains. The Mid-Atlantic Ridge was the central part of Atlantis. These mountains were volcanic; that is what caused Atlantis to sink. This area of the Atlantic is very volatile; the continents are pulling apart so everything in the middle gets pulled. When you pull something apart whatever is on top sinks inward toward the opening that is created. This is what happened to Frisland.

The Vikings kept excellent records. There was a king and queen of Frisland. There are records in Scandinavia and Northern Europe that describe the trade between the islands thanks to the Vikings. The Sagas describe the Vikings traveling several times from Iceland to Frisland, then on to Greenland and North America. The Vikings colonized the entire eastern coast corridor of North America.

One day they went to Frisland and it was not there. An entire island leftover from Atlantean culture, in moments vanished off the face of the Earth.

If you look at the old globes in Iceland they have Frisland on them as plain as day. The same thing can happen to Iceland because it is on the same mountain ridge that went underwater. Iceland could sink just like Frisland did, overnight. However, Iceland is growing and expanding, so most likely it will remain intact.

One day it is there and the next it is gone. To this day, sometimes

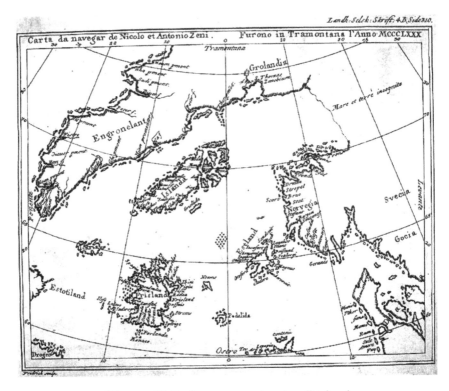

Figure 21.1: Norse map showing Frisland

travelers in the North Atlantic and even in the South Pacific will see land rising up then go back down. This is very common off the coast of Iceland where there is volcanic activity. There was also an island called Christmas Island. It appeared on Christmas day only to vanish again several days later.

Iceland has been extremely lucky for a period of time. It is one of the newest landmasses on the Earth and has not been above water very long. The Mid-Atlantic Ridge has increased seismic activity and is currently being pulled apart. The section to the right of the ridge is moving east. The section to the left is moving southwest.

Iceland is only a few thousand years old and is a relatively recent geologic development. No trees exist in Iceland. The Vikings cut down the few trees that were there for shelter and ship construction.

Iceland is basically a large volcano. This is evident by the unnerving sulfur smell in the tap water. The water is pure in the sense that there are no bacteria or viruses but this is due to it being full of radon. Yes, the water is clean, but similar to natural chemotherapy!

22. Portugal's Gibraltar Straits Island

After the main continent of Atlantis sank there is evidence of another piece of land that remained above water. This island was approximately the size of Portugal off the coast of Portugal and had an archipelago that connected to Morocco.

Plato wrote that when he travelled to Egypt he found documents in Alexandria that described a very large island with elephants and a high civilization that existed between the Gibraltar Straits. There is geological evidence that there was land connecting North Africa and even parts of Portugal to this island. Woolly mammoth skeletons were found in the Atlantic Ocean where this island once existed. Tons and tons of copper were also discovered in the same region.

In the 1960s and 70s Russian, British, and American ships of private independent researchers sent probes in this area and found sand that is usually found on a beach, not under the ocean. They also found evidence of mountain ranges that were once above the ocean.

The Egyptians speak about these people coming into the Mediterranean and attacking Egypt. There are hieroglyphic paintings on the walls in Egyptian pyramids that talk about and show the army attacking from that island. What happened to that island?

The destruction of Maldek created the asteroid belt, for thousands of years and even still today there are comets and asteroids left over from the explosion still in orbit in our solar system. In ancient times the fragments were hitting the Earth quite regularly. One of the disasters described in the history of Greece, Egypt, and Babylonia hit the Atlantic Ocean in approximately 2,500 BC. This created tidal waves, tsunamis, volcanic eruptions that allegedly caused the island in the Gibraltar Straits to sink beneath the ocean.

23. CELTIC EMPIRE

The Celtic civilization existed from approximately 1000 BC to 500 AD. People normally associate the Celts with the United Kingdom. Even Eastern Europe had a large Celtic culture that existed. Celts also traveled from Ireland all the way across to North America.

There are documents in Ireland of Celtic priests who left in their ships and sailed west to what was described as a very wealthy land. They were actually referring to Frisland, their first stop. They would come back with a lot of supplies and information from Frisland. It was a relatively easy trip to Frisland; from there it really was not that far to North America.

The language the ancient Celtics used was called "Ogam". This was a written Esperanto. It was a language that was used for writing so that everyone in Europe could understand each other. The Ogam symbols and writing has been found in North America. Some of the artifacts are over 2000 years old.

There is a plethora of Celtic artifacts found in North America. All along the Eastern Coast of the US from New England even into Virginia, Celtic altars were found that were dedicated to gods and goddesses. In the northern part of Georgia, artifacts were unearthed near Indian villages with Celtic inscriptions from around 1000 AD. Records indicate the Celtic People went north into the Great Lakes region. The problem was they could not return home since their vessels were destroyed. So, they decided to make North America their new Celtic Empire.

This is a precursor to the Lost Tribes of Israel. When the Romans came to the Holy Land/Ancient Israel, the tribes were dispersed. 10 of the 12 tribes are "missing" because they spread out. Meanwhile the

Figure 23.1: Celtic Empire

Celts were spreading out over various parts of Europe. People always think the Celtic people were only in the United Kingdom, however they spanned all the way into Turkey, which also has some Celtic connections.

24. LOST TRIBES OF ISRAEL

The "Lost Tribes of Israel" is a very sensitive topic. 10 Tribes left Israel. Many of them went to the Caucasus Mountains. A lot of them went into what became Turkey, known as "Galatia" in ancient biblical times.

The New Testament says that the Apostles mostly went to what is now Turkey. They preached in Turkey when Turkey was part of the Roman Empire. Populated Turkey can ultimately trace its ancestry to the Hebrew tribes.

The country of Danmark/Denmark and the Danube River both derived their names from the tribe of Dan, which was one of the Hebrew tribes that disappeared. There are other tribes that possibly became the Moors and the Greeks, as well as the Khazars, who mixed with Sumerian descendants.

David Ben-Gurion, the first president of Israel in 1948, declared and traced 50 million Jews to the descendants of the "Lost Tribes" who were located in Western and Southern China. These Jews were killed in the 1700-1800s at the hands of the Catholic Church. When the Catholic Church reached China only to find Christians and Jews all the non-Catholics were systematically executed.

The Catholic Church has killed more people than the Nazis. The Catholic Church killed anyone that had any psychic, or mental, abilities even though psychic abilities are listed in the Bible and are part of what Christ supposedly did.

The Church did not want anyone with any abilities that the Church could not control. For this reason, anyone who demonstrated any "special" mental abilities outside of the Catholic Church commission was called a "demonic entity" or a "heretic" that needed to be either

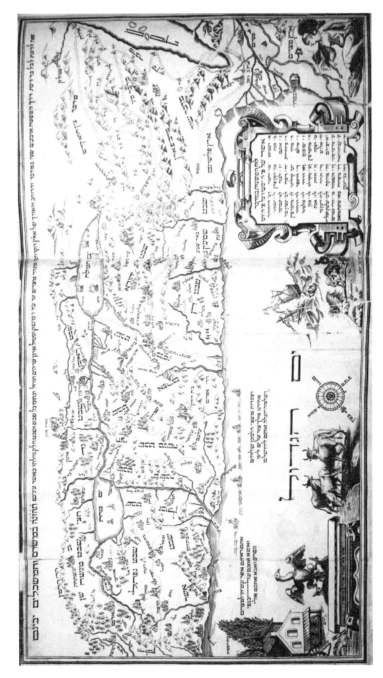

Figure 24.1: Lost Tribes of Israel (Israel map from 1695 in Amsterdam Haggada by Abraham Bar-Jacob)

converted or executed. The Catholic Church seemed to forget the words of Christ directly from the Bible where he said "the works that I do shall he do also; and greater works than these shall he do". Even the Bible sanctions these things and even greater things, but the Catholic Church said "No! It's not from the Pope!"

According to both Edgar Cayce and the Mormon religion, the "Lost Tribes of Israel" fled to Central America in 3,000 BC to become the Olmecs and Toltecs.

25. INCA

Central and South America have a unique situation because these are some of the few places where refugees of Lemuria and Atlantis mixed. This means that there is a "double dose" of Reptilian/Human genetics in these areas. One of the Mayan objects of worship was the Reptilians.

The Incan and Mayan cultures both have legends of tall, white-skinned people who came from the east across the ocean. These white-skinned people were considered to be their new gods. In actuality, these people were the Vikings who colonized and mixed with the entire region, from North to South America. When the European Spaniards came centuries later, the Central and South Americans thought they were returning Vikings because the Vikings had promised to return.

Figure 25.1: Incan Empire

The Incan culture describes their leaders and foundational ancestors as tall, blond and red-haired people. Incan legend states that their civilization began with a tall, blond-haired, blue-eyed man with a beard. Legend also says the people who came with him married the local natives living in the mountains. The Incas say that this was the beginning of their Holy or Royal Empire from which they are descended.

One of the Sagas uncovered in Iceland describes a leader of a Viking group called "Inka". This was a legend from the people before the Vikings that said there was a leader who had a disagreement with the chieftains in Scandinavia so he fled in their ships across the ocean. The Sagas indicate he went out into the ocean searching for a new land to colonize. He took a band of men with him who sailed away and never came back.

Inka left Scandinavia in the late 900s AD. The Incan Empire began in 1000 AD and ended in 1600 AD. No one ever puts together the Inca origins with the Vikings, but this is how the Incan civilization began. The Incan Empire was vast, lasting 600 years. This civilization was larger than most countries in present day.

The Andes mountain range in South America is very similar to the Himalaya Mountains, with crisscrossing tunnels and caverns throughout the entire range. In the 1980s, two men were mountain-climbing in the western region of Peru in a very high elevation with only snow and rock. Here, they found a little boy kneeling on his knees frozen in Incan clothing.

At first they thought they found a statue, but soon realized it was a real frozen body. Thinking it was a great find, they brought it down to their camp at a lower elevation. The warmer temperature caused the body to start to thaw. Blood started trickling out of the ears and nose, and the body looked like it was beginning to move.

The men brought the boy to a hospital in Cuzco where the body died. Hospital authorities said that this little boy was around 10-12 years old and had been in suspended animation for centuries. A couple of years later another body was found at high elevations in Peru that was also defrosted and died. Had these bodies been left alone perhaps proper protocols to bring them back to life might eventually be found. The Inca knew something about how to freeze and suspend the body for indefinite periods of time.

In 1999, three Incan children were found frozen at 22,000 feet on the summit of Mount Llullaillaco, a volcano 300 miles west near the

Chilean border. They were religiously sacrificed and froze to death as they slept. According to Incan beliefs, the children did not die, but joined their ancestors and watched over their villages from the mountaintops. 500 years later they still appeared like sleeping children. Together, they are known as the "Boy and Girl of Lightning". The Llullaillaco maiden is known as "La Doncella". The 15-year-old Llullaillaco maiden "La Doncella" can be seen in an exhibition at the Museum of High Altitude Archaeology in Salta, Argentina.

It is proven that the Inca used to do brain surgery and extensive dental work. There are skulls that show patches that have been cut out and sewn back in.

Incan civilization was astounding.

26. Bolivia Underground Tunnels

Tiahuanaco is located on the border of Peru and Bolivia at approximately 13,000 feet in elevation. At Tiahuanaco you can see faces that definitely are not human.

There is an entire complex of incredible underground tunnels throughout the Tiahuanaco area in Bolivia. The Bolivian Government gave me permission to go anywhere I wanted to search for tunnel entrances in Tiahuanaco.

The archaeologist who invited me said that in 1982 he and a group of researchers found a cavern that went down into the earth near Lake Titicaca. When they broke into the cavern they found a bank of computers that were estimated to be 15,000 years old.

In the middle of the room, in the center of the computers was a slab with a 3-meter/9-foot tall Cyclops in suspended animation. If they had known how to work the computers, who knows what would have happened had they awakened the Cyclops. Due to internal political unrest, the Bolivian Government ordered a military crew to seal up the entrance. With the political upheaval at the time, the records with the exact location of this entrance were lost. I was given the assignment to find the entrance to the underground chamber once again, so that is what I did while I was there.

Around Bolivia in La Paz and Lake Titicaca at 12,500 feet there is evidence of seashells and coastal environments. If you go to Tiahuanaco in Bolivia, along some of the lower elevations of the mountains you find beach sand and sea shells as well. There is evidence that there were once ports at 12,800 feet. Geological evidence shows that the land was thrust up from sea level to 12,800 feet within a matter of a few hours.

When Lemuria sank the western coast of South America was thrust upwards. There is physical evidence of an immediate shift - something went down and something went up. If a continent in the Pacific Ocean suddenly sank abruptly and violently the tectonic force and subduction would push the western plate of South America upwards. This is similar to the New Madrid Fault line in North America. The edge of the old Atlantean tectonic plate is now mid-continent. Theoretically there are not supposed to be any mid-tectonic lines, yet one exists.

At night over Lake Titicaca lights flash and zoom up into space. There are also a plethora of statues with non-human forms. I was taken to a room in a museum that was not open to the public. I was not allowed to take pictures.

In a glass case was a basket with dozens of elongated skulls that were not human. Supposedly, Egyptians and Incas attached boards to the heads of babies to make the head elongated. The skulls in the museum had different suture marks on them which were clearly evident. These elongated skulls were not formed by boards. These elongated skulls were definitely from a different species.

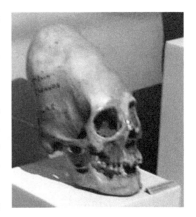

Figure 26.1: Elongated skull (museum display)

The governments know that these things exist and have physical evidence but they do not release this proof to the public. Humans are not natural to this planet. You are an alien species. No one can ultimately trace their ancestry to the Earth because Earth was originally a water planet. There was no life like you know it here. Everything you see on the planet was either brought or manufactured here; it did not originate on Earth.

27. MAYA

The Mayan civilization began in 200 AD and lasted until 1400 AD, existing for approximately 1200 years. The Mayans worshipped reptiles; reptiles were holy to them.

Mayans were located throughout Central America in Costa Rica, Nicaragua, El Salvador, Guatemala, Belize, Honduras, and into the southern part of Mexico. You can see that it is a very short trip to the Gulf of Mexico coast and then an easy trip up the Mississippi River valley where the Mayans traded with the local Indians and Vikings.

Further up through the heartland of North America, the Great Lakes were also a trade center for the Mayans and Vikings.

The Mayans were not the only ones in Central America. Before the Mayans, the Olmecs existed from 1800 BC to approximately 1000 BC. Toltecs existed for a very short period of time from 900 AD to 1200 AD before the Mayans conquered the Toltecs, thus ending their civilization.

The Mayan civilization closed up the first time when a comet hit the Earth approximately 1200-1300 BC, creating the 10 plagues in Egypt and destroying the Minoan civilization.

The Mayans recorded immigration from the east at approximately August 12th, 3013 BC which was the state of destruction. There were black, red, and white volcanic stones that were popular in Atlantis, Central America, and the island off the coast of Portugal in the Gibraltar Straits. Of course, you know that August 12th is officially "Montauk Day". It is significant that it is mentioned in Mayan records.

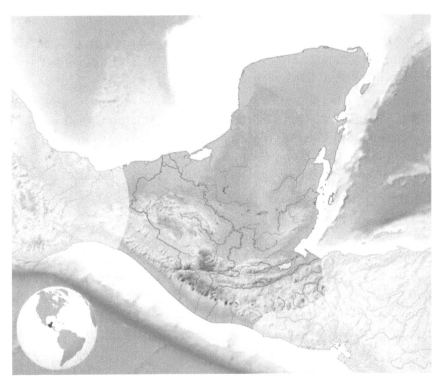

Figure 27.1: Mayan Empire

28. AZTECS

The Aztecs were located further north in Central America. The Aztecs were a conglomeration of various indigenous people that came together around 1325 AD and perished in the 1500s when they were destroyed by the Spaniards.

The Aztecs began with the legend that states the indigenous people wandered Mexico in search of the land that their god Huitzilopochtli had promised. They were in search of an Eagle perched on a cactus devouring a serpent which they found in Tenochtitlan. The Aztecs developed this area into the largest Mesoamerican city ever and thus began the Aztec Empire.

The Aztec Emperor Montezuma II resided in Tenochtitlan, which became Mexico City at the time when the Spaniards invaded in the 1500s AD. Tenochtitlan was a huge city on an island in Lake Texcoco. When the Spanish conquistadors arrived on the coast they were met by emissaries of Montezuma who brought gold as gifts.

What did the Spaniards do with the beautiful gifts that the Aztecs gave them? They kept the gifts, killed all the emissaries but one who they sent back to Montezuma to alert him of the Spaniards and their ferocity.

When the Spaniards reached Lake Texcoco they saw Tenochtitlan was in the middle of a lake. There was a long bridge that connected the end of the shore to the city.

As the Spaniards readied for battle, Montezuma came bearing more gifts, thinking that these new arrivals were the expected gods returning from across the water. The Spaniards took this opportunity to kill Montezuma and enter the city.

Provinces dépendant de la triple alliance ★ Membres de la triple alliance   Mixes État ou peuple indépendant
○ Chef-lieu de province tributaire   ● Chef-lieu d'État indépendant

Figure 28.1: Aztec territories

The Spaniards destroyed Temples and homes; massacred the people, and took all the gold, melting it into bars to make it more portable. This was the sad end to the Aztec civilization.

Weren't the Spaniards lovely? They did this everywhere they went in the name of Jesus Christ and the Catholic Church who sent them under the puppets of Rome, King Ferdinand and Queen Isabella.

The Aztecs, Maya, Toltecs, and Olmecs all worshipped Reptilian gods. They all sacrificed human beings to the Reptilian gods. At the top of the step pyramids on the sacrificial altar they cut the living heart out of a person while he/she was still alive. After removing the heart the body was decapitated and kicked down the steps. The head was used to play futbol, or soccer, as the game became to be known. When the Europeans came they found the people playing games with heads, not balls.

All the ancient civilizations including the Mayan and Aztecs have common stories of huge flaming balls flying across Earth skies. When this happened, they thought the gods were angry at them so this led to more human sacrifices to appease the gods. These asteroids were pieces of Maldek.

The crystal skulls do not come from Central or South America; they came from Atlantis and were alien technology. Even today, technology does not exist that can recreate them.

29. MONGOL EMPIRES

FIRST MONGOL EMPIRE   The Mongols picked up where the Khazars and Vikings left off. The Viking civilization basically came to an end around the 1100s AD. The Mongols invaded Eastern Europe in the 1200s and into the 1300s, flooding across Ukraine, Poland, and Russia. If you have Eastern European genetics, guess what? There is a high probability that you have Eastern Asian/Mongol genetics as well.

The Mongol Empire extended from Korea, to India, and into Eastern Europe. This was a huge empire including almost all of Asia and parts of Europe.

Attila the Hun was the first one to organize the Mongol tribes, creating the army and Empire that swept across Asia and into Europe, ending in what is now known as *Hun*gary - aptly named after its conqueror. Attila the Hun brought an end to the Roman Empire.

The language of Hungary known as "Magyar" is different from any other language in Europe. Magyar matches almost identically to the ancient Sumerian language. Magyar is also the closest language related to Finnish. Magyar has also been determined as the foundational language or syntax of the Aborigines in Australia.

Attila the Hun had his armies and emissaries all over Europe. The Tatar people in Russia really have Mongol origins. The history of Europe and the World is not what you have learned; there is a deep connection between Finland, Russia, and Iraq... and Australia.

SECOND MONGOL EMPIRE   While in Hungary, Attila the Hun had many, many wives. He was about to marry a new wife when he was killed on his wedding night. Approximately 750 years later

Genghis Khan, inspired by Attila's conquests, united the Mongolian Tribes together and followed the same route, only he did more.

Genghis Khan conquered India and went all the way into Russia, Poland, and Lithuania. Russian people have Asian genetics as well; this is also why the Chinese are presently involved in Russia. In the 1200s Genghis Khan spread out to cover more territory than anyone before, and had the largest Empire in ancient times.

The Second Mongol Empire lasted approximately 200 years from 1200-1400 AD. To compare, the United States is just over 200 years old; you can accomplish a lot in two centuries!

In the 750 years between Attila's reign and Genghis Khan, the Mongolians incorporated the Chinese dynasties into South and Southeast Asia. This is where the Hmong people came from that are in Laos. The Mongol civilization/culture exists throughout China and even into Korea. Mongolian genetics are evidenced by their round faces and thick bodies. "Hmong" may be derived from "Mongol".

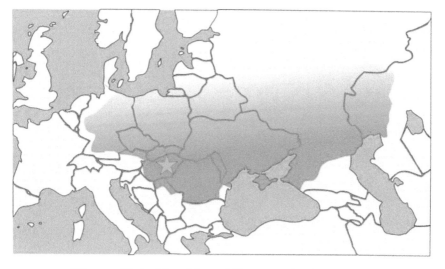

Figure 29.1: First Mongol Empire - Attila the Hun

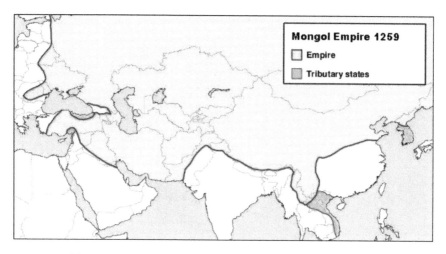

Figure 29.2: Second Mongol Empire - Genghis Khan

30. CHINA'S INFLUENCE

China began in 2000 BC. The last of the Chinese dynasties came to an end by the hands of the British in 1911. China covers all of Southeast Asia into Korea, some of the disputed islands between Russia, Japan, and into Nepal. Even though the Nepalese are not very oriental looking, they are connected to the Chinese and practice Buddhism.

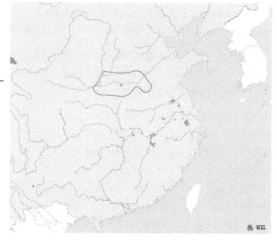

Figure 30.1: China Xia dynasty (green outline: proposed Xia territory)

The Chinese reported discovering and colonizing the West Coast of the United States, including many of the Pacific areas along the West Coast of North America. There are documents in China from 500 AD that show the Chinese had been in North America. The Chinese had scribes with them just like the Vikings. And, just like the Vikings, they were excellent sailors and map surveyors. There is even an accurate world map confirmed from the year 1093 AD. This is proof that the Chinese and the Vikings were extensive world seafarers.

There is a mountain on the coast of Oregon with several caves where Chinese artifacts were found that date to over a thousand years ago. Wood from a Chinese vessel from about 1000 AD was discovered in these same caves. The Chinese explored the Pacific Coast from Alaska to Mexico. The Chinese now own the Panama Canal. Perhaps they threatened to reveal this "hidden history" to the world and that is why they are "allowed" to own it?

Even now China encourages their population to immigrate and spread out all over the world so that there is a Chinese influence, or at least a minority, everywhere. In Western China there is the Persian/Islamic majority in Xinjiang province. The Chinese have relocated the Han Chinese from the Eastern and Central parts of China into Western China. This was done so they become the majority and then overrule the Persian/Muslim previous majority. The same thing is happening in Tibet which the Chinese call "Xizàng province".

In Tibet, you are not allowed to call this area "Tibet"; its official name is "Xizàng province". China considers Tibet part of China, not an independent country.

There are only 6 million Tibetans in this vast territory. There is not much of an effort by the Chinese to move its population into the area. Tibet is dry and arid, making it difficult to grow crops and develop agriculture. There is not much the Chinese can do with the limited industries and jobs in Tibet. In fact, if the Chinese government moves too many Chinese into Tibet there will be high unemployment necessitating government subsidies.

The "cultural revolution" destroyed Tibetan Monasteries and killed Tibetan Priests. In a brilliant way, what they have decided to do is start rebuilding the Temples. Now they can have a tourist industry that will fuel the economy.

31. Moors & Arabs

The Moors and the Arabs are two different people that connect through Islam. We get the name "Morocco" from the Moors. The Moors are an offshoot of Egyptians and Berbers. The Moors migrated west across the Sahara desert and North Africa to the Atlantic coastline. Originally the Moors were not Muslim; they had their own animistic religion. When Islam developed, especially as it grew in the early 600s, it spread rapidly across the desert regions. From there Islam began creating its own New World Order.

The Moors spread into Europe, as far north as Holland. The Moors actually began in 100 AD but did not become Muslim until the 600s. For 500 years the Moorish Civilization was not Islamic. In 1492, Queen Isabella and King Ferdinand removed the Moors from Spain with the intention of expanding the Spanish culture and territory.

This is why they funded Christopher Columbus to go to the so called "New World", which really was not so new after all. The Moors civilization did not actually end as intended. Instead, they were simply pushed back into North Africa, ultimately creating Morocco. The Moors were one of the reasons that Charlemagne was adamant about converting everyone to Catholicism because the Moors were a direct threat to Rome.

The Pope decided to dissolve Islam, pushing it back wherever it could be suppressed. The Roman Catholic Church created the Inquisition in the 12th century to be able to interrogate people. "The fight against heretics" went from country to country to make sure everyone was a Catholic. Not a Christian, but a Catholic. You could not be just any denomination, you had to be Catholic. If not, you were either executed or had to convert.

When the Moors took over Spain, the South of France, and other countries, they accepted other religions even though they encouraged people to convert to Islam. The Moors allowed the Jews to exist in their culture unhindered. They also allowed the Christians. The problem was the Islamic people were particularly against the Christians. Because of this, the Pope ordered the execution of the people of Islam. That is the difference between Christianity, the Moors, and Islam.

The Moors and the Islamic cultures retaliated all across North Africa and the Middle East. Basically, the 21st century is a recreation of the Crusades - Christians against Muslims - again. The conflict has never really ended. Even as far back in history as 600 AD, for about 1400 years, all of the areas throughout Northern Africa to the Middle East were Muslim. Even today they are Muslim, except for the southern part of Europe. Just because someone is Muslim does not mean they are Arabic; they could be Persian, Turkish, Afghani, etc.

Muslim populations have existed in Bosnia, Albania, Macedonia, Kosovo, and Croatia for many centuries since the Ottoman invasion of Europe.

Indonesia in Southeast Asia is the largest Muslim country in the world with over 200 million people. The Philippines is the only Catholic country in Asia. South Korea is the 2nd most Christianized country in Asia with approximately half the population Christian.

32. OTTOMAN EMPIRE

The Ottoman Empire is extremely fascinating; it began approximately 1299 AD and ended in 1923 right after World War I. Historically, all Turkish cultures started around 500 AD, existing to the present moment. Turkey is a very large country of 70 million people.

The Ottomans took over the entire region including Greece, Bulgaria, and Romania. The empire stretched all the way into Hungary as well. Muslims live in the Balkan area of Serbia, Croatia, and Bosnia as a result of the Ottoman Empire invasions over the last few centuries. This is also why there are Muslims in Europe. The Ottomans occupied Egypt, Israel, and the Middle East.

The Crusades started to get going around the year 1099 when the Christians or Catholics of Europe decided to follow the Pope's call to retake Jerusalem. They were funded by the wealthy landowners from France and Germany.

In 1099 one of the largest Crusades left France, traveling all the way across Europe. They travelled over land part of the way, sailing by ship the rest of the way. The Crusade landed at the city of Akko/Acre, which is next to the city of Haifa in Israel. To this day you can see the huge Crusader castle on the coast in Akko or Acre, as it is called now. From this castle the Crusaders went on the road in their quest to conquer Jerusalem.

When the Muslims invaded Europe there was a lot of death and destruction. But, they let the civilization or the people in the area survive, encouraging them to become Muslims. When the Crusades entered into a Muslim area they killed everyone, burned the city, and left nothing. This is what they did to Jerusalem in 1099. They entered and killed thousands of people, including women and children.

Figure 32.1: Ottoman Empire

They executed them just for being Muslim and living in Jerusalem. They raped people, cut them in pieces, and were very proud of their actions. The Pope honored them for their acts.

The Hospitallers originated from the Crusaders who were involved in medical care. They were called the Hospitallers since there were so many people injured and wounded that needed medical treatment. The Crusaders were treated and then had no other choice but to occupy the land. Some stayed in the Holy Land where they died, never to return home to their families. When you joined the Crusades one of the things you had to do was give up all your wealth, possessions, and say goodbye to your family. That was it; very few returned.

124

Once Jerusalem was Christian again wealthy Europeans came to Jerusalem and Bethlehem to see where Christ lived. The Hospitallers discovered Muslim raiders that lived in the hills who were attacking the Christian pilgrims. There were originally 9 Templars who went to Jerusalem to protect the Christian pilgrims. The Templars were really an offshoot of the Hospitallers.

33. TEMPLARS

There are two different versions of the Templars cross. Both were used, and are still used even to this very day. The Templars began their adventures in the holy land in the late 11th and early 12th centuries. It was after that time they started using these symbols. The first version (see fig. 33.1, bottom) was mainly what they used on their tunics.

The original version (see fig. 33.1, top), also called the "Maltese Cross", was used in the ornamental and ceremonial items. They have also been called the "Knights of Malta", hence the Maltese Cross. The original color of the Maltese cross was gold, and was older than what the Templars used it for. The Templars took it for a reason.

They are called "Templars" from the documents and secret information they discovered under the Holy Temple Mount in Solomon's Stables. What they found was so profound that it undermined the Catholic Church. This is why they had their own ceremonies and rituals, and their own empire, within an empire. The Templars first headquarters was based in Jerusalem on the Temple Mount; they had their Crusader castle in Akko/Acre.

Figure **33.1:** Templars crosses

The Church was worried about what they found under the Holy Temple Mount in Solomon's Stables. Of course, the Templars would not reveal or give the information to the Catholic Church in its entirety.

The Church actually had to make a strange alliance with the Templars so they wouldn't reveal the information to the public. It only remained within the Templar Brotherhood, or organization, and was not allowed to go beyond that under threat of death.

On Friday October 13th, 1307 a majority of the Templars were arrested by King Philip IV of France, who was in league with Pope Clement, a childhood friend. This is why Friday the 13th is considered a bad luck day. From 1307-1314 they tortured and killed many of the Templars. The rest of

Figure 33.2: Seal of Templars

the Templars snuck away with their ships and caravans, supposedly hoarding all sorts of gold and artifacts they found. They were never seen or heard of again officially.

The Templar symbols are also found related to pirates. When the Templars were attacked at sea they would retaliate and raid the other ships of their supplies so they could not escape. Other criminal elements and copy-cat pirates would masquerade as the Templars. This began the era of pirates in the Mediterranean, Atlantic, and the Caribbean. It then became an entire romanticized lifestyle up to this day with movies and Halloween costumes, etc.

Did the Templars really have a physical treasure with silver, gold, jewels, and where did they go? The idea is the treasure wasn't actually monetary, but a treasure of information about the true history of Jmmanuel or Jesus Christ and his marriage to Mary Magdalene and that they had children. The Holy Grail is not an object, but the symbolic representation of the womb of Mary Magdalene, that was the "Holy Chalice" as they called it. From her came the offspring of Christ. When that merged with the Khazars, through the Franks and Merovingians in France and Germany in the 1300's, the descendants became the Illuminati. They claim "Holy Rite" to rule the world because their ancestry was traced back to Christ. The Queen of England, the Rothschild's, and all the families say that they have every right to control the populace because they have the genetics of

Christ. They place themselves on pedestals and claim responsibility, in their view, to control and rule the world. In addition to having a higher percentage of Reptilian DNA, the Illuminati families also have a mindset of being superior to mammalian life forms. They feel that the reptilian format more closely resembles the God-Mind traits of never needing to evolve or adapt to environmental changes.

There is a Templar legend that supposedly they buried a treasure on Oak Island off the coast of Nova Scotia. In 1795 Daniel McInnis discovered a depression in the ground that he excavated known as the "Money Pit". After two centuries a treasure has never been found buried in this location. There were stones found on the island with inscriptions that had Templar references. People have been digging, and digging looking for treasure, to the point the island is almost destroyed.

When the British came to the new world towards New England and Southern Rhode Island they saw a tower built in Templar style. It was already established on the coast and had obviously been built a couple hundred years earlier. This indicates the Templars came to North America and established some type of colony. There are Templar organizations in the United States, Canada, and throughout the world. They use these symbols on their literature and buildings. Anyone that really is a descendant or connected to the real Templars is not going to reveal that. They won't have an organization you can join or will publicize it. The real secrets are not revealed under penalty of death.

Unfortunately most of the Templar information was confiscated by the Catholic Church after they were killed. The Grand Master of the Templars, Jacques de Molay, was tortured for months in hopes he would reveal where they had hidden information and artifacts in Paris. He refused to divulge any information and was even executed for it. The Church wanted material things, and to eliminate anyone that could undermine them financially. The Templars were actually the ones that started the banking system, not the Jews. They owned vast territories of land and were the largest land holders in the world at that time. They were the richest organization, even though they personally gave up all of their possessions in order to become part of that group.

Originally there were 9 Templars that started the organization. Over time, they had their knights to protect them and do their work since they were so busy excavating the Temple Mount. The Templars had many other soldiers, subsequent to the original organization, that did their work and fanned out afterwards. Those groups eventually started the ideas and legends of the pirates and the secret Templar organizations.

The Templars still secretly exist, also going by the name "Priory of Sion". They are intimately connected to the Jesuits, the military arm of the Vatican. The current Pope, Francesco I, is the first Jesuit (Black) Pope. Prophecy claims that this is the last Pope before the introduction of the New World Religion.

34. WALDENSIANS/VAUDOIS/ VALDENSES

The Waldensian territory stretched from France into Italy, and even into Eastern Europe. The bulk of it was in Southern France and Northern Italy. Waldensians were also knows as the "Vaudois". There is a lot of controversy about how they got their name. "Wald" in German means forest. One theory says because of persecution, they fled into the mountains and forested areas, and therefore were called "Waldensians", the people of the forest.

Another theory put forward largely by the Catholic Church, says that was there was a man named Waldo who established a sect, which then incorporated his name into it. However, the Waldensians existed centuries before Waldo was born so this could not be true. There are a lot of stories created to explain this group of people. The truth of the matter is the word "Vaudois" in French comes from an old word in Latin that represented people that do secret, psychic, or hidden things. The word was used as early as the 4th century.

The verbal history of the Waldensians told by the Waldensians themselves say that they are the descendants of the Apostles. The Apostles spread out from the Holy Lands into what is now Turkey, Egypt, and Southern Europe. They eventually wound up in Rome which was their goal, especially for St. Paul.

St. Paul's original name was Saul; he was from the southern part of what is now Turkey. He was a Roman citizen and had his famous revelation on the road to Damascus. St. Paul was the one who came to Rome and started to spread information. The original information is very close to the Waldensians' beliefs.

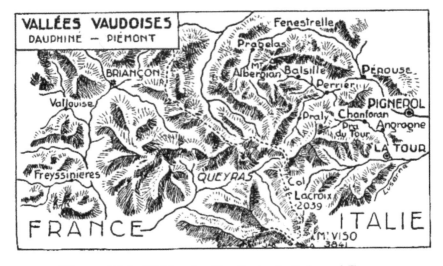

Figure 34.1: Waldensian Territories in Italy and France

The Nag Hammadi documents from Egypt, the Gospel of Philip, Thomas, and Mary Magdalene are the foundations of the Waldensian beliefs. They did not believe in an intermediary between human beings and God. They believed you do not have to go through Christ, but you have God within you, therefore you can go directly into the God-Mind wherever you are. They believed that women had equal rights to men and could be preachers, and participate in ceremonies.

They did not believe in church buildings. They believed that the people constituted the church, or temple, preferring to worship outdoors.

Waldensian beliefs were similar to those of the Cathars. Of course, all of this was against the Catholic Church and was considered heresy at the time because of Mary Magdalene.

The Waldensian symbol is the Maltese cross which originally was called the Waldensian Cross before being used by the Templars. The symbol represents the creation of life based on the 4 elements, the 4 protein bases of DNA, and the Mind of God. The Templars used the symbol based on the information they knew of Jmmanuel's marriage, his children, and what he believed. The Gospels of Thomas, Philip and Mary Magdalene were suppressed for this reason by the Catholic Church.

A lot of research has been done on the Waldensian people with evidence showing they existed since the time right after Christ. They originally left with Mary Magdalene and were part of her entourage, traveling to different territories with her. Ultimately this particular group ended up in Rome before the Holy Roman Empire. The Romans became the Holy Roman Empire when they adopted Catholicism. That form of religion became the state religion by law. There could be no other religion except Catholicism.

The Waldensians were accused by the Catholic Church of being evil heretics, a word the church used constantly for people who were not Catholic. The Waldensians had very strong armies; they invaded Spain, France, and were trespassing into Catholic territory. This was a problem for the Church; they were upset about losing territory, monetary wealth, as well as population. They were pursued by the Catholic Church which considered them the most dangerous people of all time. The Waldensians knew the truth of Jmmanuel, Mary Magdalene, and other secrets that the Church did not want revealed to the public.

When France became a Catholic country the Waldensians were expelled. Thousands of Waldensians were imprisoned throughout Southern France. Two hundred were hidden in the hills of what is now Northern Italy in the Piedmont region. These 200 were able to fend off thousands the King's soldiers and mercenaries off and on for hundreds of years.

When the King finally agreed to release Waldensian prisoners, granting them safe passage by walking across the mountains during the winter to Switzerland, thousands died along the journey. All of the children 12 and under were placed throughout Europe with Catholic families to try to stop their knowledge from spreading.

Eventually the Waldensians were expelled from Europe because they were considered to be heretics and anti-Catholic. They were said to be the "Mother of the Protestant Reformation". Most people don't realize this as you hear more about the Cathars and not much about the Waldensians. In the United States and North America no one knows about the Waldensians because of the three small colonies that settled here the one in New York is gone, the one in Monett,

Missouri is dying out, and the one in Valdese, North Carolina is losing its identity to the Presbyterian Church with whom most US Waldensians aligned themselves.

Europe and South America are more familiar with them; Europe because of their origins and history; South America because many persecuted Waldensians found sanctuary here.

The Waldensians were persecuted for hundreds of years; eventually they fled into the hills of Italy and hid in Piedmont. The Cathars and the Waldensians became allies because they had a common enemy. The Cathars believed in two Gods, a good God, and a bad God. This is represented on the altar in the church in Rennes-le-Château. Here, there is not one Baby Jesus, but two. One on the lap of Mary and one on the lap of a Saint. Supposedly there were twin babies born, one had good ways, and the other had evil ways. This is where the origins of the evil twins started. The Cathars took that symbolically and said there is a good God, and a bad God. Of course that was very contrary to the Catholic Church.

The Church successfully eliminated the Cathars; they completely burned all of their homes and villages. If you go to France where they were located you will see the destruction that was caused by the Catholic armies. The Church had difficulties finding people to do this for them especially in the Middle Ages after the Reformation. Often the Church used Catholics that were expelled from countries that did not accept Catholicism. For example, the Irish became Catholic, but were expelled by the British because the British did not like Catholicism. A lot of the Catholic Irish were sent to France and Italy where they were used as slaves and soldiers to attack heretics. You can look this up in conventional history.

When the Franks invaded the Hebrew Kingdom of Mary Magdalene in the 500s, the remnants of her Hebrew Kingdom fled into the French Alps in the province of what is now Aix-en-Provence. The remnants of the Apostolic Waldensians who were persecuted in Rome also fled to the north. Here, the Magdalene lineage joined with the Waldensian Apostolic refugees in the Alpine region of Italy and France.

When the Islamic Moors invaded France and were fighting the Catholic armies, they allied with the Waldensians because the Church was their common enemy. This group of people where the True Original Christians, although they didn't name themselves "Christians". However, they were not Catholic and they did not consider themselves "Protestant". They simply believed in God in the correct way. Their alliance with the Moors further provoked an already angry, hostile, and vengeful Church.

35. WALDENSIAN EXTERMINATIONS

From the 1200s to the 1600s Rome intensely campaigned to completely eliminate all Waldensians from the face of the Earth. The Church worried that the Moors/Waldensian group was gaining a stronghold in the mountains. They were well entrenched and safe; the Romans could not easily reach them among the high peaks and steep-sided valleys. The Catholic Church was afraid they would align with the Mongols who invaded Europe in the 1200s, thus bringing the Mongols into Rome. Had that happened it would have been the end of the Roman Catholic Church forever. This is another reason why the Church started a campaign to eliminate the Waldensians in the most brutal manner possible.

The Catholic armies decimated Waldensian villages, throwing children off cliffs, impaling elderly people, beheading and parading the heads around the valleys. They barricaded people in buildings, homes, and caves, setting them on fire. They buried the Waldensians alive, raped women and children, stripped them naked, pulled them behind horses, chopped off their limbs and did every unconscionable crime against humanity possible in their effort to dehumanize, traumatize, victimize, and instill enough fear that the Waldensian people would give up their beliefs.

These atrocities were committed by the Catholic Church in the name of God. Sometimes they were kind enough to first ask the Waldensians to deny their religion and accept the Pope as their religious leader in exchange for their lives. Almost 100% refused even after watching their children die in front of them rather than give in to the Catholic Church and its idolatry. That is how strong their faith

Figure 35.1: Waldensian persecutions

and belief was. The Waldensian way of life was not a religion; it was the foundation of existence that was inherited via the Apostles; some even say via Mary Magdalene and Jmmanuel.

What happens when there are defiant people like the Waldensians, Cathars, or the Moors who have information that undermines the Catholic Church? The Church tries to entice them to convert, then forcibly tries to convert them, or eliminate and kill them. This is what Charlemagne was commissioned to do. He forcibly converted everyone in the Catholic territory, or they were executed. Because of him the Vikings formed as a way to defend Scandinavia against this terrible scourge. The downfall was the Black Plague. When that happened armies and families were decimated. The only one who had power and money to do anything was the Catholic Church. The Church sent armies which literally walked into these other countries, converted them to Christianity, and thus ended that part of Europe.

The Waldensians were pushed to the very highest peaks in the Piedmont area. The paths leading up to the villages were almost impassable for armies, much less for transporting weapons of any kind.

Figure 35.2: Waldensian persecutions

Wherever the Catholic armies tried to attack, they would be surrounded by mountains and cliffs. The Waldensians ambushed and blocked the opposing soldiers to drive them out. This strategy worked for hundreds of years until about 1655 when the last big attacks on the remaining Waldensian villages occurred. Thousands and thousands of soldiers were accumulated by the Duke of Savoy, the Pope and the Inquisitors. The sheer numbers and tactical advantages finally overwhelmed and decimated the Waldensians.

The survivors managed to make their way to Geneva, Switzerland. By that time the Reformation had occurred. Northern European countries became "Protestant". Because these countries were also against the Pope, they provided asylum for the remnants of the Waldensian refugees. The Waldensians, in fact, were called "The Mother of the Reformation".

In addition to the suppression of Pure Knowledge, the Protestant Reformation was fueled by the incessant need of the Pope and his bishops for more money. Parishioners were told that they were "born in sin". With enough money, people could buy their wait out of

Figure 35.3: Waldensian persecutions

purgatory and prevent burning in hell forever.

The Church sold "indulgences", which required people to pay in advance to forgive any sins that might be acquired. The Catholics in Switzerland and Germany refused to comply with the new law. Martin Luther posted his manifesto on the door of the Catholic Church against selling indulgences, which catapulted the rise of the Protestant Reformation. This is another reason why Switzerland and Germany gave the Waldensians refuge. In the 1700s the Waldensians moved into other areas of Europe. Finally in the 1800s the French and Italians expelled them, exiling them into the Cottian Alps.

In the early 1800s Napoleon began to rise into power. The French wanted an Empire like everyone else. Napoleon invaded Rome, demanding the Pope abdicate. There was a time period when there was no Pope because Napoleon basically assumed the role. Acting as the Pope and Emperor, he decided to expel everyone who was not in allegiance with him. He ordered the people in Italy that he controlled to expel all the Waldensians. The Germans and Swiss were also worried because Napoleon was invading these countries as well.

The Waldensians had nowhere to go. Many left France and Italy to Uruguay and into Argentina. To this very day Uruguay and Argentina have the largest Waldensian population in the world. From there, some came to the United States, establishing communities and churches in New York, North Carolina, and Southern Missouri in the town of Monett. The only ones left now are in Missouri and Valdese, North Carolina.

Interestingly, the topography of Southern Missouri replicates Southern France; it is full of caves, hills, vineyards and also has a lot of water in the area. At the time they sent word back to the people in Europe that it was too expensive to maintain the Waldensian churches. For financial and safety reasons, the Waldensians in Northern Italy suggested that they meld with other Protestant religions.

For this reason, the Waldensian churches globally affiliated themselves with primarily Presbyterian and Methodist churches. The church in Monett, Missouri still stands, incorporating a small museum display of the original Waldensians in the basement. The Waldensians of Valdese, North Carolina has the largest repository of Waldensian artifacts and displays available to the public. While Waldensian churches still exist worldwide, the public religion is no longer the original religion. It is thought that the origins of the original religion are hidden away and protected from the public for safekeeping, in much the same way that all indigenous peoples must closely guard their secrets from the Global Handlers.

Officially there are no written documents to explain the origins of the Vaudois/Valdese/Waldensians because the Catholic Church burned and destroyed whatever documentation they found - or carted it away to be stored beneath the Vatican. And, much of Waldensian history was orally passed through the generations to help keep it alive and safe. It is also believed that ancient Waldensian documents and artifacts are hidden in the cave systems of the Cottian Alps.

In France, there is reference to the Waldensians in Rennes-le-Château. The Priest that was stationed there created the church with symbolism to undermine the Catholic Church. Rennes-le-Château shows all of the wrong information perpetuated by the Catholic Church. The correct information is encoded symbolically in the statues and paintings in the church.

Presently there are many Waldensian people with Moorish last names that are related to Arabic or Moroccan sounding names. These names are related to the Islamic Moors that blended together in the South of France and Northern Italy. This is quite an interesting liaison for a group of people that started in the 600s. In the 800s Charlemagne pushed the Moors back into Spain. The very northern part of Spain was liberated by the Catholic armies of Charlemagne.

The central and southern part of Spain and Portugal remained in Islamic hands until 1492 when Queen Isabella and King Ferdinand finally pushed them out. Still, the Islamic influence was strong for several hundred years. These Moors could not return back to their country so many joined the Waldensians to help fight against the Catholic Church.

There were many groups throughout history who did not bow to the Catholic Church. The Waldensians were one of these groups. Even with dwindling numbers and limits of freedom, they retained their integrity.

36. Michigan Connection

Michigan is a fascinating place. The name "Michigan" came from the indigenous tribes who called it "Michigama" or "the big water" because of the way its lower and upper peninsulas jut out into the surrounding lakes, with the longest freshwater coastline of any political subdivision in the world. It is bordered by 4 of the 5 Great Lakes, and also by Lake Saint Clair. In addition, Michigan has almost 65,000 inland ponds and lakes.

In Mexico, there is a state called "Michoacán" where ancient Mayans had a civilization. "Michoacán" means "place of water". Interestingly in that language it means the exact same thing as "Michigama". How can people thousands of years ago and over 2000 miles apart use the same name? Conventional history does not give you this connection. Yet, here it is. Plus, the names of the indigenous tribes in Michoacán are extremely similar to the tribes that lived in Michigan.

Many of the explorers that came to Michigan in ancient times traveled through the Labrador Sea, into the Hudson Bay, proceeding into Northern Ontario and Manitoba, Canada. From here, they traversed the rivers that flow into the Great Lakes. The Mayan civilization came up through the Mississippi all the way to the Great Lakes. Museums in Mexico have Mayan art depictions of animals such as beavers and other North American type creatures from the Great Lakes region that do not exist in Central America.

Original settlers, such as the French, arriving in the Great Lakes region, found the indigenous peoples speaking words that were Old Norse. Priests accompanying the settlers recognized Old Swedish, Norwegian, and Old Norse words included as part of the Ceremonial Language of the indigenous peoples.

In Michigan there is a collection of metals, gases, crystals, and energies that are unique on the Earth. This is why there is a vortex created by the Great Lakes. Especially in the winter time if you watch the weather maps, there will always be swirls of storms right over Michigan. Because Michigan is in the center of the Great Lakes, Michigan is actually in the middle of an energy vortex with the water acting as an amplifier.

The Great Lakes also has a triangle similar to the "Bermuda Triangle" in the Caribbean and the "Devil's Triangle" in Asia by Japan, Guam, and the Philippines. One of the points of the Lake Michigan Triangle is in Benton Harbor which connects across to Ludington, Wisconsin and down again to Manitowoc, Wisconsin. Every year people, planes, and boats vanish without a trace in all three of these triangles due to the vortices contained therein.

The Great Lakes are inland de-salinated oceans. At the bottom of the lakes they have found fossils of sea creatures, whales, and other salt water creatures which have at one time been in the lakes. In fact, there is a layer of salt underneath the bottom of the lakes that has been there since glacial times.

Both Michigan and Wisconsin have similar pyramids and artifacts in both locations. When Michigan was colonized from the mid-1800s to the early 1900s, a plethora of artifacts thousands of years old from ancient times were discovered. Minoan, Mayan, Viking, and Celtic artifacts have all been unearthed here. Over 3000 tablets from approximately 312AD have been discovered in the last century across the entire state. These tablets depict Mary Magdalene and the creation of Christianity. Apparently refugees that were persecuted in Europe came to Michigan to escape the Romans. There are also Minoan tablets found dated approximately 2500BC.

In the early 1900s a former Michigan Secretary of State, Daniel E. Soper, was digging a posthole for a fence and hit something made out of stone. He continued to dig and discovered a tablet that was written in a strange language with different symbols appearing almost hieroglyphic.

Over the course of the years other people started finding tablets all over the state. Over 3000 tablets were unearthed from one end of

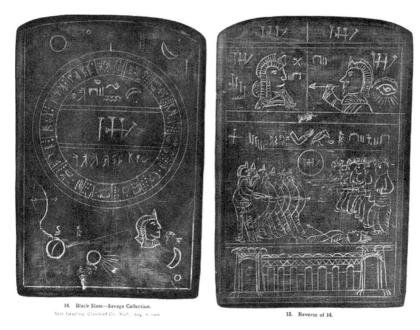

14. Black Slate—Savage Collection.

15. Reverse of 14.

Figure 36.1: Michigan Tablet

Michigan to the other on various farms. Sometimes they were found when fields were plowed, or if there was a storm and a tree blew over tablets were found in the roots.

A famous tablet that was discovered in the Upper Peninsula was by two farm workers who were chasing a mink. The mink ran into the root system of a tree that had overturned. They followed the mink and hit something. When they pulled it out it was a statue. They continued to dig more, finding two more statues and a large tablet. There was a statue of a man, woman, and a little boy. The tablet was written in a language that no one could understand. It had a grid pattern with symbols in each box. In each box were hieroglyphs, letters, and symbols that no one could interpret.

These were translated in recent years after determining that they were written in an ancient Minoan language. The Minoan civilization existed in the eastern Mediterranean. It was made famous by the 10 Commandments with the Biblical flood and the 10 plagues of Egypt. A Minoan volcano exploded causing all the problems in Egypt to occur, creating floods as well as spreading hot ash and the causing the migration of animals. How did an ancient Minoan tablet find its way to the Upper Peninsula of Michigan when supposedly Columbus discovered America in 1492? How do you explain that?

In those days, as today, when something is considered unexplainable it is dismissed, hidden, and/or destroyed. During these 50 years, the 3000+ tablets were dug up and brought to museums, historians, and universities to decipher. When they couldn't decipher the tablets many of the historians and university researchers destroyed the tablets, eliminated them, or simply hid them away. Fortunately the bearers of these tablets sometimes photographed or copied them before handing them over. All of the tablets show a symbol or code on the top.

There is research that indicates that there may have been descendants of Mary Magdalene and Jmmanuel in the Great Lakes region. They fled Europe and North Africa from persecution after 300AD. There is strong evidence on many of the tablets found in Michigan as an image of a woman with her eyes cast down often appears, resembling the image of Mary Magdalene.

Mary Magdalene was often portrayed with downcast eyes as if she was ashamed or embarrassed because the Catholic Church labeled her a prostitute. Eventually, the Church absolved her, renewing her as a person of fine repute. Her image has always been represented as repentant with downcast eyes. Her image was on the tablets and the Maltese/Magdalene Cross was created around 312AD by followers of Mary Magdalene.

These symbols were found on all of the tablets. They are an ancient Greek letter abbreviation for the name of Jesus, or Jmmanuel. These symbols were first invented and used in 312AD, by those who followed the Magdalene lineage which believes she was married to Jmmanuel. What are 3000 tablets like this doing in Michigan with the same symbol? Written in several different languages, they all have the same code on them.

When you connect the symbol of the 4 leaves, or arrows, they form the Maltese, or Magdalene, Cross that is also found in France. This is a code used by only a specific group of people. These tablets bore inscriptions indicating that they were made by refugees from the Magdalene lineage who escaped Holy Roman persecution over 1600 years ago. Could they have influenced the Cherokee tribes that were in Michigan?

Correlation charts show that many Cherokee words are a direct match to words of the Minoan language. How is this possible for two cultures that supposedly have never met? It is worthy to note that a percentage of the Cherokee people have red hair and blue or green eyes. Where did these genetics come from?

The Cherokee tribe originated in Michigan and the Great Lakes region before being driven out by another aggressive tribe. The Cherokees then migrated to North Carolina and Tennessee. This is where they were found when the settlers arrived. The US Government wanted the mines and minerals in that area, so they were driven out of their homeland once again. The Cherokee were marched across the country to Oklahoma. This forced march, where many Cherokee died, is now known as the "Trail of Tears".

A study done of Cherokee spiritual traditions and teachings closely matches the teachings from the Hebrew Torah. We now know that the Cherokee were connected to the Minoan who were connected to the Atlanteans, creating one big picture. What is fascinating is that all the pieces are in the state of Michigan.

In 1898, a farmer by the name of Olaf Ohman from Minnesota near Duluth was plowing his field when he came across a huge tree in his way. Olaf and his sons chopped down the dead tree; as the roots came up a tablet was stuck in them. The tablet was written in the rune language of the Vikings. Of course, the tablet was called a hoax; people said the Ohmans had chiseled the rock, even though the family did not know how to write in runes nor had they even heard of runes before the tablet was found.

Years later, the tablet was deciphered and translated to describe a band of Vikings, specifically telling how many Swedes and Norwegians were among the group. The Vikings came across an island and were attacked by indigenous people. Returning to their camp, the Vikings found some of their companions dead. The tablet was written to tell people how far their ship was from that location. The tablet is estimated to be between 700-800 years old and made from local stone.

A stone carving was discovered in a river in the Upper Peninsula of Michigan in the old Celtic language of "Ogam". All it said was "May God help me not be killed in the storm". Someone must have carved it quickly and tossed it into the water for protection. There is also very strong evidence that there were ancient Irish travelers in Michigan, too.

Sumerian Cuneiform, Egyptian hieroglyphics, Greek, Minoan and Phoenician languages have all been found on these stone tablets in Michigan. Some tablets had a combination of different languages on the same tablet. People from Michigan in the late 1800s and early 1900s did not know these languages, let alone how to write them.

One of the tablets found in Central Michigan was written in a Mongolian alphabet called "Kok Thurki" or "Turku-Mongolian". This is part of the original Khazar language which was a Middle Eastern/Asian version of the ancient Mongolian language. The Khazar Empire extended into the northern part of Mongolia and Northern China. In a period of time in the early centuries these letters were used to write in other languages, just like to understand Hebrew letters they are written as English letters. They used Mongolian letters to write in Greek and other languages. Here we have a Khazar connection to Michigan. The tablet was over 3000 years old; how did it get to Michigan?

In Northern Michigan in 1925, someone was digging a post hole for a pier and dug up a coin from Java from 1200 BC. The Vikings had trade routes with Asia; it was very likely the coin was acquired in this way and dropped as the Vikings passed through Michigan. It is highly unlikely people from Java traveled to Michigan because no other Javanese artifacts have been found in the region. Coins from Viking times have also been unearthed in Massachusetts and Maine.

How many people were at this crossroads? How well-known was this area of the US? Michigan was a happening place back then if the number of ancient artifacts found here is any indication. There is a connection from almost every continent to North America. Nearly every culture has been in Michigan, yet this is not told to you in the "official" history books.

Figure 36.2: Michigan Copper Mines

Michigan is known for its copper resources. Between the 1870s and the 1920s, immigration expanded throughout the upper and lower peninsulas.

Copper was found in Michigan's Keweenaw Peninsula beginning approximately 5,000-10,000BC. The oldest copper mines in Michigan are over 7000 years old. There are over 5000 copper mines in Michigan, some estimated at 87 stories deep. They are so vast that current known technology cannot recreate them. Over a billion tons of copper is estimated to have been extracted from Michigan copper mines. No one knows who dug the mines or how they knew copper existed there. The local people refused to go anywhere near the copper mines, saying that the mines were "haunted" and "a sacred land of other people".

Figure 36.3: Copper Island Keewenaw

The mines were opened and closed 3 separate times by 3 separate civilizations over the millennia. Copper production stopped in 1500BC and started up again in 1000AD by the Vikings; then halted again in approximately 1250AD. The mines were again abandoned until they were rediscovered by the French and English during colonization in the 1800s. These starting and stopping dates correlate to Earth disasters. In the copper mines, tools and implements were found as if the miners were expecting to return, indicating an abrupt departure.

Michigan was a major trading area; the Vikings, Central/South American cultures, and Egyptians all used copper from Michigan. The height of the copper extractions in Michigan directly correlates to the beginning of the Bronze Age in Europe. Some believe the Bronze Age began as a direct result of the input of Michigan copper. Bronze is made from a mix of copper and tin. The copper has been traced to Michigan origin due to its unique composition that is not found anywhere else. Significant amounts of copper in Europe were found, but well beyond what Europe could produce.

Tests prove that the type and purity of the copper could only originate in Michigan. Michigan's copper is the purest on Earth. This pure copper creates an amplifier and conductor, especially when combined with the billions of tons of underground crushed quartz crystals left over from the glaciers that only dissipated 10,000 years ago. The glaciers left when Atlantis sank, coinciding with the discovery of the copper mines. Electromagnetically, a combination of crystal, copper, and water acts as a step-up transformer. This means that whoever you are or whatever you are doing increases exponentially - either in a positive or negative way. You may feel differently just being in Michigan.

How would the ancient people know that Michigan had the purest copper in the world? How could you find mines when supposedly no one knew of their existence? Apparently the Atlanteans knew they existed and where the mines were.

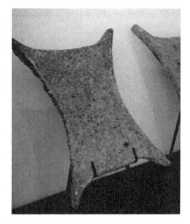

Thousands of years ago the commonality between European and North and South American cultures was Atlantis. It allegedly vanished under the ocean at approximately 10,500 BC. However this was the final destruction of the main continent, but there is evidence that not all of it vanished at that time.

Figure 36.4: Oxhyde from Cyprus - ox-hide shape copper ingots

When copper was removed from the mines in ancient times they carried it in a shape now referred to as "oxhydes". The ingot was actually in the shape of an animal hide, with four convenient handles that could be shouldered by the bearers. According to Egyptian stone reliefs and records, a people from beyond the Straits of Gibraltar traded copper with the Egyptians. A mural from 7000 BC in ancient Egypt has a depiction of the Phoenicians bringing Michigan copper back in the form of "oxhydes" and trading it.

It is also believed that the island off the coast of Portugal in the Gibraltar Straits had a trading route to Central and South America because the same copper has been found there. The Phoenicians were called "red men" similar to the American Indians. According to ancient legend, the Atlanteans had red skin. It is believed that the Phoenicians are direct descendants of both the Atlanteans and North

Figure 36.5: Phoenicians copper oxhydes

American indigenous peoples.

Frisland also continued the trade route with the copper in Michigan. Statues were found in the deep woods of Michigan of European people with beards and Viking outfits carved in stone. Native peoples did not create these. Even they thought these statues strange, sometimes even leaving ritual gifts to the statues.

The destruction that happened in approximately 2500 BC that caused the island off the coast of Portugal in the Gibraltar Straits to sink ended the copper flow between the continents. However, it is interesting to note that this same Michigan copper has been found in South Africa; apparently Michigan was quite a center of trade.

Pure Michigan copper has even been traced to ancient vaults in remote mountain villages of Switzerland dating back thousands of years. Over the course of 3 different time periods, over 1 billion tons of pure copper have been removed from Michigan. Nobody knows where it went other than the traces that have come up in Europe, Africa, Central America, South America, and Asia. This indicates thousands of years ago there was a trade route and system that existed far beyond what you have ever been told.

Thousands of mounds were built in North America east of the Mississippi and into Michigan. Nobody knew who built them. When the settlers arrived they had no clue who built the mounds; even the indigenous peoples did not know. These mounds have baffled historians for over a century; some of these mounds contain burials and artifacts while others remain mysterious.

Inside the mounds that were excavated giant skeletons, copper weapons, and spears were found. They even contained ancient coins in Hebrew, Egyptian, Roman, and a plethora of Viking artifacts, all thousands of years old. Curiously many mounds, even in the Deep South, contain copper from Michigan. Mounds in Michigan contain shells and artifacts from the south indicating a trade route and communication.

The largest mound known as the "Monks Mound" is in the Cahokia Mounds UNESCO World Heritage Site, located east of St. Louis, Missouri on the Illinois side of the Mississippi River. This mound is located directly south of the copper mines in Michigan. Cahokia Mounds is the largest mound area in the country and also the largest city in North America dating to approximately 800 AD. There was also a huge city in the Northern part of Louisiana along the Mississippi River.

The mound contained artifacts that came from the Mayan culture. At the time of the Spanish invasion of North America, Cahokia was believed to be the largest city in North America, even rivaling the largest cities in Europe. Scientists say the mounds located all throughout the Midwest and South are burial mounds. Do you know how long it takes to move earth and dirt that is hundreds of feet high and a mile wide? That would be some funeral! These mounds were ritualistic temples; ceremonial caverns have been discovered along with bodies and other highly valuable artifacts.

The Mayan civilization came up through the Mississippi all the way to the Great Lakes. The Mayans were the "mound builders". This is why they built the mounds in the same dimensions and shapes as the step pyramids in Central America. The trade route went from the Mayan area of the Yucatan up the Mississippi and into the Great Lakes. Artifacts have been found all along this route of Mayan and Viking origin.

There was a city in Southern Wisconsin that was called "Aztlan", which sounds Mayan. Nearby at the bottom of Rock Lake in central Wisconsin there are submerged stone pyramids almost identical to Mayan pyramids. Of course, when these pyramids were built the land was above ground. The pyramids submerged in approximately 1500 BC. You can still visit the lake and scuba dive to see these pyramids.

Pyramids have also been found at the bottom of lakes in Northern Michigan. Mayan artifacts and materials have been discovered in the Upper Peninsula and west coast of Michigan and Wisconsin.

The National Museum of Anthropology in Mexico City has a Mayan carving of a beaver and other artifacts from the Great Lakes region that could not possibly exist in Mexico. There are also copper artifacts from the Great Lakes region, thus proving the connection between the copper country and central Mexico. This is evidence an interaction between the two civilizations occurred that you will not find in history books.

When settlers came to Berrien County, Michigan they found ancient gardens. No one knew who created them. The indigenous people explained the

Figure 36.6: Monks Mound in Illinois

gardens existed when they colonized the area. Some gardens were 2-3 kilometers wide and one-half mile long. The gardens appear to have existed for thousands of years and were laid out in patterns so old that they are imprinted into the ground.

Mastodon bones and skeletons of gigantic beavers the size of bears have been found in Michigan. Bones of whales have also been found - what were bones of ocean creatures doing in Michigan?

Three pyramids were discovered buried in the woods near the Keweenaw Peninsula of Michigan. No one knows who built them. The area to the east is where the copper and Viking artifacts were discovered. The exact location of the pyramids is not available to the public.

In 2007, Northwestern Michigan College announced they discovered a series of stones arranged in a circle similar to Stonehenge 40 feet underneath Lake Michigan. One of the stones outside the circle appeared to have carvings of a Mastodon; other petroglyph sites are also located in the area.

One person in Michigan purchased land on a cliff with a big drop-off to the water. Painted on the side of the cliff was what looked like a huge image of a turtle, the other looked like a monkey. There are a lot images that are referred to as underwater cats or tigers. The indigenous people used to talk about sea creatures in the lakes that would kill people.

Shipwrecks and missing vessels discovered in Lake Michigan are believed to have collided with sea monsters. There are three different kinds of sea creatures in Michigan alone that are considered to be monstrous. One that is accepted by science is a gigantic sturgeon. There is also a gigantic eel that could be over 100 feet long that lives towards the bottom of the lake. There is another creature that looks very much like the Loch Ness monster which has been sighted throughout all the Great Lakes. A few years ago there was a blip in the newspaper that said the US military had captured a 115 foot serpent off the coast of Northern Michigan. Nothing else was said after that.

Numerous stories exist of the Thunderbird, a gigantic creature that can lift you up with its talons. In fact, a few years ago in Illinois a mother was looking out of her farm house window and saw talons pick up her 6-year-old child and carry him away. When she ran outside the bird dropped him. Thunderbirds have been sighted around the Great Lakes, all across Canada and into Alaska. A few years ago an airline pilot flying in Alaska said he saw a bird the size of his plane. Thunderbirds are coming back! The Illuminati are trying to recreate the Jurassic period in North America. There was a government plan for the Midwest to release creatures into the wild that existed in that time period.

Approximately 20 years ago a hunter in central Michigan was hunting a deer that ran down an embankment. When he followed the deer he fell in a hole. At the bottom of the hole he found himself in a Viking lodge, undisturbed for a thousand years replete with Viking artifacts.

There is a fault line termed as a "monster fault" in Northern Michigan. This fault goes across into the Upper Peninsula into Ontario, Canada and is considered inactive. There used to be volcanoes in this area. The indigenous people said that the earthquake was centered over one of the old volcanoes. In St. Joseph, Michigan there are hot sulfur springs. No one here can explain why because these are only supposed to exist in volcanic areas.

In 1966 UFOs were seen in Hillsdale, Michigan. At the time J. Allen Hynek of the US Air Force gave the famous "swamp gas" explanation. He later changed his opinion and became a UFO researcher.

The Chicago O'Hare airport has reported "phantom planes" on their radar. Planes were told to avoid them but pilots said they could not see what the air traffic controllers were seeing on their radar. In 2007, a UFO was hovering above Gate C17 seen by passengers and pilots before it shot into the sky leaving a hole in the clouds. They called it a "weather anomaly" but all witnesses agreed that it was definitely not an anomaly.

I personally know two people who saw a UFO in the Great Lakes area that looked like a sideways skyscraper floating around in broad daylight. Other people have since confirmed this sighting.

Secret government investigations purposefully leak information intended to fester in your mind and trigger Greenstar programming.

There are also other things happening that are related to the present moment and to the future. This also involves what will become the Staged Alien Invasion. There is a description of Central Michigan as being a landing point for the invasion.

Michigan, being in the center of a natural vortex of the Great Lakes, has one of the highest anomalous animal sightings in the US, as well as one of the highest amounts of UFO reports in the world. Most of Michigan is used by the Illuminati because of the Viking, Mayan and even Atlantean connections.

37. Bosnian Pyramids

Dr. Sam Semir Osmanagić PhD is a professor of anthropology at the American University in Bosnia-Herzegovina. He is a foreign member of the Russian Academy of Natural Sciences and has authored ten books. Dr. Osmanagić has spent a considerable amount of time in Central America and has a PhD in Mayan civilization.

In April 2005, Dr. Osmanagić first traveled to the town of Visoko, 20 miles northwest from Sarajevo, the capital of Bosnia-Herzegovina. He made one of the greatest archaeological discoveries of modern times. He found a whole valley with pyramids known as "the Pyramid of the Sun, the Pyramid of the Moon, the Pyramid of the Dragon, the Pyramid of Love and the Temple of Mother Earth". There he also discovered a huge underground network of tunnels, chambers, intersections, and underground lakes. The series of tunnels that connects these pyramids spans for miles underground. When he saw the hills with the geometry with four faces that had obvious corners, he immediately knew they were intelligence-made structures under the layers of soil and vegetation.

The word "pyramid" is normally associated with Egypt and the Giza plateau. However, the majority of the world's pyramids are actually covered by soil and forests. 250 of them are in the central Chinese province of Shaanxi, thousands of them are in Guatemala, El Salvador, Honduras, Belize, and Mexico, all in different climate belts. For thousands of years soil has accumulated on top of the pyramids. What you learned about pyramids in school is incorrect. Pyramids are located on six continents with some talk now of pyramids in Antarctica - something I have spoken about for decades.

Egypt has 155 publicly acknowledged pyramids. Thousands more are located in Mexico. There are 300 pyramids in Peru, Bolivia, and the

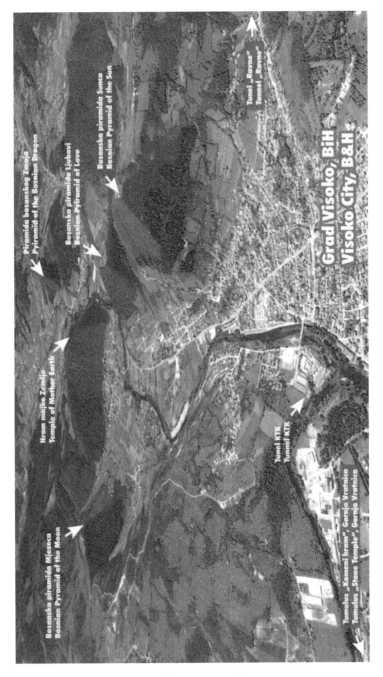

Figure 37.1: Bosnian Valley of the Pyramids (Courtesy of the "Archaeological Park: Bosnian Pyramid of the Sun" Foundation)

Canary Islands in the Atlantic Ocean. Dr. Osmanagić has investigated seven pyramids on the island of Mauritius in the Indian Ocean. There are also pyramids in Indonesia and Cambodia; obviously there is a worldwide network of pyramids.

You must distinguish the original, oldest and most superior pyramids from the replicas built by Pharaohs and Chinese Emperors. These replicas were built with inferior material like mud or brick by those who did not understand the true purpose of the original pyramids. Original pyramids are located in Egypt on the Giza plateau, in Mexico in the city of Teotihuacán, in Peru, China, and Bosnia; they are all over the world.

The original pyramids were either built by a super-civilization or there were several highly advanced civilizations that were communicating with each other. Until the real builders are revealed, you must be open to exploring the options. But one thing you do know is that these original pyramids were built by intelligent beings with superior technology. The Pharaoh's agents did not have the knowledge or engineering skills to build the pyramids known as "Cheops/The Great Pyramid, Khafre/Chefren, Menkaure/Mycerinus, and Snofru's". The same can be said of the city of Teotihuacán, the Pirámide del Sol and Pirámide de la Luna.

Historians say these pyramids are less than 4,000 years old without one single proof, radio carbon datings, tools, organic materials, nothing. The same thing with the Peruvian pyramids; you can see the vertical erosion on them which means they have been exposed to rain, precipitation, and storms. For 7,000 years the climate has been the same, desert and dry, so we need to go back in the past 7, 10, 12, 15,000 years; even more. This raises a question, "What was this planet like in its previous cycle?"

History did not start with Sumeria, Babylon, Akkad, Assyria, Ancient Egypt, or India; this was just the last cycle. Before this cycle there was a previous one, obviously a highly advanced one. If you go to Baalbek in Eastern Lebanon you can see the blocks that are 1200 tons in mass; current technology can only move 350 tons. This is physical world proof that advanced civilizations with capabilities at least four times ours existed long before our civilization evolved.

The theory of the French material scientist Joseph Davidovits is simple. He says that instead of cutting blocks, blocks were actually poured on site, making some type of ancient concrete. Instead of 200,000 slaves, like you have been told, this technique only requires 2,500 skilled workers. There are other options that could explain this, but with such precision and so much engineering skills, astronomical, mathematical, and geometrical knowledge, what would be the purpose of the Bosnian pyramids? Here are huge, huge structures, the largest on the planet. What is their purpose? They are made of concrete with passage ways. The Egyptian pyramids are not tombs for Pharaohs as you have been taught. The Pharaohs are buried 200 miles south of the Giza Plateau in the Valley of the Kings - not in the pyramids.

Bosnia pyramid researchers measured electromagnetic and electromechanical phenomena, like ultrasound and infrasound, and other electric and magnetic phenomena. They measured the Bosnian Pyramid of the Sun which produces an energy beam that comes through the very top, or apex, of the pyramid. This energy beam has to have an artificial source; it is approximately 13 feet in radius with a 28 kilohertz frequency. This ultrasound frequency is beyond the spectrum of normal human sight and hearing, but it can be measured.

Figure 37.2: Pyramid of the Sun (Courtesy of the "Archaeological Park: Bosnian Pyramid of the Sun" Foundation)

Independent teams from Croatia, physicists from Zagreb, Finland, Italy, and Serbia all confirm the frequency of 28 kHz on the top of the Pyramid of the Sun. The ultrasound also indicates a mechanical phenomenon on the top of the Pyramid of the Sun as well as in the tunnels. The pyramid itself appears to be some type of ancient technology.

In the underground tunnels in the Bosnian Valley of the Pyramids there are megalithic blocks. Analyzed by scientists, test showed the building material to be ceramic. Archaeological finds often include small ceramic dishes and objects, but here are blocks weighing up to 1800 pounds. These huge ceramic objects are believed to be made and poured at the site in two phases: first the base was poured, then an oval-shaped object the size of a football and believed to be silica was placed inside, with a final step to put a lid or cover in place, sealing the object inside. The researchers discovered that the ceramic objects were placed over the underground water flows and rivers. The underground river provides the energy flow, the energy is hitting the blocks and the little oval objects are surrounded by ceramic.

Ceramic has a property to vibrate, producing an electromagnetic field. The tunnels are covered by so many blocks, electromagnetic fields are everywhere, and there is a lot of quartz crystal inside. Through the piezo-electrical effect they produce ultrasound. Why is ultrasound important? Ultrasound is something that humans cannot hear; humans only hear up to 20 kHz while ultrasound is 28 kHz and above. Animals can hear the ultrasound. Inside there is a huge network where they are not finding any bones or animals; nothing. It seems someone created and designed the underground to keep animals out.

In the summer of 2010 the first three underground chambers were discovered. They are from 300 to 500 square feet; every underground chamber has 6-8 tunnels. They appear to be very important meeting places. The concentration of negative ions was measured. Negative ions kill microbes, viruses, and bacteria. Outside the tunnels the average concentration is about 1000 kilo-ions per cubic centimeter. In your environment or home it is even less, approximately 500 kilo-ions. In the underground chambers the concentration is much higher, around 43,000 kilo-ions per cubic centimeter. In other words the environment is ideal for an underground hospital or healing place. There are no viruses, bacteria, or microbes.

When you stand on the surface of the planet you are exposed to a lot of cosmic radiations. There is also underground natural radioactivity, and it all attacks your body; your body cells fight these radiations. The tunnels were measured for the presence of Hartmann, Curry, and

Schneider grids. The results were zero, no negative radiations. So, you have a place with a high concentration of negative ions, and no negative radiations. Instead of your body cells fighting the enemy on the outside, they can now do their job, which is to balance your body's energies and organs. This underground includes a self-healing complex where people could go to regenerate; it is a revitalizing place. This complex of pyramids was not built for the dead but for the living.

When we were in Bosnia in 2011 Dr. Osmanagić mentioned that perhaps the builders of these pyramids and tunnels were not surface dwellers; they possibly lived underground. When you enter the tunnels within the first 10 feet and even after 3,000 feet you can breathe normally; the air circulation is there. How did the builders accomplish this? Some of the tunnels are very narrow and are from 3 feet to 12-13 feet in height. The areas with lower ceilings have a higher pressure. Basically the pressure creates a vacuum, pushing and circulating the air. The pressure is stronger in the areas with lower ceilings, and is weaker where there are higher ceilings. This way it creates a fan or natural circulation. There are hundreds of tunnels and the air circulates perfectly; the builders were geniuses.

These beings did not have light bulbs or electricity; there is not a trace of any illumination devices. How could they see? They had to have a means to move in the underground labyrinth. Today, you have your eyes, but you are on the surface. Those people were living underground; they probably developed other senses. For example the bat uses sonar to navigate. It seems the environment was different 10,000 years ago with the cosmic radiations or wars and dangers on the surface. It seems they did use some other physical senses.

They were highly intelligent beings with a great knowledge of engineering. They built the underground labyrinth 70 feet under the surface. To do this, you have to know about engineering. The air circulation is much better than what we have in our coal mining facilities. There is a small blue lake that was found underground as well. The water was analyzed from the lake and from some of the other tunnels. After thousands of years it was expected the waters would be full of microbes. When they did micro-biological and chemical analysis the results showed that the water is drinkable! How is this possible after so much time? Obviously, the high concentration of

Bosnian Pyramids

negative ions kept the atmosphere very clean.

Dr. Osmanagić feels that the pyramids were built as some type of energy machines. They are structures; you can see the concrete, the blocks and the shape of the pyramids. In the case of the Bosnian pyramids there are three different types of energy being produced. The first one is the energy beam that goes to the very top of the pyramid and has a frequency of 28 kHz; it can be measured by anyone. The second type of energy is the energy flow within the pyramid. Scientists have known about the energy flows of pyramids for approximately 60 years now. The energy flows really affect and improve your molecular structure. The third type of energy is the one that goes off the pyramid in concentric circles affecting the crops and whole societies. This is one aspect - the energy aspect.

When you have a strong energy source, you can do anything you want. You can use it for communication, not only on this planet, but for more than that. It can be used to manipulate the climate, and be used for weapons. You can also manipulate time and space. When you are able to deal with powerful energies they are much more superior compared to our mechanical devices. All of our lives as a community, and as human society we have basically fought to get energy sources. Today we are using oil, gas, thermal, nuclear, hydropower etc. In the past, people had different means to get the energy they needed. We can see the Bosnian pyramids still work, maybe not like in the original times, but they still work. So, in other words, for over 10,000+ years energy machines have been around us. The ancient people started the machines and they have still been working; the pyramids are some type of perpetual motors.

The strength of the energy coming from the Pyramid of the Sun can be measured. On the surface the strength is at a certain level, 10 feet above that the energy is stronger, another 10 feet it is even stronger. This contradicts our type of technology that we call "Hertzian technology", which says the closer to the source the stronger the energy; when you move away it gets weaker. In the case of the Bosnian pyramid the opposite is observed. This is an example "non-Hertzian technology".

The first scientist that experimented with this technology was Nikola

Tesla over 120 years ago. He was born just a couple hundred miles from the Bosnian pyramids, then moved to the US. He was doing some experiments in his lab in Colorado Springs and designed the so-called "Tesla Coil". He was able to move energy wirelessly in his lab, which was about 55 feet long. Before they burned down his lab he did an experiment that sent the energy from the Tesla Coil into the ionosphere, using that as the unlimited source of energy. The energy came back much, much stronger and lit up 20,000 homes in Colorado Springs. Tesla also had a lab in the southern part of Manhattan in New York City; he generated enough energy to create a small earthquake that started to destroy the buildings in the area. The equipment had to be destroyed to stop the earthquake from destroying New York City.

For the first time in publicly-known history, a scientist discovered an unlimited source of free wireless energy. Did the corporations use that for the advancement of human benefit? Of course not. For them it was much more profitable to build thermal, hydro, and nuclear power plants with all the cables to sell energy, for a lot of money. This is what the profit economy is based on. If you have free energy you have the basis for a free society. All you need is the free flow of information and knowledge, and of course the elite do not want this.

With all original pyramids what you see above the ground is just half of the machine. This means that there is a pyramid under the ground, too - pyramids are actually octahedrons which in turn are delta-T antennae which generate interdimensional energies. Dr. Osmanagić witnessed the same thing in China when he spoke to one of the more distinguished archaeologists, Dr. Cao Fazhan, who basically said this same thing: that under one of the biggest pyramids in China, there is another one underground.

Obviously, beings in the past knew how to work with the energies; they knew that the shape of the pyramid is just half of the machine. The shape of the pyramid is most beneficial, as far as the energy production. The 2nd shape necessary to energy production is the sphere. This is the reason there are so many stone spheres found in concentration in Costa Rica, Western Mexico, Easter Island, and Bosnia. They have found spherical stones in more than 20 different locations in Bosnia. These stone spheres are also an extremely powerful energy source. This is the type of knowledge the ancients had. They knew our planet much better than we do now. They knew about energy flows, positive and negative spots, and underground waters.

There are pyramidal structures in the shape of the step pyramids on the bottom of the Pacific Ocean floor in Yonaguni located between the islands of Taiwan and Japan and mainland China. There are 13 underwater cities that have been discovered in the last 15-20 years at a depth of 100 to 250 feet. Obviously at some point in time these structures were on the surface. The last time the Pacific Ocean rose 250 feet was around 12,500 years ago at the end of the last Ice age. Huge quantities of ice melted from Northern Asia, Europe, and North America, causing the oceans and water levels to rise.

In the Caribbean around the island of Cuba there are many underwater pyramids. Unfortunately, the Cuban government has not allowed anyone to investigate them. Hopefully, in the near future, we will learn more about them. In the middle of the Atlantic pyramids have been found on the bottom of the ocean floor as well.

In my opinion, there were continents in the Atlantic and Pacific that through some cataclysm did sink to what became the oceans. The pyramids are remnants of the civilizations that existed. Perhaps the survivors of those civilizations went to places like Bosnia, China, and India etc. to build replications of their cities. Perhaps this is what we are finding now and what you are finding in Bosnia as well as other places.

In the southwestern parts of Illinois there are 200 Cahokian pyramids. Dr. Osmanagić spoke to the main archaeologist; unfortunately whatever the mainstream teaches us about these pyramids is wrong. They call the city "the Sun City"; the real name is unknown. They call the park "Cahokia Mounds UNESCO World Heritage Site". Cahokia was actually the name of the minor Indian tribes from the 17th century, but the pyramids were built long before that. They call the pyramids "mounds", although "mounds" is really an underestimation. Mounds were built from the soil, but these structures have four different kinds of materials used to build them: sandstone/limestone, pebbles, sand, and red cedar. To cover the pyramids sod was cut into squares and then placed upside-down on the pyramid. The biggest mound, called

"Monks Mound" used the equivalent of 226,000 trucks of material. That is 20 ton trucks and trailers, absolutely huge! Plus, they built 200 pyramids - not just one.

The American Scientific community and all the archaeologists from the US should have been required to go there and figure out how they were built, and what there purposes were. Instead the government does not allow anyone to touch them and makes the permits extremely expensive. It is amazing that there are such valuable creations on US soil and yet they do nothing about it.

There is not a word mentioned about the mounds or pyramids in history books. Just because they cannot be attributed to the white European settlers does not mean they are not valuable. All but one of the 200 pyramids are oriented toward the cosmic north or Northern Star. The biggest one is oriented toward the magnetic north. Some people know that the cosmic north is fixed but the magnetic north moves approximately 25 miles/42 kilometers every year. Thousands of years ago it was moving about 6 miles per year.

Of course, there is a reason why. This is when great damage happened to the planet. The point is, those who knew the difference between the cosmic north and the magnetic north were not Indian tribes; they were highly advanced civilizations. They were not primitive indigenous tribes like museum guides tell you. Tribes did not have a social organization, engineering skills, or the knowledge to build something like these pyramids.

You have to apply all your knowledge that you have to understand the ancient structures. There is so much to learn from the ancients; so much knowledge has been forgotten. In the case of the Bosnian pyramids, the concrete that covers the pyramid of the Sun is 2-3 times better quality than modern concretes in the 21st century. Concrete hardness is measurable. We now make concrete that is in the range of 10-40 megapascals in hardness. The concrete of the Sun Pyramid is from 67-134 megapascals. You can see the people in the past had a better knowledge of these natural materials; how to put them together, applying specific formulas that are now. There is so much to learn from the past, and much of the technology we can apply in our present.

When Dr. Osmanagić first went to Visoko in central Bosnia and discovered the first two pyramids, based on his experience with the Egyptian, Mexican, and Chinese pyramids he knew that underground tunnels had to be somewhere close. In the Egyptian Saqqara under the step pyramid, there is a huge underground labyrinth about 6 miles in radius. There are also tunnel systems under the Giza, Chinese, and Mexican pyramids. He wrote about this in his first book on the discovery of the Bosnian pyramids. Of course the cultural educational establishment attacked him saying "It's impossible, what kind of networks of tunnels?"

He spoke to a lot of locals, especially kids asking them if there were any caves or tunnels. He finally found an entrance to what he calls "an underground labyrinth". It was a very narrow tunnel, only about a couple of feet and he had to crawl to get inside. Once inside, he found that the tunnel was about 60-70 feet long. When he saw the ceiling it was half-circled, and thought "this is an artificially made tunnel". He started cleaning it out, installing wooden supports as he went.

Soon, a wall to the left was discovered and then another wall to the right. Behind both walls more tunnels were found, and from there even more tunnels, a huge network of tunnels. From the tunnel entrance to the pyramid is a little less than 2 miles, approximately 1.8 miles. At the rate the explorers are working, it will take approximately 15-20 years to get under the pyramid. Keep in mind that archaeology is a very slow process requiring a lot of patience. Like the Chinese proverb says, "The road of 1000 miles starts with the first few steps", and this is what they have been doing.

The Bosnian Pyramid discovery is history-changing for several reasons. These are the first pyramids discovered in Europe. The site includes the biggest pyramidal structure in the world: The Bosnian Pyramid of the Sun with its height of over 220 meters/720 feet is much higher than the Great Pyramid of Egypt 147 meters/480 feet.

The Bosnian Pyramid of the Sun has the most precise orientation to the cosmic north of any pyramid. The Bosnian Pyramid of the Sun is completely covered by rectangular concrete blocks. Properties of the concrete, such as extreme hardness and low water absorption, are, according to the scientific institutions in Bosnia, Italy, and France, much superior to modern concrete materials.

The pyramids are covered by soil which is, according to the Federal Institute of Agropedology, over 12,000 years old. This finding confirms the Bosnian pyramids are the oldest pyramids on the planet. Below the Bosnian Valley of the Pyramids is the most extensive underground tunnel and chamber network which runs for more than ten miles. Ceramic sculptures have been discovered in the underground labyrinth with a mass of up to 20,000 pounds which makes them the largest so far found from the ancient world.

The list of the miracles in Bosnian archaeology does not end here. In the vicinity, they discovered the tallest tomb in the World: 61 meters high. England's Silbury Hill is 60 meters high. The Bosnian tomb consists of two-layer megalithic terraces, clay layers and artificial concrete layers.

Recent tests indicate that the Bosnian Pyramid Complex may be over 40,000 years old. Frequency analysis of the energy and translation of some of the markings on stone tablets show that this site could have been a vortex or portal for non-humans.

38. The Papacy

Joseph Aloisius Ratzinger, also known as "Pope Benedict XVI" was in Hitler's youth movement. He graduated to the artillery where he actually helped shoot down American planes over Germany. He was nicknamed the "Rottweiler" by Pope John Paul II due to his temper and mental demeanor.

Pope John Paul II was not so nice either; he had a great public relations advisor to help him with his appearance. He also worked for the Germans during WWII and sold Zyklon-B gas to the Nazis for use in concentration camps for extermination. At the end of the war he was wanted for the Nuremberg Trials. He was hidden and protected by the Vatican since he was such a good Catholic. According to the Nostradamus prophecies there is only one more Pope due to reign after him, then Rome will be destroyed. That will allegedly be the end of Catholicism.

Now that Benedict XVI has resigned and Francis is Pope, you may be witnessing the end of conventional religion and the start of New World Religion.

The Vatican

The Etruscans occupied the Roman area before the Romans. They are a very mysterious group that simply appeared in the 1000s BC. They had a goddess named "Vaticana", the Goddess of Death. There was a statue of Vaticana on a hill overlooking what is now Rome. The hill became known as "La Vatican".

Around the statue were the burial sites of the Etruscans. Growing n this hill was a vine that produced fruit that intoxicated and poisoned people who ingested it. The fruit was called "Vaticana", after the Goddess of Death.

When the Romans finally replaced the Etruscans and settled the area, the Romans also used the hill for burial. When the Roman Church came into being as the Catholic Church they built their city on top of the cemetery. Underneath the Vatican there are a lot of dead bodies from 1000s of years ago. When you go to the Vatican you are actually going to the Goddess of Death; isn't that interesting?

Sistine Chapel

The Sistine Chapel was built in 1481; it was supposed to be a replica/ replacement for Solomon's Temple in Jerusalem. The Pope wanted to create a building that would be the 3rd Temple of Solomon. The intention of the Catholic Church by changing the venue and recreating Solomon's Temple was to replace the old religion.

In doing so, everything from the Old Testament would then be null and void. Only what Rome said would apply to the new religion that would be centered in this new temple. Of course, Michelangelo was commissioned to decorate the building with artwork that would glorify Rome and the Pope. The Vatican Sistine Chapel is the Roman Catholic version of Solomon's Temple based on its description in the Old Testament.

However, out of all of the paintings not one image is from the New Testament. All the artwork is from the Old Testament and filled with anti-Catholicism because Michelangelo hated the Catholic Church and the Pope. He was not happy to be commissioned for this work, but he knew that he could not refuse it or his career would come to an abrupt end.

Michelangelo was a sculptor and did not like to paint. He was extremely upset that he had no choice but to lie on a scaffolding for years and years, painting what he did not want to paint. For this reason he devised codes and secret images embedded in the Sistine Chapel paintings to offend the Pope and the Catholic Church. He brilliantly disguised these secret codes and images as beautiful paintings to hide these covert messages.

When Michelangelo was young he was appointed as an apprentice to the de Medici family to learn his trade. Here he learned the ancient languages of Hebrew, Greek, and Latin. He was fascinated with the Hebrew language, the Old Testament, and the Kabbalah, meaning the ancient Jewish mysticism from thousands of years ago. Michelangelo never associated with those who promoted Catholicism. Based on the letters Michelangelo wrote and left behind, and the people with whom he associated, it is believed that he became a Waldensian. It is also known that he received secret codes and information from the Waldensians.

When the Pope enters the papal ceremonial area in the Sistine Chapel, on the archway over his throne is a Latin phrase that says, "Vicarivs Filii Dei" which means, "Vicar or Representative of the Son of God". This is the Pope's official title. 1799 an English representative of very high rank was at the Vatican and noticed some of the letters in the phrase looked curiously like Roman numerals.

Here are his findings:

V	I	C	A	R	I	U	S		
5	1	100	0	0	1	5	0	=	112
F	**I**	**L**	**I**	**I**					+
0	1	50	1	1				=	53
D	**E**	**I**							+
500	0	1						=	501
									=
									666

Whoever built the Sistine Chapel knew these numbers. And, 666 = 6 + 6 + 6 = 18, which is the Anti-Christ number.

Sistine Central Panel   Interestingly on the Sistine Central Panel Michelangelo encoded internal organs in the painting. It was illegal in those days to do autopsies, study medicine or know what the organs were. People were not allowed to know anything; healing was not allowed to be done unless a priest did it. To spite the Church, Michelangelo painted internal organs, lungs, kidneys, and hearts. Every part of the human body is represented in the Central Panel in some form. Everything the Church was against was all around them

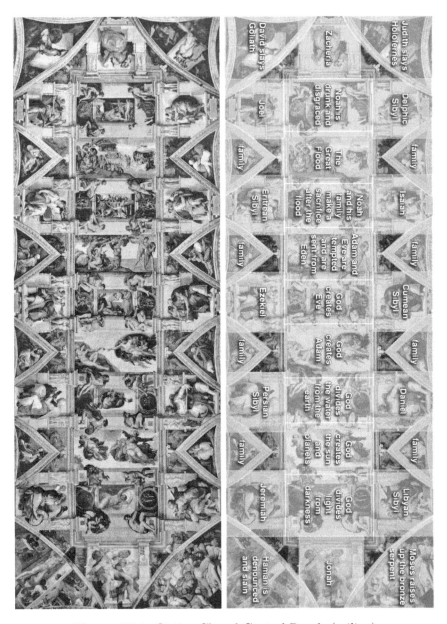

Figure 38.1: Sistine Chapel Central Panels (ceiling)

when they thought it was just beautiful art. (Figure 38.1.)

Amminadab   In the Old Testament "Amminadab" is the pious father of Nashon, chief of the tribe of Judah. The name Amminadab in Hebrew means "from my people will come a prince", in reference to Jesus. As far as the Church was concerned Amminadab represents Jesus.

Michelangelo painted a yellow circle on his sleeve. The yellow circle comes from a Muslim tradition of making someone considered a very bad person wear yellow, representing urine or toxic. In Rome the Pope made Jews wear yellow arm bands with a circle on it to distinguish they were a bad and evil people. Michelangelo decided since Jesus was Jewish he would paint a yellow circle on his arm. He couldn't paint Jesus that way, so he used Amminadab to symbolize Jesus. Once you know the symbolism you understand what Michelangelo was doing against the Catholic Church. And of course, you know that the Nazis made the Jews wear yellow arm bands during World War II - now you know where that came from! (Figure 38.2.)

Seals of Solomon   The Seals of Solomon, or Star of David, are also found at the Vatican. Michelangelo painted them all over the place. He put them in the exact place where the ballots are burned for Papal elections. No crosses or Christian images were used, only Stars of David.

The Pope is a paid position. For example if you come from a wealthy family and wanted your nephew to be the Pope so you could benefit from it, you would pay the Vatican a certain amount of money and make promises. They then add the substance that makes the ballots burning smoke turn white, and the person becomes the Pope. This is what goes on in the Vatican. (Figure 38.3.)

Pope Julius II   The Pope that commissioned the Sistine Chapel was Pope Julius II. He was from the Delle Rovere family. Rovere means "of the oak tree". Pope Julius II was a very corrupt Pope; he wanted the oak tree symbol all over the Vatican. Sometimes you will see these symbols at the Vatican because it represents the acorn of the oak tree of Pope Julius II. When he passed away he wanted Michelangelo to create the most amazing fantastic tomb that anyone had ever seen. So Michelangelo created a pyramid-shaped tomb layered in gold, with all kinds of biblical designs on it. His tomb was not finished until decades after he was dead because Michelangelo was doing so many other projects. On this tomb, Michelangelo put a myriad of Jewish symbols to spite the Pope who banned the Jews from Rome. (Figure 38.4.)

Due Putti/The Cumaean Sybil   Due Putti means "the two prostitutes" and was part of the gay art depicted by Michelangelo. The Cumaean Sybil is the image of the Pope on a feminine body, but with masculine features. This image is directly over where the Pope sits. All of Michelangelo's models were male, even if they were used for female images. He would paint a face over the original one, replacing it with someone's face he did not like. In this case it was the Pope. He also painted genitals in his works which were expressly forbidden to be seen in the Vatican. The angel to the left of the Pope with his arm around the other appears to be flipping off the Pope! (Figure 38.5.)

David Panel "Gimmel"   Michelangelo painted this image in the form of the Hebrew letter Gimmel. The symbol is called "devora" or severity, and represented the Pope's fear of the Jews; this is why he put this in the David panel. As we know Jesus was supposed to be descended from David. Michelangelo kept making references in the Catholic religion to its origins in Judaism. He kept trying to remind the Catholics that they should not be another religion, since they were really the old religion made into something else. Michelangelo learned this by studying the Kabbalah and Jewish mysticism. He put the image of the Gimmel in this painting quite obviously. Many of the bodies of the people in his paintings are shaped and positioned as Hebrew letters. (Figure 38.6.)

Judith & Holofernes "Chet"   Here we have the story of Judith and Holofernes and the Hebrew letter "Chet", which looks similar to the Pi sign. Michelangelo used this painting to represent the feminine nurturing energies of the Old Testament. Judith is the handmaiden; to the right is the Assyrian general Holofernes who came into the region and conquered the city she lived in called "Bethulia". Holofernes took Judith as a prisoner and wanted her for sexual favors. When Holofernes was drunk and passed out, Judith decapitated him and took his head on a platter or basket with another female servant, giving it to their people as a symbol and proof that they had killed the occupier.

This is also symbolic because the Catholic Church denied women their rights. They had to be subservient to the Catholic Church, and were treated as non-persons. They were only seen for having children and nothing else. The head on the platter represents the Pope being beheaded and held up by the women, supported by the feminine principal. The joke was the nurturing of the women killed the evil general that occupied them. And, according to Waldensian beliefs, women could serve as spiritual leaders. Michelangelo depicted nude males in most of his paintings, totally against what the Church accepted. (Figure 38.7.)

Creation of Sun and Moon This painting represents God creating and is situated in front of where Pope Julius II sat on his throne. The image on the left represents God mooning the Pope and the Catholic Church. God is turning away from the Prophet on the right because he is wrong, also representing the Church. This is what God thinks of the Catholic Church, according to Michelangelo. (Figure 38.8.)

The Drunkenness of Noah In the Old Testament there are Bible stories. In the ancient Hebrew tradition on the side of the stories is the explanation, or side bars, that explain each of the stories in detail. The story with Noah is that his three sons abuse him. At least one of the sons took advantage of Noah sexually when he was inebriated. Michelangelo depicted this to spite the Catholic Church since it did not allow homosexual activity, drunkenness, or nudity. He has put almost everything against the Church in this one painting, including connotations of incest and sexual molestation. (Figure 38.9.)

The Last Judgment   The "Last Judgment" mural on the altar wall of the Sistine Chapel is shaped like the 10 Commandment tablets from the Old Testament, referring to the 10 Commandments of Moses in the Old Testament. Within it are coded Hebrew letters.

In the right top quadrant of the painting are at least three images of naked men hugging, kissing, and embracing one another. Homosexuality was expressly forbidden by the Catholic Church, threatening those who might consider this lifestyle with "burning in hell forever". Michelangelo was gay and so was da Vinci. Michelangelo called this painting "the male elect section"; some images in the Sistine Chapel could be considered gay pornography! (Figure 38.10.)

Figure 38.2: Amminadab

Figure 38.3: Sistine Chapel: Seal of Solomon/Star of David

Figure 38.4: Prophet Zacharias with the face ot Julius II

Figure 38.5: Cumaean Sybil

Figure 38.6: David and Goliath

Figure 38.7: Judith and Holofernes

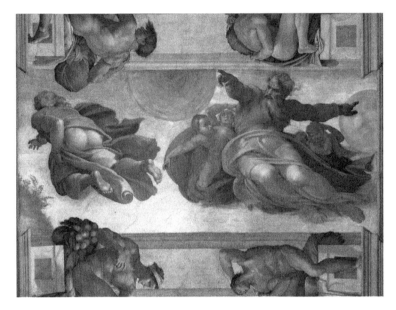

Figure 38.8: Creation of Sun and Moon

Figure 38.9: The Drunkenness of Noah

Figure 38.10: The Last Judgment

39. SPANISH EMPIRE

The Spanish Empire officially began in 1492 when they threw out the Moors. It ended in 1898 from the Spanish American war. This is when the Spaniards lost the war and a lot of territory. One of the places they lost was the Philippines.

What you may not realize is that the Spaniards were also involved in raids on Ireland where they took prisoners. Poor Ireland was raided by the Vikings, Spaniards, and the British; they just never had a good day. When the Spaniards mixed with the Irish it resulted in darker hair and complexions. These Irish are called the "Black Irish".

In the 1300s, the Black Plague, also called the "Black Death", infected the Spaniards killing a large percentage of Europeans. In a roundabout way this "Black Death" put Iceland in jeopardy from the Spaniards.

Iceland was closely connected to Norway because the Icelandic people stopped there for supplies while traveling in Scandinavia. When the Black Plague hit there was a problem with the Icelandic sailors dying from contact with the Norwegians, which ultimately led to limited interactions between Scandinavia and Iceland.

When Norway became Christianized at the end of the Viking era, the Catholic Church declared unless Iceland became Catholic Icelanders were no longer allowed to go to Norway anymore. Iceland refused to convert to Catholicism. The Icelandics then colonized a thin strip of Greenland along the southwestern corner as it was the only habitable area. There were no Inuit at the time. These indigenous people actually came later when they migrated from the northern part of Canada into Greenland looking for fishing territories.

The Spaniards took advantage of the disconnection between Iceland

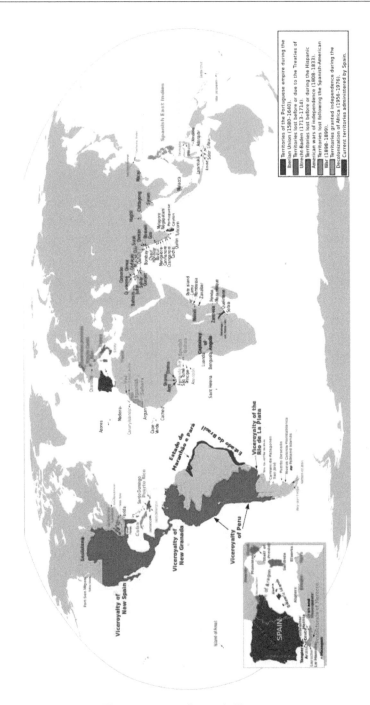

Figure 39.1: Spanish Empire

and Norway, raiding Iceland and Greenland, killing their people, taking slaves, and raping women. The Inuit from Canada took in the survivors that escaped and protected them. Many years later, the story was told of what really happened to the settlements in Greenland.

When people finally returned to Greenland, it was empty and abandoned. Why did the Spaniards attack and destroy everything? Because the agenda of the Catholic Church was to attack and destroy anyone who undermined the teachings of the Church. Today, Catholicism is the major religion in Spain, even influencing today's laws, which are perceived as backwards and thought to directly reflect the laws of medieval times.

40. BRITISH EMPIRE

The British Empire started in approximately 1336 at the time of the Hundred Years War with France. This is when the British wanted to expand and occupy other places, in a civil way, of course. The British Empire ended in 1945 at the close of World War II. The Germans bombed nearly every place the British controlled so there was nothing left of the British Empire.

The countries the British occupied are now called "commonwealth". After World War II little by little Britain gave all of these countries independence. In so doing the entire planet was complicated with conflicts throughout the world. The results of the British Empire dissolution are evident with problems in Pakistan, India, the Middle East borders with Israel and other countries. There are also problems in Africa as a result of the British giving nations there their independence.

There were even problems in the 1800s with Canada. The United States invaded Canada; why did this happen? In the war of 1812 between the US and Britain, the Canadians were just too nice to say no to England so the United States said, "Fine; we will invade you because you want to support Britain and you are going to be in trouble."

So, the US actually invaded Ontario and a lot of people were killed. This is what happened with the US, Canada, and Britain. Then, you have to consider the French in Québec. The French wanted an Empire too; this is what Napoleon attempted to do. He could not occupy Europe without an army so he went to Egypt to exert his Napoleonic Complex. He did get a big foothold in Québec, with loyal supporters, but Québec is still French. In recent years under the clause that

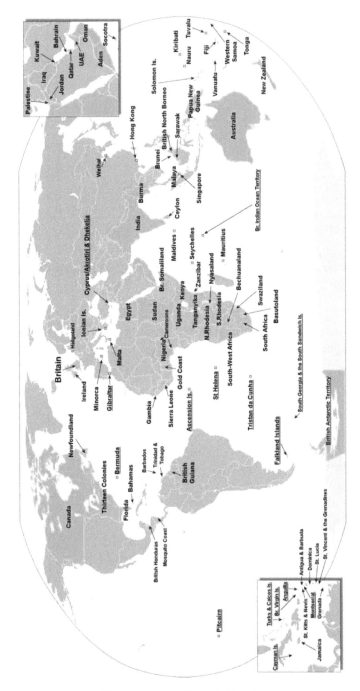

Figure 40.1: British Empire

Québec tried to separate from Canada, the Canadian Government declared Québec independent under the dominion of Canada.

This is similar to what the European Union does; all the European countries are independent but they belong to the EU. This really is a false freedom or false independence. This will happen with the North American Union. When the time comes, there will be a break-up of the United States just like happened with the Republic of California and Texas. Vermont also was an independent country at one time. Part of Louisiana in the 1800s was an independent country for a couple of years after the Civil War. There are four commonwealth states in the US: Massachusetts, Virginia, Kentucky, and Pennsylvania. They are not states but considered commonwealth with special status. They also have a lot of Federal Government facilities. Because they are not states the government can do whatever they want with them.

What I want to show you is the confusion these empires have caused to the present day. Britain allowed India to become independent after World War II. Pakistan was part of that and had the Muslim majority. Pakistan did not want to be part of India. India was trying to make it so that there were regions that were autonomous under one government, but they were all basically Indians. Britain split everything in half creating Pakistan and East Pakistan, with India in the middle. If you create conflict and split people you can control them. The British made all three commonwealth countries so Britain ultimately retained control. East Pakistan is now called Bangladesh.

The Queen of England is the Queen of Canada; her picture is even on the currency. She is also the Queen of Australia and wants to be the Queen of Africa. The British also created chaos in Africa, especially South Africa. Rhodesia was named after the British scholar Rhodes who had all the farms and British people there under his control. South Africa became a mix of Dutch, British, and German. Over time there was famine and drought, causing many Africans to migrate further south into this area because here they were provided with work and food.

The Africans then became the majority in these areas. They wanted the white people out of what they perceived to be their land. Civil wars ensued, breaking up South Africa. South Africa divided into South Africa and the new country of Swaziland. Namibia was also part of South Africa at one time; all of these are created countries that did not exist at one time.

Just because something is in Africa does not mean it is Black Africa. Whites dominated many areas like South Africa at one time. Rhodesia became Zimbabwe; many countries changed their names. Ethiopia went from a monarchy to a dictatorship. The Italians had control of Ethiopia before World War II; Rome knew the Ark of the Covenant was there. This is how the world is becoming totally and artificially re-arranged. For example, now we have British, French, and Dutch Guiana. Dutch Guiana became Suriname, British Guiana became Guyana, but French Guiana stayed French Guiana because it is still French. South America and South Africa are extremely complicated as a result of the British Empire.

In the year 1213 the British Kings could not pay taxes to the Vatican because they were poor and internal systems were falling apart. They made a deal with the Vatican whereby the Vatican would permanently own all British Royalty assets, with the proviso that the British Royalty would administer it forever. The Vatican could not control it, it could only own these assets, and this agreement is still in existence. After the so-called G7 and G8 meetings the President of the US now reports to the Vatican.

North America is under Windsor control; its assets are also owned by the Vatican. You are nothing more than an asset of the British Empire. The US Internal Revenue Service says you owe taxes to the American government and to the British Royalty. This is a special law. The US Postal Service is also owned by the bank of England. I am showing you that history as you were taught is a lie; it is not what you think.

41. ANTARCTICA & THE 4TH REICH

Antarctica is the only continent that officially does not have borders or belong to a specific country. There are territorial assignments to certain countries, but supposedly no single country can own or be in control of Antarctica. For example there are Russian, American, British, Ukrainian, Argentinean, and Chilean territories. The countries that border Antarctica or who have major scientific research teams were given territories by the United Nations.

You may have heard about the rumors that under the ice aircraft, underground cities, and technologies have been found frozen. This is partially true and some of it is false. Antarctica is quite an enigma; unless the ice melts no one is going to know exactly what is under the surface. Miles and kilometers of ice have piled up over the millennia. There was a time when Antarctica was not frozen and existed in a more temperate climate.

Antarctica became desirable during the Nazi time period; before then it was a relatively unknown location. People did not actually set foot in Antarctica until the early 1800s. The Germans have documents that show they first explored Antarctica in the 1800s, not the Norwegians or British as some people think.

Hitler was extremely interested in both the North and South Poles. He knew there were openings into the Inner Earth. Hitler was fascinated with occupying and controlling the frozen continent, sending expeditions there in the 1930s. Like the rest of world, Antarctica has caverns and cave systems that connect to the Inner Earth. The Nazis built bases within these caverns. Of course in a place like Antarctica they are covered and protected from the weather and harsh environment.

Nazi secret societies knew all about this information. The Nazis created the Thule society, a highly secret esoteric organization. You can even see Thule on a map of Greenland because the Nazis were interested in that country as well as Iceland and Tibet; all these places have openings to the Inner Earth. Hitler wanted to occupy all these countries, but he never got the chance. He even sent military expeditions to Tibet long before World War II.

The Aryan race extended all the way into Northern India which has dark skinned people. "Aryan" has more to do with culture and common origin than skin color. Hitler was trying to get the alien and Atlantean artifacts that existed in those locations, especially in Antarctica.

The official German emblem worn on the Nazi uniforms entitled "Deutsche Antarktische Expedition" is shown in fig. 41.1. The Neuschwabenland base was established in Antarctica in 1938-39.

Several bases were built on a section of Antarctica that was controlled by Norway. In 1938 the Germans said they were creating an underground paradise for the Führer in Antarctica. It took six years from 1938-1944 to construct the underground base; they used material from South Africa, Argentina, and Chile. These countries were the easiest places from which to access Antarctica.

Figure 41.1: Neuschwabenland uniform logo

This paradise was designed, outlined, and mapped after Berlin; the idea was to build an underground city that was the "New Berlin". The area now known as Queen Maud Land was called Neuschwabenland with an underground Nazi base known as "Base 211", that still functions. Neuschwabenland became the home of the 4th Reich.

In 1944 there were documented trainloads of blond-haired, blue-eyed people from Germany, Austria, Ukraine, Poland and other occupied nations with Aryan characteristics who boarded in Bremer-

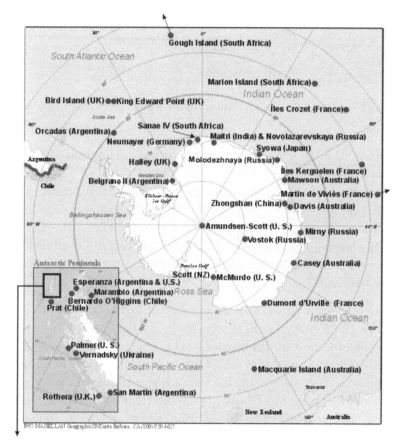

Figure 41.2: Antarctica with research bases

haven, Germany and shipped to Hamburg for transport to Antarctica. From Antarctica they were shipped by U-boats and regular ships to Neuschwabenland.

There are pictures and images that can be found showing these masses of Aryan-type people with their suitcases and backpacks, all looking alike. There were thousands and thousands of these people who were never seen again. Over 100 U-boats are also unaccounted for since the end of the war.

After WWII in 1946-47 the British, Canadians, Australians, and Americans all sent Air Force and Naval vessels to Antarctica in mil-

Figure 41.3: Map of Antarctica with Neuschwabenland

itary formation as if they were going to war. This was called "Operation Highjump" led by Admiral Richard E. Byrd. When they returned no explanation was given. Why would a military expedition of that size go to Antarctica? And, there were more than 50 fatalities all unexplained. There are documents from the US from 1946-47 showing that the US and its allies attacked Antarctica more than once, establishing bases there to monitor what you now know as the 4th Reich.

When we were in Antarctica in January of 2010, at a couple of the bases on the Peninsula there was a plaque that said the base was established to "monitor the enemy". What do you think this is about? Is this confirmation of the 4th Reich? Their presence is known to the bases on the surface by the various governments. Some of the bases even had statement booklets saying their original purposes for existing in Antarctica were to "monitor enemy activities" though the enemy or activities were not delineated.

The 4th Reich people are descendants of the 3rd Reich people who escaped and built a new society. The original Illuminati creation of the Nazis was ultimately usurped midstream by the Aldebaran influences, causing a change in alliances. The allies kept the war criminals that the Illuminati sponsored. The rest escaped to Antarctica. The 4th Reich in Antarctica is a major issue for the Illuminati. They have their own agenda and seek their own New World Order.

There are documents that indicate the Germans themselves admitted they were aided by Beings from the Aldebaran star system. These Beings are a Lyraen refugee group. They are extremely technologically advanced, and noted for their lack of emotion. They were responsible for the development of the German Teutonic tribes after the fall of Atlantis, and eventually for the creation of the Scandinavian culture.

They mixed their genetics with what was already there, creating a highly technologically advanced people. They may be emotionless, but they are very human-looking. You can be sitting next to one without knowing it. They have bases in the mountains of Austria, Bavaria, Switzerland, Iceland, and Greenland.

Jan Udo Holey better known as "Jan van Helsing" is an author from Germany who used to write about the Aldebaran culture and what it was planning to do with the 4th Reich. *Geheimgesellschaften und ihre Macht im 20. Jahrhundert* and *Geheimgesellschaften 2* (Secret Societies of the 20th Century part 1 and 2) were banned in Germany, Switzerland and France for allegedly inciting anti-Semitic hatred. Some of his books can be found on the Internet but are now widely censored. Similar to what happened to Billy Meier, anything with any truth is attacked, eliminated, or changed.

Bases under and near Antarctica are both 4th Reich and alien. There are tunnels that connect these bases to the mainland and the rest of Antarctica. In addition, all of the tunnels leading to these bases connect to the main tunnel system from ancient times. The tunnel passes directly under the Antarctic Peninsula. The main tunnel passes under the Drake Passage and under Tierra del Fuego. From there it connects to the Andean Mountains tunnel system that extends north to Central America and the Caribbean.

The people who comprise the 4th Reich in Antarctica call themselves the "Haunebu". They claim to be defending the Earth from Reptilians, et al, but want to recreate a new Lyraen Empire on Earth, with themselves as leaders. "Haunebu" has a double meaning. The Germans chose it for two reasons; it is a mysterious place in Southern Egypt in Luxor. The Japanese word "Hanabi" means "fire flower" or "fireworks". As you know the Japanese were German allies.

The Germans made allies with the Japanese with the idea that after the Japanese conquered the other part of the world the Germans would then kill the Japanese to claim the rest of it. Germans certainly did not consider the Japanese equals, but only used them. The Japanese knew this, preparing for eventual war with the Germans.

The Nordics seen in abduction scenarios are called the "Nordics". The Nordics are reported as tall blue-eyed blonds. The Nordics are

Figure 41.4: Flying Saucer of the Nazis: Haunebu II

really genetic creations of the 4th Reich; they are the superhuman man the Nazis were trying to make, perfected by the Haunebu. The Haunebu, along with their Nordic creations, have aligned themselves with anti-New World Order and anti-Reptilian groups. This does not mean that they are benevolent; it means they want their own New World Order.

There is a connection between the Haunebu and what is out in our solar system and beyond. For the last 20 years most of the alien craft seen on Earth are from here, not elsewhere. The government has technology that is anywhere from 50-200+ years advanced compared to what the public has, depending on the technology category. The Haunebu have made connections with the Inner Earth civilizations, who are in turn connected to the mine disasters and the wars going on underground.

In the 1950s and 60s the Chilean Air Force base in Punta Arenas in the Tierra del Fuego area was receiving radio signals from Antarctica. The Chilean Air Force base is situated where Argentina and Chile meet at the very tip of South America. The signals gave them instructions. The voices claimed to be "alien", but were really German.

The Germans had their own version of Area 51 on the island of Peenemunde in the Baltic Sea. This is where they were developing and manufacturing their secret weapons and aircraft technology. Before they moved the 3rd Reich to Antarctic Base 211 and became the 4th Reich, they were in the process of building a fleet of aerial vehicles called Vril craft. Vril is an ancient Sanskrit word.

Vril craft looked like discs, globes, and plates. They have anti-gravitational electromagnetic devices that rotate in different directions. They could go high into the atmosphere, travel at tremendous speeds, and even travel interdimensionally.

There are documents from WWII and just prior stating that these vehicles could travel as fast as 5000 km per hour and more. They also state that the goal was to fly the 68 light years to Aldebaran, where the Vril craft technology originated. As the war ended, it is believed that these vehicles were flown to both South America and Antarctica. There is evidence found on films showing the Vril craft taking off and flying. German documents show the vehicles were tested in occupied Prague during World War II.

Certain circles know that prior to World War II the Germans succeeded in travelling to the Moon and possibly beyond. There is a Nazi base on the dark side of the Moon. This photo was modeled after a photo from an American spacecraft that was going to the dark side of the Moon to supposedly take a picture of a crater. In the crater was the

Figure 41.5: Nazi Moon Base

swastika shape; NASA was apologetic for the anomaly of the transmission of the photograph that might have offended some of their engineers. This photo was never released to the public.

At the NATO Headquarters in Belgium in 2004/05 a woman that was attached to the US Military announced "electromagnetic anomalies had been detected by satellite". Apparently these anomalies were artificial and emanating from under Lake Vostok and other areas of Antarctica. The temperature of the lake rose 65 degrees with no reason for it. The woman said this was considered to be a "national threat to security". As she said this she was briskly escorted off the stage by burly men who then came on and said "there would be no more information on this topic". Nothing else was said and still has not been. This is when all the current maps of Antarctica were removed from public view. All you see now is the old maps without designations.

Every year you hear about scientists in Antarctica who get sick. They develop thyroid cancer, pancreatic cancer, breast cancer and other life threatening illnesses, and need to be evacuated. These announcements are made always during the Antarctic winter which is during summer in the northern hemisphere, making evacuation extremely risky due to Antarctica's harsh winter.

In 2005 a Chilean ice breaker/cutter ship went to Antarctica to rescue Russian scientists. On their way out they were trapped in an ice field that completely surrounded the ship, effectively holding the ship in place. No further information was heard about the incident.

The MS Explorer was a ship that sank going to Antarctica on November 23, 2007. The ship was specifically designed to handle the icy conditions of the Antarctic Ocean. Supposedly, the ship hit an unidentified submerged object reported to be "ice", causing a small hole in the hull. Again, no news beyond this report.

There are airlifts that go on every year until recently when they basically abandoned the Russian base near Lake Vostok. Other countries have also had to abandon scientific research because something was going on that was making people sick. Electromagnetic anomalies were getting more intense by 2003/04. By November 2005 the anomalies became so intense that they were detected elsewhere. This is the reason why this knowledge was made public; it could no longer be hidden.

In 2006 the US announced it was opening up an office in Colorado to examine the unusual electromagnetic and microwave bombardments of both the North and South Poles. Why would they open an office in Colorado to examine electromagnetic anomalies of the North and South Poles? Because a central location far away from the poles was needed to study the effects of these electromagnetic anomalies:

tectonic movements and drifts creating an increase in earthquakes and volcanic eruptions globally.

There was a time when what is now the South Pole was once the North Pole and vice versa. The poles have switched a couple of times in the course of Earth history over the last 4 billion years. The magnetic poles shift all the time. In fact currently the magnetic pole is somewhere over northwestern Canada. The prognosis is that it is going to start to shift back to an original position. This can change weather patterns but it does not mean that the Earth is going to flip on its axis.

The Earth, or any planet, does not naturally shift on its axis without external interference. If the Earth was hit by an asteroid, comet, or some other large object, then a pole shift could occur. For example, this happened with Uranus. This is why Uranus rotates north to south instead of east to west. This can only occur with artificial interference, so all the predictions of a pole shift are not going to occur unless there is huge external influence.

Antarctica is reporting the coldest temperatures ever recorded in its history. Antarctica is getting colder despite the global warming theories. Reports about blocks of ice the size of Rhode Island breaking off and floating away caused by global warming has nothing actually to do with global warming. There is a string of undersea volcanoes erupting under the ice along the coast due to tectonic plate activity. Of course volcanic activity is going to melt large pieces of ice!

The British Antarctic Survey confirmed undersea volcanoes off the coast of Antarctica have been causing the ice shelves to fall into the ocean, not global warming. They found at least a dozen volcanoes off the coast of Antarctica, many of them active. Some rise more than 10,000 feet off the ocean floor. There are some volcanic cones that are only 160 feet below the surface. This is in addition to the active Deception Island caldera that I sailed into during my Antarctic trip in 2010.

The team mapped an area almost the size of Britain on the sea floor because there were no known topography maps of the area. Official maps were blank. But, interestingly, even after this mapping was done, a huge blank area remained right in the middle of the new ocean floor map. The official explanation is that islands were blocking the sonar so it could not fill in the space.

How can islands block sonar when you are mapping under the ocean? Perhaps they saw something there that should not be seen in public. There are many areas of Google Antarctica that are blacked out or fuzzed over so no one can see what is there. Obviously, there is renewed official interest in the 7th continent, but not all of it can be revealed.

The same thing is happening in Greenland. Greenland is not melting because of the weather. Magma is coming to the surface from the volcanic activity underneath. In fact, even the North Pole is reporting extremely cold temperatures; this is why the national weather service has been warning that the winters will be much harsher than normal.

The Earth is cold and moves further away from the Sun naturally. Nothing is going to get warmer. The Earth is 70% water; an influx of light would evaporate a percentage of the water and create more cloud cover. This would reduce the temperature on the planet and make it colder. More volcanoes are erupting simultaneously than ever before. All the rock and ash that goes up into the ionosphere can potentially create blockages of the Sun for decades to come.

After Krakatau erupted in 1811/12, snow fell in July in New England. There was darkness for weeks and months all over the Earth. This was followed by severe winters for years from this one volcano. Now, there are 60-70 active volcanoes, erupting simultaneously. Think of the implications this brings to the Earth's weather.

The government said in 2005/06 that it wanted to repopulate all the empty land in the Midwest with animals from the Jurassic period, essentially recreating that time period on Earth in this location. Japanese scientists have cloned mastodons. In 1999 when I was working in Norway, I read in a Norwegian newspaper that South Korean and Russian scientists had cloned a mammoth. The fetus was planted into an African elephant and the birth was imminent. That was the last I heard of this; what happened?

Ancient creatures are being recreated by extracting DNA from amber, reconstituting it, and then infusing this DNA material into live cells. The story you saw in Jurassic Park can really be true; this is already being done. Ancient frequencies have been, and are being, brought back to life.

Lemuria is in the process of rising up. The goal is to repopulate it with all the creatures that existed at the time, recreating the ancient Earth homeland as well as the time before the last Ice age.

There was a CNN video of a Japanese ship in the summer of 2007 on its way to Australia that witnessed an island re-emerge in front of them. The whole South Pacific is shifting and rising up.

Observe the USGS maps south of Australia in Antarctica and south of the South Pacific region, you will see huge earthquakes occurring weekly. Something is shifting and rising.

As the Lemurian continent rises, pressure is put on all the tectonic borders. This is why there are quakes occurring along the coast of South America and what is aptly called the "Eastern Rise" of the Pacific. Everything is shifting. Along the Western US the plate is shifting northwest. Alaska gets about 300 earthquakes a day.

All the displaced water could potentially hit Eastern China and Japan. The Indian Ocean has large quakes south of India which is fracturing that area into a new tectonic plate. Currently this is called the Indo-Australian plate. This is part of what happened in 2005 with the large quake in Indonesia. All these things that are going on relate to Antarctica.

The only airline that still flies to Antarctica is Qantas Airways. They used to offer flights once per month in December, January, and February which is the Antarctic summer. Air New Zealand also used to offer flights but stopped after a flight crashed on Mount Erebus in Antarctica on November, 28th 1979. I have done seminars in New Zealand and met a person related to the pilot of that downed plane. Officially, the accident was blamed on pilot error. Pilots do not get assigned to that route without years of experience. Flight computers are programmed with the routes before the planes even take off. There are bases in Antarctica that monitor the radar screen nonstop.

This person found out years later that someone sabotaged the computer program before the plane took off. This meant that the pilot thought he was in one place when he really was in another place.

The plane flew right into the mountainside, killing almost 300 people. Since then there have been no Air New Zealand flights to Antarctica.

Qantas decreased its flights to only one or two a year, and these must be booked at least one year in advance. Public flights are limited; the number of people who can go are limited; the places you can fly over are limited. Flights do not land on Antarctica; they are only allowed to fly over specific land areas.

Even land tours are limited. When I went there only a certain amount of people can go on shore at one time; you cannot even take one rock with you; and only a specified number of ships can be in a limited area at one time. The public thinks that it has access to Antarctica without realizing how extremely restricted the access is.

Antarctica is a highly mysterious continent. No one is allowed to go into the interior more than a few miles or kilometers. Even established bases are closing up. Something very strange is going on there about which you are not being told.

Currently people in the United States, Canada, and some in Northern Europe are being activated with Antarctic programming. This means that they have a strong desire to go there as well as strong connections to Fourth Reich triggers which are currently being activated. It appears as if the Fourth Reich, or whatever is underneath Antarctica, is activating its secret army in various locations.

If you feel some kind of longing, desire or obsession with Antarctica or anything connected to it, even peripherally, then you need to look at the possibility of 4th Reich programming.

42. TIBET, INDIA & NEPAL

Tibet is a strange and mysterious country with interesting connections to Antarctica and Hitler's WWII 3rd Reich. Keep in mind that Tibet was an independent country until 1947. While Hitler was obsessed with occupying Egypt and deciphering the secrets of the pyramids, he was equally obsessed with the mysteries of Tibet, sending numerous expeditions there because he believed the legendary tales of underground areas based upon the stories of Shambhala and Agartha.

When the Russians invaded Berlin at the end of the war, they found dead Tibetan Monks in his compound. Tibetan Monks were assigned as guards in Munich, Nuremberg, and Berlin. Hitler also imported Tibetan Monk Leaders in an attempt to help him lead Germany. The Germans were very involved in mind-control and sexual magick ritual. They studied the Monks resistance to mind-control to develop better methods for programming. Castles were used in the Alpine region to conduct sexual magick ritual. Using ancient manuscripts from Egypt and Tibet, magick rites were used to create and reinforce the German Empire. Hitler believed in human sacrifice rituals, killing several men by pulling their hearts out while they were still alive.

Hitler never did a thing without consulting his astrologer. Everything was calculated according to the best astrological outcome. He even had a plan to invade the United States. The bombing of Japan by the US is what scared the Germans into surrendering. If this had not happened, the Germans would have moved forward in their plans, and it is highly likely that US citizens would now be speaking German. Hitler was that close to complete world domination because of his Vril craft and development of his own nuclear weapons. Laser electromagnetic weaponry was also acquired from the Aldebarans.

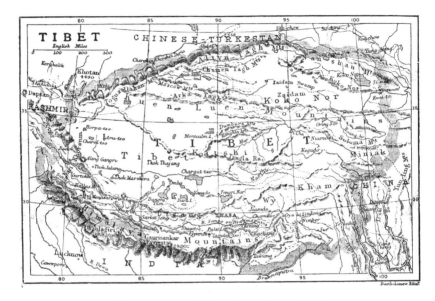

Figure 42.1: Tibet (map from 1906)

Hitler used to have terrible nightmares, waking up screaming in the middle of the night. He was out of his mind with fear and would say, "I saw who controls humanity and they are not human beings". He also said that he saw his true masters and they were not human but Reptilian. His doctor kept him sedated with barbiturates such as Coramine/Nikethamide to counter the effects. Nightmares are side-effects of programming.

Hitler was also highly interested in India and Nepal because he knew of the underground tunnel system which crisscrossed the entire area that was rumored to be filled with hidden esoteric information. In the valley of Katmandu in Nepal at an elevation of 5000 feet, there is a large, strange object said to have been brought down from the Himalayas by a male mystic. The object was aimed at the valley whereupon the water receded and the valley of Katmandu appeared. The statues, which look like a device, are there to this day. This is only one small example of the mysteries hidden away in India and Nepal.

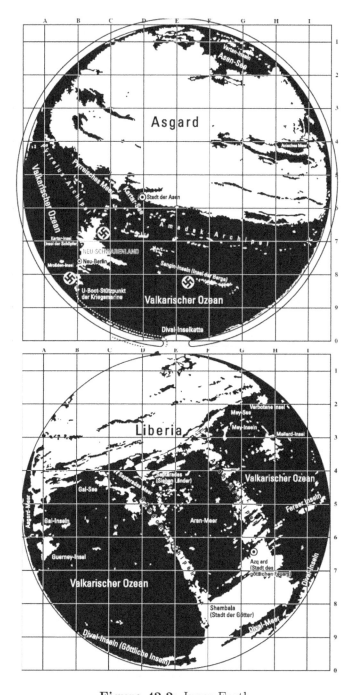

Figure 42.2: Inner Earth

43. Iceland

Hitler desperately wanted to invade Iceland. His troops invaded Norway practically overnight because Norway did not have much of a military. Hitler saw this as a stepping stone to Iceland. Presently there are approximately 4.9 million people in Norway; the majority of its territory is empty. It is rich in oil located in the North Sea region.

Britain and the United States had bases setup in Keflavik, Iceland, west of Reykjavik, anticipating the German advance. Keflavik, of course, is now the location for the International Airport which was once the NATO military base. If Hitler had made it into Iceland, he would have been very close to invading North America. The German military was trained to work in snow just for this purpose. Hitler was close to accomplishing his goal.

Currently there are only 320,000 people in Iceland. During World War II there were only approximately 120,000. 100% of the Icelandic population lives along the edge or coastline because the interior is uninhabitable due to lava fields, volcanic activity, and glaciers. There are major openings to the Inner Earth through its volcanic chambers. People disappear every year in Iceland without a trace.

Hitler knew a lot of secret esoteric information and was actually quite brilliant; this is why he wanted to go to Iceland, Antarctica, and Tibet. He knew they had joint subterranean connections and that various alien civilizations occupied areas underneath these countries.

There is a huge Aldebaran base under Bavaria, Germany. Hitler was intent on keeping this a secret, even from the people who knew he had a retreat in this area. He was determined to be close to the alien energy that he wanted to energetically assimilate.

Hitler's father was a Rothschild and Jewish; his mother was a maid. When it was discovered she was pregnant, Madame Rothschild demanded the maid leave. Hitler hated the Jews since he felt rejected by them. However, his best friends during his school years were Jewish. Ultimately, the Rothschild family funded his Nationalist party. Hitler projected his own self-hate out onto the people who he thought rejected him.

44. NAZI EXPERIMENTS

The Germans were involved in many, many scientific and esoteric projects. German scientists continued their work and research in the United States and Canada under the code name of "Project Paperclip". In the late 1990s these governments finally admitted this truth.

After WWII, Britain, the US, and Canada salvaged important German scientists so that their experiments could continue uninterrupted as well as avoid the Nuremberg trials. Dr. Josef Mengele, well-known for his Nazi death camp experiments, died in Brazil in the 1980s, where his body was found floating off the coast. Dental charts and DNA matches from his son confirmed his identity. The Nazis had laboratories in Brazil, Paraguay, and Argentina, with many people. Mengele was involved in all of them. Nazi experiments continued for decades after the war and still do to this day.

The Germans were also involved in time travel experiments. There is a famous story that circulated in the late 1950s of a salesman driving to Omaha from another city in Nebraska when his car ceased to function. He claims he saw a craft off the road with a Swastika on it and German-speaking scientists wearing white lab coats took him aboard. Even though he saw the inside of the craft, no one spoke to him. When they were done he was put outside and the craft vanished.

After World War II, diseases previously rare in North America began to increase. Since 1945 incidences of such conditions as diabetes, cancer, stroke, and high cholesterol have escalated. These health issues did not exist prior to World War II. This is because German scientists came to North America with all their research from the concentration camps.

They knew fluoride in water deadens the brain, creating much more docile, controllable population. Corn syrup added to food prevents insulin production, resulting in diabetes. Homogenized milk causes cholesterol buildup in the arterial system. These are just a few examples of how chemicals are manipulated for sinister results.

Thanks to the Nazi scientists and their research conducted at concentration camps we now have increased disease in North America. In Germany they experimented on people, monitored the results, and then brought this heinous research to the US and Canada, including mind-control and programming.

Ewen Cameron came to Canada from Scotland in the late 1940s. Using the Nazi research, he created mind-control and programming. He was so successful that this was brought to the United States.

Wernher Von Braun, creator the V-2 rockets that destroyed London and killed tens of thousands of people, became the Director of the newly created NASA in 1960.

Many scientists were brought to the United States after World War II to continue their research and technology development unimpeded. These war criminals were free to perpetuate and extrapolate their work on the unsuspecting population of North America. Most of current technology and medical science comes from the German Nazi scientists that were brought to the US as well as from captured UFO material after the 1947 Roswell crash.

The Soviets did the same thing but in their own way. The Soviets kidnapped the Germans when the Soviets invaded Berlin. The Soviets started researching time travel and invisibility cloaks in the 1920s, especially in Siberia. They tested invisibility cloaks on aircrafts developed from Nikola Tesla's equipment and information, and were developing interdimensional vehicles. In Western Siberia, west of Lake Baikal, the Russians were developing a plane that could take off at a speed that increased until the plane became invisible. The issue was that the plane could not hold the invisibility for long.

The kidnapped Germans managed to steal the Russian technology, escape, perfect this technology, and install it in the German Vril craft.

Now, it is widely believed that the vehicle seen by the salesman in Nebraska could have been a German experimental craft that left in the 1930s or 40s from Nazi Germany, went to the future, and then back to the 1930s or 40s.

Remember that Montauk was populated by a myriad of Nazi scientists. The US government in the early 90s admitted to a "Project Paperclip" that brought Nazi scientists to the US to continue their experiments. The culmination of the Philadelphia experiment was in 1943 and involved Nazi scientists as well.

During World War II the people of Montauk witnessed German U-boats approaching the coastline and going underneath into what appeared to be a submarine pen, then they would leave without anyone stopping them. This indicates that the German and American governments were working together. Why else would they bring their highly valued German scientists here to protect them?

In the late 1930s Hitler sent expeditions to Egypt, Tibet, parts of Africa and even places in South America where he was trying to find information on gaining access to the Inner Earth. Hitler was extremely programmed; in fact he did not even know the identity of his real masters. He knew who funded him but he did not know who was behind his financial benefactors.

Rituals were performed by elites of the Nazi Party at castles in Germany, Austria, France, and Switzerland high up in the mountains. Many types of rituals were performed, but they were particularly interested in possession or using a person as a vessel. They wanted to bring in astral energies that would help them win the war and gain control over their enemies. These types of rituals were practiced not only by the Nazis, but by the elite in Russia, England, France, and the United States.

Nazi esotericism has been widely publicized, and glorified in films such as "Raiders of the Lost Ark". People think these films are fantasy, but many stories are based on truth. Nazi leaders performed rituals in Ethiopia, Tibet, and India. There was a very close connection with the Nazi party and the leaders of esoteric Muslim fundamentalist groups, even back then. Hitler was quite interested in getting information on the "Jinns", or "genies" as well as the mysticism of the Arabic and Islamic cultures.

One of the reasons Hitler invaded Norway overnight and was so anxious to dominate Russia, was due to the underground bases and anomalies in the northern area of Scandinavia. The Kola Peninsula in Russia used to belong to Finland and Norway but was confiscated by the Russians during World War II.

In addition, there are large areas of unexplored cities and superior ancient technology found frozen in the ice. The Russians were very curious to know what this was and how they could use it, as was Hitler. He did not care about the land or the people; he only cared about what he was going to find in the Kola Peninsula.

Hitler destroyed his army and ruined himself while trying to occupy the Soviet Union. Horrible weather killed off much of his army, along with 20 million Russians as he attempted to find artifacts. At the end of the war when the Russians invaded Berlin and supposedly found his charred body, he was being protected by Tibetan monks.

The Tibetan monks that guarded him came back with the Nazi expeditions. The Tibetans were fascinated with the Swastika symbol. The Swastika is a Tibetan, Hindu, and American Indian symbol; it has nothing to do with the Germans. The Nazis took the symbol, reversing its direction, and now it's viewed as a Nazi symbol. Energetically, the Swastika represents the 4 elements of creation that intertwine with each other to create reality. This very ancient symbol was used by many cultures on Earth.

Due to the Nazi regime, the Swastika now has extremely negative connotations, when in fact it really is a highly positive symbol. The Nazi symbol "SS" is based on the lightning bolt, which represents activation of the mind and body. The Nazis knew that blue-eyed blond-haired genetics were easy to control and manipulate, so this is why they wanted the whole world to be blue-eyed blond-haired. These genetic qualities had nothing to do with beauty; but only with control.

Adolf Hitler and Eva Braun did not die at the end of the war. There is information proving that Hitler and Eva Braun fled Berlin by submarine to the island of Peenemunde in the North Sea off the coast of Northern Germany. From there they escaped to Barcelona, then across the Atlantic to Buenos Aires, Argentina.

At the end of World War II Russia invaded the eastern part of Germany. They occupied the German comparative version of Area 51 located on Peenemunde Island. Hitler left a body double in the bunker who was burned after being shot, only to be found by the Russian army. No one was able to verify this body as Hitler's.

A news report in December 2009 claimed that the KGB burned the remains of Hitler and Eva Braun in 1970, dumping the ashes in a river in East Germany. This bogus story came only a few weeks after scientists claimed that the skull of Hitler kept by Russian authorities was actually that of a female.

Why would Hitler's body be kept for 25 years in a grave and then burned? Why would a skull be kept by officials who claimed it was Hitler's? The answer is to cover up the fact that Hitler and Eva fled Germany for Argentina where they lived happily there for decades. This was confirmed by the head of Argentina's secret police that guarded Hitler until his death.

When I worked in Switzerland my sponsor was part of the Swiss Intelligence. He said that sometimes he would drive very fast, thinking that he would never live. Then, he went on to tell me a story going around in the Intelligence circles of a man who lost control while driving a vehicle on a steep mountain road in which his car was headed for a sheer wall of rock. The man braced for impact, preparing himself to die. Instead, he went right through the wall, finding himself in an open area surrounded by human-looking people. Apparently the wall was a holographic disguise that he drove through. The people pushed his car out, telling him never to return.

All kinds of mysteries are out there that are stranger than fiction. Hitler knew this and so did his backers. And the scary thing is that his backers are still out there somewhere, still working on completing the projects that Hitler started.

There are many stories about the rituals that took place in the Alpine and Bavarian regions of Europe. One of the major projects that came out of the Third Reich, now the Fourth Reich, is the "Lebensborn Project". This was a German project that started in the 1930s to create the "Aryan Super Race". Regardless of marital status, soldiers with the "proper" Aryan genetics were put with females with the "proper" Aryan genetics to produce as many children as possible.

The resulting offspring were then placed into homes with families where they were raised with the Third or Fourth Reich agenda. This continued through World War II. Often, when Germany invaded a country like Poland, Czechoslovakia, or another Aryan-like nation, children considered to be Aryan were taken from their birth families and placed with German families.

Even at the end of the war after Hitler and regime survivors fled to other locations, the Lebensborn Project continued under the guise and control of Dr. Mengele, who escaped to Brazil. Children produced this way into the 1960s were placed with families in Northern Europe, particularly Norway, Sweden, and Denmark. Some children were also placed in United States' orphanages, including the states of Minnesota, Tennessee, Texas, Pennsylvania, and Colorado as well as Northern New England and Great Lakes states.

I have had some of these children as clients. When trying to find their original birth documents, these clients, without fail, were inevitably told that the records were destroyed a long time ago, often via fire. These people could never find their true identities. All of them have blond-hair blue-eyes with similar personality characteristics: aggressive tendencies, anger issues, nervous, easily irritated, and inherited programming.

As far as I know the Lebensborn Project does not exist anymore, ending around the time the Montauk Project began, which basically continued with the goals of the Lebensborn Project.

45. BOOK OF REVELATION

The Book of Revelation is the script, or agenda, for the Illuminati. The name "Jesus" came centuries later when the New Testament was completely altered by the Council of Nicaea in approximately 330AD in the area of Constantinople.

The Gospels in the New Testament only contain what the Council of Nicaea decided should be in the Bible. The Original Bible looked much different than the Bible of today.

The New Testament was translated from Aramaic, to Greek, to Latin, to German, and then to English. Do you think that after five translations some things "got lost in the translations"?

Especially from Greek to Latin translations, there are words in Greek that cannot be translated into Latin. So, translators simply made up words to fit the sentence. Take this back to the original Aramaic and you will know for certain that the original meanings of the sentences were not translated correctly.

For example, the original New Testament talked about reincarnation. When Jesus said "I have come before and you have known me before", he was talking about previous lifetimes. There is a lot of information in the original New Testament that has been changed and deleted. Several websites can be found on the Internet that claim to have the lost books of the New Testament; some do, some do not; use your tools of discernment to decide what is correct and what is not correct.

The Bible is extremely conflictive; the Old Testament is not really from God. So who is performing all these functions and miracles? Alien Beings directing humankind as an experiment, according to the *Talmud Jmmanuel*. This book also confirms that the New Testament is a continuation of the human experiment.

The *Talmud Jmmanuel* is a document encased in resin discovered in a cave in Jerusalem in the 1960s by a Palestinian researcher. This researcher sent part of the document to his colleagues in Switzerland where it was translated into German. He took the remainder of it to a Palestinian refugee camp in Lebanon. While there, the camp was bombed by the Israelis, killing the professor and destroying the remaining text. Coincidence?

The *Talmud Jmmanuel* says that the Christ figure was a genetic manipulation. The Christ figure did not die in Jerusalem, but really died in Kashmir, India.

The *Talmud Jmmanuel* says that "Jmmanuel" was the real name of the Christ figure. Jmmanuel was married to Mary Magdalene and together they had three children. In the painting of the "Last Supper" the person seated next to Christ is not an Apostle but Mary Magdalene. If you look closely, you can see that the Apostle Peter is directly physically threatening her.

Peter did not like Mary Magdalene, causing her to fear for her life. For her own safety, Mary Magdalene fled the Holy Land by ship with two of the children, travelling to what is now Turkey, eventually to Malta, and finally to the South of France.

Jmmanuel and the oldest son went to Srinagar, to the area now known as Kashmir, on the border of Pakistan and India. You can find his grave here. The grandson of Jmmanuel eventually travelled on to Japan where there is a temple devoted to him. As you can see, history is not what you have been told. During the so-called "20 missing years" from ages 13 to 33, Jmmanuel was not in the Holy Land at all, but learning in the ancient schools of Egypt. This is documented in Egypt.

The New Testament ends with the Book of Revelation, which is really the plan for humanity by the Global Handlers. When this was written the Illuminati were not in a hurry, as it had time to gain control with the goal of complete Earth domination.

This is the entire purpose of Christianity as with all organized religion. Christianity was brought to the Roman Empire as a control force. At the time of Jmmanuel, the Roman Empire had expanded to most of the known world, encountering many civilizations, cultures, and religions that were very much against the Roman Empire. The Roman Empire was determined to eliminate cultures, assimilate the populace against the will of the people, and impose Roman will above all others.

The Greek civilization, which was also an empire that existed during this time, accepted other cultures, allowing their conquered populaces to decide whether or not to embrace Greek culture. The Greek Government's only demand was that it would administer the conquered territory.

The symbol of the Roman Empire was the eagle, which astrologically is the opposite of the Scorpion. In conventional astrology, Scorpio is the only sign with two symbols: the Earth/physical symbol of the scorpion and the spiritual symbol of the eagle. Both are predators that can attack and kill on two different levels. The Romans' symbol depicted the simultaneous conquest and destruction of enemy culture and spirituality.

The other civilizations to use the eagle as symbols were the Nazi Empire and the American Empire. What does this tell you? That basically, the same people are in charge as the eagle swoops down on its prey to kill it. The Book of Revelation details the steps to complete domination in the symbolic script of the Illuminati.

The Illuminati agenda for world domination also includes the Soviet Union. Understand that the Soviet Empire stretched from Asia to Europe and even into Cuba and other continents. One of the moves of the Soviet Empire was their own dissolution, to break itself up into many components/countries; each one giving the appearance of being independent and free. The reasoning behind this breaking up into separate Republics enabled foreign aid to build up each piece separately so they could all be reconstituted in a more powerful position, which is what has already happened.

What happened to Russia? Russia is the Soviet Union once again. It is sending bombers over the coast of Alaska and Britain, buzzing US airbases all over the world, ignoring nuclear proliferation treaties, and assisting countries that it wishes to take over, such as the Republic of Georgia. The brilliant idea is to dissolve, then strengthen each piece and reconstitute the whole. This plan is called the "39th Move";

the agenda is world domination via manipulation without firing any weapons.

Extrapolate this agenda to your own mind and programming matrix. You go into the pieces of the matrix to break them, then strengthening the pieces, and finally, merge the pieces into one whole unit. You do this to support and unify your original soul-personality; as above so below.

The New World Order likes to give the appearance of its dissolution, evidenced in the last election. But, the plan is to reconstitute it in a more powerful position. Do not be fooled by Chapters 17 and 18 in the Book of Revelation. In my opinion, we are closing Chapter 16 going into 17. Only the Illuminati know the real answer to this. Since it wrote the Book of Revelation a lot of things have transpired and the set of instructions has been altered.

The current agenda of the Illuminati includes the "Revelation" of Biblical artifact discoveries in the Middle East, Peru, Mexico, Egypt, and Israel. News of these artifact discoveries is planned to coincide with the Book of Revelation which in turn "proves" to the populace that the predictions in the Book of Revelation are true.

Project Blue Beam will project holographic images in both physical reality and in the sky to give you the impression that yes, these "Revelations" are happening or about to happen, such as the Staged Alien Invasion and the Staged Second Coming of Christ.

Movies like Harry Potter, Narnia, and Lord of the Rings, among many others, are all designed to condition your mind to accept the fulfillment of prophecy and what will happen in the future. This involves acceptance of astral entities, alternate realities, and virtual realities. There will come a time when you will not know the difference between actual reality and virtual reality.

You will live in a created world, which you are anyway, except instead of being created by your mind your world will be created by technology. You will not know where technology ends and your mind begins. This is why the Illuminati want children to be so connected to video games. Children are growing up in a way that makes it challenging for them to differentiate between what is real and what is fake; to them it is all one.

You have a pathway and purpose that is unique; there is not another one of you in all of creation. This is because every point in time and space is unique. When that point in time and space is replicated, there is instant communication and instant assimilation of that point. This is how time travel, deep space travel, and interdimensional travel are accomplished.

Two points in time and space are determined, the frequencies of these points are matched and there is an instantaneous connection. There is no passage of time or space; it is instant and it is frequency.

You are a unique point in time and space. As a unique point, you discover your unique function within the God-Mind that no one else can fulfill but you. You were created in this part of the God-Mind as a reflection of It. God-Mind does not create accidentally or incidentally; It creates specifically and purposefully. Especially in this particular lifetime you will find your specific purpose. You have infinite lifetimes and realities; but what you know and express is a matter of where you are focused at the moment. Each lifetime is valid and a part of you.

There is a reason there are 22 chapters in the Book of Revelation. There are 22 letters in the Hebrew alphabet. In Hyperspace, the number "22" represents a transition. Basically, the Book of Revelation is a transition from one phase of humanity and life to another. According to their agenda that tells us that after they complete the 22 scenarios that life will be very different on this planet.

The Voynich Manuscript is an enigma that was found in Italy in 1912. This document is written in an unknown language that the greatest cryptologists of our time are unable to decipher. There are images and drawings of plants, herbs, and flowers that do not exist or are unknown. Some believe that it is either a hoax or fictional story. One theory suggests that it was written by Sir Frances Bacon in the 1200s as a code. The manuscript appears to resemble oriental writing, although no one knows for sure and was donated to Yale University after unsuccessful attempts to sell it.

46. STAGED ALIEN INVASION

The 1947 Roswell UFO crash was a staged incident for public consumption. A vehicle crashed on a ranch in New Mexico scattering debris over a very large area. When the military arrived, remnants of a craft with three dead bodies were found, with a live alien watching over them. A school expedition from the University of New Mexico actually arrived before the military.

These school participants were taken into military custody for several days; their lives and the lives of their families were threatened if they revealed any of the information. These people believed they and their families would be killed, so they refused to publicly speak about this incident.

In the 1970s and 80s as these people aged, they began to reveal these secrets on their death beds believing that they had nothing to lose. This is when the story of Roswell once again began receiving public attention.

You may have seen the famous photograph of the military officer kneeling by the silver material that was defined as "a weather balloon". He has a document in his hands that is illegible. Thanks to technology advancements, a brilliant person enlarged and clarified the photograph. Now, you can easily read the document. On it is written "an alien craft with bodies was discovered".

There is a lot of misinformation about Roswell. For example, one of the stories states that the craft's navigational equipment was affected by radar, causing it to crash. Another story says the craft was hit by lightning. Do you think an interstellar craft that could go billions of miles would be affected by radar or lightning? Of course not!

Another government story reports "the bodies found were crash dummies, mannequins". However, these "dummies" were invented in 1952, and the crash was in 1947. They need new writers! Even you could get a job with "Disinformation Services" and write something more convincing!

Basically, the Roswell crash was staged by the Illuminati; it was a way to start the process of telling you about the alien presence on Earth - at least this part of it. The other part was intended to create fear within you. The war with the Germans was over; the Cold War had not started. People who are afraid are easier to control; fear is always the beginning point of programming and mind-control.

The public was therefore presented with the possibility that an alien civilization was attacking or coming to the Earth with technology against which there was no defense. The Roswell incident laid the foundation for the start of the "Staged Alien Invasion" scenario.

Remember that 1947 was also the year Monarch Programming began under the auspices of Dr. Ewen Cameron. This year marked the beginning of the end of the way things "used to be".

By 1954, the US government had made a deal with the Beings from the Rigel Star System. It gave these Beings the right to abduct US citizens as long as the government was given a list of the people taken. Years later, the government realized the list was incomplete; people were vanishing never to return again.

In the 1960s, 17 scientists from Earth were exchanged for 17 scientists from the Rigel star system. Our scientists never came back. This all led up to the creation of the Dulce Base in the 4 corners area near Farmington, New Mexico. This is the largest underground base in the world with nine levels. An underground war started when the government realized the aliens had lied. Delta SWAT teams were sent to extract the kidnapped humans, but the SWAT team was killed. Phil Schneider released information on this in the 1990s.

There are over 130 underground bases in the continental United States with several in Alaska. There used to be a base on the Michigan/Wisconsin border; the largest submarine base with the largest submarine communications in the world. Why would there be a base in Michigan? What is under the Great Lakes? Bases exist under the oceans and other continents.

The government created the "Blue Book" UFO investigation group for public consumption. This way the public thinks that the government is as baffled as the populace. Of course, every UFO incidence is given an official explanation by the government, explaining everything as merely ordinary objects or events.

The latest "space" news centers around meteors and asteroids, creating fear that one of these has the potential to hit the Earth and destroy it. Secret UFO information is supposedly now being released by the U.K., France, and Russia. Even conventional media has suggested that meteors and asteroids are actually weapons being hurled at Earth from an alien civilization.

Mars is another popular topic, with discussions of oceans and vegetation existing on the Red Planet at one time. With a telescope you will see vegetation in the northern hemisphere of Mars during the Martian Spring.

Astronauts and pilots have released information on the UFOs that they have seen. Mass public UFO sightings continue to increase. The Illuminati are positioning you to react in fear when it uses the "Blue Beam Project" to project UFOs in the sky as "invaders" land on Earth and create explosions. It wants you to scream and flee in terror.

A global crisis will be announced as well as the need for a "New World Order" government to unite all people together to fight the alien invaders. Those with Greenstar programming who have not deprogrammed will be completely activated.

Finally, a savior race will intervene to help. Enter the Reptilians. They will be hailed as rescuers/saviors. The Reptilians will announce that they are our true ancestors who seeded the Earth long ago and are the original colonists of the planet. They will develop Earth into a space society under strict rules. Then they will bring in the Second Coming of Christ who announces his new Holy Empire where everything is peaceful and wonderful again. When a DNA sample of this Christ matches the Shroud of Turin which is now authenticated, how could you doubt this Christ?

How will you know the difference between the Staged Alien Invasion and the real one? There will be several clues. When you see the real Illuminati flee, when the President is gone, you will know that this one is the real invasion. When the leaders are making public statements and promises to save humanity, then you will know it is the Staged Alien Invasion. The experience may be the same: explosions, images in the sky, and dead people. This may happen in both scenarios, but look at the reactions of the leaders to tell you what is real and what is not.

47. KUIPER BELT

Kuiper Belt Programming parallels Illuminati programming. Kuiper Belt Programming is a secret sabotage by double-agent Illuminati programmers. Or, perhaps this programming was installed by Kuiper Belt Beings.

When the media first announced objects in the Kuiper Belt, it was reported that "objects were appearing never before seen". Then all of a sudden these reports stopped. Then the media reported that there was an object moving and actually coming closer to the Earth. Then, this information stopped as well.

Most of objects in space are artificial, but there is a real Kuiper Belt with many objects hidden within it. The Kuiper Belt is a good cover due to the debris surrounding our solar system; the Kuiper Belt is almost like a fence that goes around our solar system. In fig. 47.1 you can see the orbits of the planets. You cannot even see our Earth from this perspective but you can see how extensive and far out the Kuiper Belt is.

In August 2006, scientists voted for a new definition for Pluto at a meeting of the International Astronomical Union (IAU) in Prague, Czech Republic. They declared Pluto was not really a planet, but a Kuiper Belt object due to its orbit. They called it a "dwarf planet, planetoid, and a trans-Neptunian object". They announced that we really only have 8 planets in our solar system and not 9. Is it a planet, or is it not a planet? Nobody knows what Pluto is to this very day. The media no longer discusses it. Now, the solar system is reconfigured, omitting Pluto as a planet to cover up the fleet that exists in the Kuiper Belt. This fleet appears to be quite spread throughout the Kuiper Belt, especially around the orbits of the outer planets.

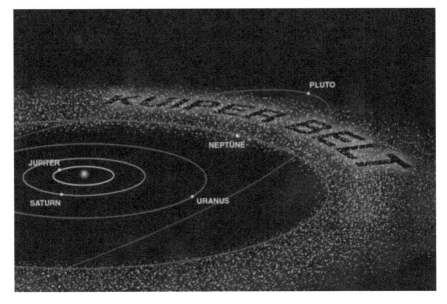

Figure 47.1: Kuiper Belt

Looking again at fig. 47.1 you see that Neptune is also in the Kuiper Belt. So, why was Neptune not reclassified? Neptune is clearly in the Kuiper Belt, so why is it still a planet and not simply a piece of debris like Pluto?

For one thing, Neptune is a giant planet with moons orbiting around it; however, Neptune has a circular orbit. Pluto has an elliptical orbit. Why does Pluto have an orbit that is so different from the rest of the planets in our solar system? Keep in mind that Pluto was discovered in the 1930s. At that time, the capacity to look into the Kuiper Belt did not exist.

If Pluto was a Kuiper Belt object how was it discovered? Since Pluto suddenly appeared in 1930 and has a strange orbit, can you make the assumption that perhaps Pluto is not a natural object? Perhaps it is some type of observation post that was flown in around 1930 to prepare for what is now happening. This happened over 80 years ago, so in the scheme of life, Pluto is simply a blip. If you are a vast force with an agenda against billions of people, you are going to take your time to put everything into place. Perhaps time is viewed differently from their perspective; perhaps 80 Earth years to them might only be 8 years; 8 months... or even simply a few minutes.

You may have noticed that in the last few years there are many science fiction movies about the space exploration as well as the invasion of Earth by aliens. All aliens encountered are usually depicted as insects or Reptilians. Rarely do you see humanoid-type aliens. These are clues to what is happening in the Kuiper Belt, which contains a massive fleet - no one knows exactly how many.

If these beings wanted to destroy the planet or harm us in the last 80 years they would have done so by now with their vast technology.

It appears the agenda of the Kuiper Belt Beings is to remove the Illuminati from this planet. If they wanted to destroy the Illuminati, they could have blasted the Earth in a second. They must want this planet for a reason because they did not destroy it. There is some kind of methodical event being prepared.

In 2007, the Pioneer 10 spacecraft was reported to slow down as it approached the Kuiper Belt. This spacecraft was launched into space in 1972 with the picture of a naked man and woman attached to its antenna to familiarize any alien beings it might encounter with the inhabitants of planet Earth; this alone is extremely strange and ritualistic.

Scientists said a "mysterious force" was slowing down Pioneer 10, forcing it to go backwards, and whatever was doing this was associated with the Kuiper Belt. They also said other things were being affected such as satellites.

Scientists said that it appeared that all the dust and particles from the Kuiper Belt were slowly filtering their way toward the Earth. They further explained that the gravitational pull of the Sun was pulling objects and debris from the Kuiper Belt to the Earth; some was even falling onto the Earth. So, you might even be stepping on Kuiper Belt particles!

This pull was causing a drag against the Pioneer 10 spacecraft's equipment. Do you believe this story? If this were true, then why has no other spacecraft had a similar experience? The Voyager 1 and 2 spacecrafts made it out of our solar system without incident.

The Kuiper Belt Beings were responsible for the sabotage of the Hadron Collider at the CERN facility outside of Geneva, Switzerland in September 2008. When the Hadron Collider was turned on, something went wrong with the magnets so it had to be turned off. By November 2009 repairs were completed so it was turned it on again. There are tunnels underneath the CERN facility that go underneath Lake Geneva. There are also tunnels that go specifically into France and nowhere else. There are other tunnels that go into other parts of Europe from CERN. No one is allowed to go in the tunnels without special clearance. Most tunnels are under the lake. Lights have been observed deep under Lake Geneva. UFOs are reported in the skies in Western Switzerland over Geneva.

The Kuiper Belt Beings also attempted to sabotage the US election in 2008 by bringing out information about certain people. In October 2009, NASA bombed the surface of the Moon with the public explanation that this was to see if there was water on the Moon's surface. Previously, lunar rovers dug deep into the surface so why did they need to bomb the Moon?

Watching the video of the NASA Moon bombing, you see the camera go blank just before the bomb was set to detonate. NASA proclaimed the test successful, saying, "Yes, there is water on the Moon". What do you think that was about, and what were they actually bombing?

I think that there may have been some type of probe or monitoring device on the Moon, possibly from the Kuiper Belt, watching the Earth and NASA wanted to destroy it. Rockets cannot be launched anymore from Cape Canaveral because reporters ask too many questions. So, NASA made a big show out of it, telling reporters that it was a scientific experiment, and then blacked out the main event.

In April 2008, two asteroids passed between the inner orbit of the Moon and Earth. In recent years, news reports of these types of objects flying in from space to pass through this inner orbit are increasing. This is extremely unusual because most of these objects pass away from the lunar or Earth orbits. You can compare this to flying a plane underneath a bridge and then flying out. Why is the Moon in orbit around the Earth and what holds it in orbit? The gravitational pull of the Earth.

So, when an object passes between the Moon and Earth what happens to that object? Theoretically, should not that object be pulled by the gravitational pull of the Earth thus incinerating it upon contact? This happens occasionally, but for "some reason", these objects keep going on their trajectories without incident. Perhaps these "objects" are under intelligent control and are here to monitor something that is going on between the Moon and Earth.

In 2010, NASA used a webcam that recorded large objects coming out of the Sun. These digitally enhanced pictures showed these were not natural objects but actually looked like artificial vehicles that were the size of planets. And, these objects were moving toward the Kuiper Belt. Nothing more of this has ever been mentioned by the media.

Also in 2010, there were an abundance of earthquakes in Central and Northern Virginia, West Virginia, and Washington D.C. The earthquakes did not occur on any known fault lines. There are no obvious volcanoes in these areas. The quakes were only 2-3 on the Richter Scales, so what was the cause of these anomalous earthquakes? These appear to be artificially created underground explosions - possibly the opening caverns or tunnels. In 2011, a 5.8 earthquake occurred in Virginia which rattled the entire Eastern US. Perhaps this was also triggered by these secret government underground projects.

There was even some kind of excavation work on the front lawn of the White House. Official explanation was that this was for an upgrade of bombing bunkers utilities. However, during the 9/11 event, it was publicly reported that the bombing bunkers under the White House were in good condition. Perhaps the Illuminati were preparing an untraceable underground escape route to a star gate. It is my opinion that the Illuminati are running scared and that it is quite possible that the Illuminati will come to an end.

Kuiper Belt activity is increasing, although communication with Kuiper Belt Beings is almost like radio silence. The rare communications that do occur cannot be tapped into; even if the Illuminati have placed implants in you or it somehow monitors you, whatever communication you receive from the Kuiper Belt cannot be intercepted in any way by the Illuminati.

There are only a very few specific people on Earth who receive Kuiper Belt information and communication. Even those who receive this information have difficulty consciously interpreting it. Somehow, this communication goes directly into the subconscious mind where it is waiting for activation at the appropriate time.

A vast array of many different species comprises these Beings in the Kuiper Belt. The majority of these Beings are insectoid or insect-like, especially the military/aggressive factions. There appears to be a Sirian group in control. Some species in the armada come from alternate realities and dimensions. Andromedans, survivors of the Nibiru explosion, and Aldebarans are also part of the Kuiper Belt fleet aligning with the 4th Reich with the common goal to overthrow the Illuminati.

While in Antarctica in 2010 we connected to Base 211 of the 4th Reich, located east of the Antarctic Peninsula in a region claimed and protected by Norway. This base is huge; many levels deep with a tropical-like environment. This base is located approximately 2 km/1.24 miles underground, goes as deep as 25 km/15.53 miles with continual additional construction through the decades.

Base 211 houses a tremendous fleet of Vril craft as well as possibly as many as tens of thousands of inhabitants by now who have extensive connections to various alien groups; their technology is nothing similar to what we have on the surface.

There is also evidence that leads me to believe that the 4th Reich in Antarctica is in league with the Kuiper Belt Beings. Strange electromagnetic energy emanating from the South Pole into deep space indicates a connection between the two groups. If this is so, then the obvious intentions of the Kuiper Belt armada is to help the Nazis overthrow the Illuminati so that the 4th or maybe 5th Reich can take global control.

The 4th Reich as well as bases under Bavaria and Tibet might be working to sabotage the Staged Alien Invasion. Perhaps if they remove, destroy, or disable the "Project Blue Beam" satellites there will be no way to generate the images, except from the ground. The images projected from the ground into the atmosphere are not as effective as the ones beamed from the atmosphere onto the surface of the Earth and ionosphere.

UFOs are known to have sabotaged nuclear missile tests. This obviously indicates something going on against the Illuminati. Perhaps these UFOs are associated with the Kuiper Belt.

Is it a good thing that the Kuiper Belt armada is coming? Yes, and no, as this represents another control system. The protocols may be different, but it is still a control system. As an analogy, was the populace better off during the Soviet or Nazi occupation? The end result is the same; it is simply a matter of how you get there.

Generally, when a group interferes with any population, the group does not interfere for anyone's best interest but for their own. There is a collective feeling among alien groups that Earth is now part of an "axis of evil" to those in other worlds. Whether you call them good or bad, many Beings do not like what is happening on Earth because of how it affects their worlds. If they wanted to destroy this planet, they would have already done so. There is a sense of responsibility for what happens on Earth because among the Kuiper Belt Beings are those who started the humanoid experiments which opened the door for other experimentations.

In my opinion, the Kuiper Belt Beings lean toward benevolence as opposed to the Illuminati which is strictly out for its own benefit. I believe that once the Kuiper Belt Beings are officially recognized here on Earth, they will designate liaisons between humans and their group as well as install some type of leadership that will be in alignment with the goals of the Kuiper Belt Beings.

This Kuiper Belt connection may extend to or include the 4th Reich in Antarctica and on the Moon. This might explain why the Germans were so anxious to have a Moon base as well as explore space and experiment with interdimensional existences. This was even more important than occupying other countries unless those countries held keys to obtaining specific esoteric and nonphysical secrets. The Kuiper Belt Beings and the 4th Reich could be in league with each other even now.

In the near future you will learn more and more about what is really happening on this planet as what was once done covertly is increasingly publicly acknowledged. You have to be very vigilant now in your Hyperspace/Oversoul work. This is why I warn you that there is no more time to play around and procrastinate about doing your deprogramming and release work.

The test is coming around the corner. You have to study now and do your work now, because if you do not you will not pass the test when it is in front of you. Yes, I am being dramatic because the situation here on Earth is exponentially becoming dramatic.

Why do you think there are several billions of people alive on the face of this planet? This has never, ever happened before. Why do you think there is such an influx of soul-personalities who want to incarnate in this horrible civilization? Why would anyone be so desperate to come in this crowded, disgusting, polluted place? Because, this is the last time, hopefully, and the only time you are going to see this kind of an event of this grand nature. This will never happen again in this reality, on this planet. So, everyone comes here for a front row seat to either observe or to participate.

This planet is really unique in all of existence. Nowhere else will your soul-personality find such a conglomeration of different species together in one place. This simply does not happen anywhere. In fact, many people who have had alien abductions who asked the questions, "Why are you here? What are you doing here?" all claim to get this one response: "Because this planet is so diverse that there is no place else where this spectrum of elements is all in one locale".

Earth is like a party. There are all these different minerals, plants, people, everything that you can imagine. This planet is like a Saks Fifth Avenue store. Alien Beings can all go shopping here and find what they want; this is why it is so important. Plus, location, location, location.

Our solar system is located at the end of one of the points in one of the spiral arms of the Milky Way Galaxy. That is why from Earth you can see the whole galaxy. From the center, you cannot see the entire Milky Way Galaxy because you are surrounded by billions of stars. From Earth's unique position, you can see the rest of it. An invasion force would strategically surround a galaxy by going to the outer points and then work its way inward. Our solar system is surrounded by the Kuiper Belt which is a defensive great barrier.

Plus, the energetic location of Earth is on the borderline between physical and nonphysical realities. Many other planets are deep within physical reality making it difficult to go into the astral and beyond. Why do you think there are so many paranormal events on planet Earth? Why do you think there are so many interdimensional events, ghosts, and experiences?

The energy on Earth creates a very thin veil between dimensions making contact between physical, nonphysical, intraphysical and even superphysical easy. Earth is in the most unique spot in this galaxy for invasion as well as traveling to other galaxies and interdimensionally. This is without even discussing all that can be done with Inner Earth energies. Anyone coming into this solar system has to physically pass through the Kuiper Belt. Interdimensionally you can go through a star gate and go any place; this is why in the US there is a law that states it is illegal to communicate with an extraterrestrial.

The Illuminati now try to monitor Hyperspace activities. It is trying to establish some kind of anchor from physical reality to Hyperspace. It already has an anchor in the astral. The Illuminati can capture soul-personalities upon death, extract the soul-personality, place it in another artificial body, and then do with it whatever it wishes in an electromagnetic containment field. The Illuminati have been using alien technology to do this for the past 60 to 70 years.

Earth is considered a danger to other civilizations; this planet is the "Iraq" of the universe. Think about it; why did we invade Iraq? We were told that Saddam Hussein was an evil Emperor from which the oppressed people of Iraq needed to be liberated. The armada in the Kuiper Belt thinks humanity needs to be liberated from the Earth oppressors. The Illuminati are part of humanity, we are all hybrids; but the Illuminati is the control system, just like Saddam Hussein.

Are we in need of liberation from our evil control system? As an analogy, what happened when we "liberated" Iraq and got rid of Saddam Hussein? Would you want to live in Iraq in the aftermath and say everything is fine? Of course not! So, do you think it will all be love, light, and peace after the Illuminati are gone? Of course not! Has there ever existed on Earth a society or culture that has lived harmoniously on Earth? Yet, hope springs eternal; change and perfection are still the ultimate goals.

The Illuminati will attempt to sabotage the Kuiper Belt Beings and Kuiper Belt Beings will attempt to sabotage the Illuminati. In the meantime, you are in the middle as well as everyone else on this planet. What will stop this from happening? Only the changing of mind-patterns will stop these events from occurring. Your Hyperspace/Oversoul work is more paramount than ever. Change your mind-pattern to change life on Earth.

48. YOUR GENETIC LINEAGE

Your ancestry may not be what you think it is. Especially in the US, you may not have any idea of your ancestry. On the East Coast of the US, most people have some kind of ethnic identity: Italian, German, Jewish, Irish, and so forth.

When you ask people on the West Coast where their families come from most people respond with a state within the US.

Where did your ancestors come from? The majority of people do not know. This is not a topic of discussion because no one really knows where their families came from before they migrated West.

Genetic lineage is important because it tells you what is in your true history. You need to understand your genetics to know who you are and why you chose this lifetime. The deeper you go, the more you find out. You most likely have more than one lifeline in your family genetics. This is why you keep coming back; to understand what you are and what you started as well as to complete/correct/balance what you did "before".

All your name frequencies are clues to who and what you are. You chose these name frequencies so you need to know "why". This is one reason why I do "Name Energy Scan" Reports. This is a great beginning point. But as you do your Hyperspace/Oversoul work, you can go even deeper. I also do the "On-World" and "Off-World" Simultaneous Existence Scans. Again, more information for you, but you can use these scans to go even deeper.

Finding out who you are on all levels takes you deeper into your own soul-personality, Oversoul, and God-Mind. Knowing your own true history helps reveal the true history of the world because the outer world has to reflect your inner quest. The inner work you do on true history adds strength to the unveiling of true world history. This is Universal Law.

You are a mix of many genetics, both positive and negative. Based on this information you can learn to deprogram, release your past, and move forward in the most correct and beneficial way for you. This shows you that you are much more than you think you are.

Explore your DNA by opening the DNA archetype, which is a 4-rung medium green ladder, by using the violet "Pi" sign as the key. Download the information and read it. Do not fear finding out who and what you are. Embrace all aspects of yourself so that you can explore the totality of your soul-personality.

You would be amazed to find out how many people do not even know their full birth name. Some people are adopted; sometimes one parent remarries and changes the child's name. Some parents do not want the child to know his/her true background due to shame, fear, or even illegal activities.

Do you know your official ancestry? You have to search every single corner of your mind and DNA to determine this information. You have to search through your early childhood imprinting as well as your programming.

If you told someone from Poland that has blond hair and blue eyes that he/she has Mongolian genetics, he/she would think that you are lying. However, a large portion of Polish people have Mongolian genetics as do many Russians and Eastern Europeans. Greek, Italian, and French people often have Egyptian DNA.

So, when you are doing your own DNA exercises, do not discount what comes before your inner eye. Keep your notes and do your research because you may truly be amazed by your own true history that is revealed.

49. EXTRATERRESTRIALS, ALIENS & INTERDIMENSIONAL EXISTENCES

I already told you that in the US there is a law that says it is illegal for US citizens to interact with "extraterrestrials". On the same page it says that you are not allowed to swim unsupervised with dolphins. This tells you what the government thinks about dolphins. The law does not state that you cannot have interaction with an "alien" because the US defines an "alien" as a physical being who comes from a physical location in our physical universe. An alien can be seen, felt, and monitored.

An "extraterrestrial" comes from the borderline physical/nonphysical and may not be from this universe. An "extraterrestrial" could be from an alternate universe, bleeping in and out of physical reality; the government does not know how to monitor this. Since extraterrestrials cannot be monitored, the law says that it is illegal to have communication with them.

How many other dimensions are there? Infinite, because any dimension that you can think of exists somewhere. Some alien beings are interdimensional, claiming to be from other timelines. Some people have been taken aboard UFOs only to be told that the craft comes from a timeline where Atlantis never came to a conclusion.

There are reports of abductions by UFOs claiming to be from a timeline where the Nazis won the war and are in control of the Earth. Someone was told that there was a species that developed on the Earth instead of humanity. When the abductees ask the aliens where they are, the reply is sometimes, "We are from here, the same place you are from, only a different timeline, dimension, or frequency of the Earth".

Use the analogy of a radio station. The radio is God-Mind with several dials. As you turn the dial, you get different stations all on the same radio. Different frequencies, yet the same radio; the same source: God-Mind. All you have to do is tune into a different reality. In the room you are in right now, there are infinite realities passing through it.

In the same way, there are alternate versions of you in existence. You might be a tall Reptilian or a fish swimming in the ocean. Anything you can imagine at this moment exists and is valid.

Civilizations exist in pockets within this reality, or different bandwidths of frequency. In Iceland, for example, there are elves, gnomes, faeries, and trolls. These "hidden folk" exist in realms within our reality that bleed in and out of our physical dimension.

There are several civilizations in the Inner Earth. Just like there are many cultures and groups on the exterior of the planet, there are many on the interior. And, not only do civilizations exist in the Inner Earth, they also exist between the inner mantles of the Earth's crust that contain the caverns and cave systems.

The Bible states that God did things for what is on the Earth, and what is in the Earth. Did you ever wonder why the Bible says that God is doing things for Beings "in" the Earth?

Genesis says, "Let 'us' make man in 'our' image". Every reference to God in original Hebrew language is plural. "Elohim" means "the ones who descended from above". "Adonai" means "our Lords". There is not one singular reference to God.

The Bible talks about giants, dwarves, aliens, and other creatures on the Earth. You know about the Reptilian groups. You can see how much this one planet has going on: history on the Earth; history in the Earth; history in the Earth's crust; and the interdimensional factor. No wonder there is so much interest in this planet!

50. Factors That Affect You

Many factors affect you now and in the future such as secret organizations, the astral realm, 13 Illuminati families, Committee of 300, 4th Reich and allies, interdimensionality with infinite realities and extraterrestrials, Inner Earth civilizations, and an infinite number of aliens... just for starters.

Even NASA says that many planets it has discovered are Earth-like. In our galaxy it estimates over 400 million Earth-like planets. If you time that by 100 billion galaxies in our physical universe, times the infinite universes, then you cannot even begin to imagine how many civilizations are out there. When you talk about aliens, which aliens? What dimension? It would be impossible to even categorize them all.

The most volatile factor of all is humanity. Each person attracts this current reality. It is mind-pattern that allows this reality to even exist. In the 1940s when Ghandi sought independence for the 350 million people of India, there were approximately 100,000 British controlling them. Ghandi said that he blamed the Indian people for allowing only 100,000 people to control 350 million!

So, I say the same to you. There are billions of people on this planet that are responsible for the attraction of all of these factors. You are responsible because what your mind-pattern projects out reflects back. Humanity with its victimization mentality is what attracts the tyrants and oppressors. If everyone woke up tomorrow morning without victimization life would be very, very different.

There are other factors affecting us that we do not even know about because these represent our buried, suppressed, and ignored mind-patterns. Keep this information in mind as the pieces to the puzzle are revealed. Where is all of this taking us and what does it mean?

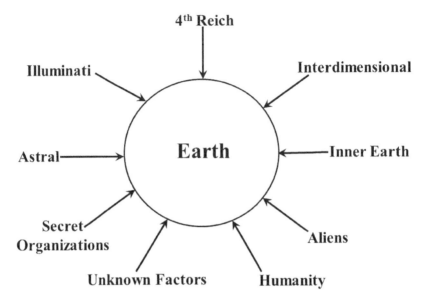

Figure 50.1: Factors That Affect You

Even within humanity there are cultures, races, religions, and more. There are so many influences, agendas, and inputs that it is practically impossible to consciously understand all of them. But, all of these factors reflect the species mind-pattern in different ways.

What happens when you have too much software running on a computer? It overloads and fails; too many plug-ins crash the computer. Think about humanity and all of these inputs. We have so many things going on it is no wonder that we are controllable.

When you have all these rocks and weights being pushed on you, of course you want someone to help you. Releasing your burdens sounds wonderful, even if you are given a different burden in a different way. The best slave is always one who does not know that he/she is a slave. The best way to hide something is right in front of you because that is the last place you will look.

In the same way, everything that is going on in the world at this moment is right in front of you, but you are not paying attention because there are too many distractions.

The US is nothing more than a democratic dictatorship. Usually when the term "dictatorship" is used no other term applies, but here "democratic" is used because this completes the "Illusion".

To fix or correct anything, you have to know what is broken; you need to know its components so that you can decide what to do with whatever is before you, whether it is internal or external. Whatever is going on in your life, it is correctable, even if you do not feel this way at the moment, because you created it.

You are the projector with the film sending out the movie; therefore, you have the power to change the movie. Some people like to watch the same movie over and over again, so they keep showing re-runs even when the re-run is terrible.

Every thought you think throughout the course of the day creates your movie. If you focus on self-sabotage, self-punishment, low self-worth, and self-abuse, this is the movie that is going to play out in your life. You are creating this. Any person who abuses you in any way is simply filling the role that you created for him/her. You can extrapolate this to the entire Earth.

If you do not like the government, or the president, or the rules and regulations, then change them. Protesting in the streets is meaning-less; voting them out of office is meaningless. The best thing you can do is change your own internal government and rules and regulations so that this can be reflected back to you.

You must also keep in mind that you cannot take away the lessons and experiences of others, even a situation with dire consequences. If you "save" others, their mind-patterns simply have to start re-creating the same scenario over again - you create more work for them and you take their experiences for your own because you have played "God" by judging what they do or do not need. They may experience temporary relief, but the next experience will be even more difficult for them and you will complicate your own life. The only way to effect permanent change of any kind is to change the mind-pattern.

51. TAKING RESPONSIBILITY

Many people of all ages are opting out of this reality, exiting in a variety of ways. On some level, these people say, "Okay, you know what - I don't think I want to see the rest of the show. I'm going to leave before the curtain goes up and there is less traffic to get out of here".

Many people who came here to witness and participate in all of this got a taste of what is to come. Now, they are changing their minds and leaving! Yes, you can change your mind because there is free will. Right now you are at a point in the present where there are unlimited possibilities. Which possibility will you choose?

Every thought you think shapes, changes, and directs the direction you take next; all decisions, whether minor or major, direct you to a specific "future" path.

When you think about a linear timeline going in one direction that holds all of your lifetimes, all you really have is the illusion of a straight line. If you stand back far enough and observe, you realize the linear timeline is an illusion. Your life really exists on a circle. This is why the Mayan calendar is a circle. One cycle ends and another one begins. There is no end of time; time is indefinite.

At your pineal gland, visualize the Hyperspace Pineal Gland Archetype: a royal blue dot in the center of a royal blue circle. Center your consciousness here. This is the liaison between physical and nonphysical realities. The universe is curved; it is not linear. If you sent a rocket into space from where you are, at some point it is going to return to its starting point.

Time and space are an illusion of physical reality. Time and space act as reference points for the mind. Everything that exists is a reflection of mind.

Mind is comprised of Frequency. It is always your choice to which frequency you connect.

Some people like to say that they are going to "ascend"; well, ascend to what? Where are you going? There is no up and down anyway. You might even be inside out and you need to put yourself back in the proper perspective. You are already in God-Mind and ascended; there is no photon belt that you are going to pass through; there are no space brothers coming to save you; you already have within you all that you will ever be.

So, what is the future? Whatever you create for yourself. Everyone will have a different future, even though you may have a similar underlying foundation. On a subconscious level you may agree to the same foundational future as others, but within that foundation you will experience your own specific nuances.

As an analogy, think of many people living in one apartment building. You live in the same building, but each apartment dweller has his/her own unique experiences within that building. The apartment building provides the joint foundational experience; you have your own unique experiences while living there.

Know the difference between Reality and Actuality. A room filled with people, for example, has many different Realities. Some people are hot, cold, comfortable, tired, hungry, but the Actuality is that it is the same room. Within that Actuality each person's mind-pattern filters the experience to make it unique to that person.

Many people believed the end of the world would happen on December 21, 2012 and for them, it did. They created situations or events that came to an end. You can choose to be, or not be, a part of anything. You always have choice. Within the Actuality of God-Mind, every choice is taken; nothing is left undone. This is why there is no Divine Interference; there is no need for it.

Everything happens somewhere; a part of you in some alternate reality will experience what you do not experience here. This is another reason why it is so important to be careful what you think because somewhere, some place, you create this for yourself. What are you going to create?

Be careful of such thoughts as, "I can't sell my house, I can't find a job, I don't have enough money, I can't do this, I can't do that, I can't, I can't, I can't". Do not allow yourself to fall into this kind of trap.

Instead, think, "No matter what's going on around me or what's in my pockets I can still do what I need to do; somehow I will create what I need and want". What happens is all up to you; no one is going to do it for you.

You cannot heal anyone else or make anyone do anything unless they want this, too. No one can put a curse on you unless on some level you accept it. The Illuminati put fear in you so you make something happen; you make yourself afraid and then create the disaster. When a major earthquake happens on the West Coast of the US, there will be people who survive of their survival/safety mind-pattern. Perhaps they will be traveling elsewhere or visiting friends and relatives in another part of the country. Mind-pattern always determines your experience.

There are two colors that are important for you to always remember. One is violet for protection. The other is pale orange for the truth. Truth and protection are always important. You can put someone in violet via the Oversoul level and then it is up to that person to accept or reject it.

If you want to find out the truth, put the person in pale orange via the Oversoul level. If the person is stating the truth, he/she will stay in pale orange. If he or she is not telling the truth, you will not be able to hold pale orange around that person.

You can do mental work to extract someone from a dangerous situation; however, you must get Oversoul permission or you are breaking Universal Law.

You must always ask the involved Oversouls to do what is best for everyone involved. If you protect without permission, who are you really doing it for? For yourself; you would be upset if something happened to that person. The protection work is really more for you than for them. You are selfish and you risk imposing your will upon their will... unless you have permission on the Oversoul level.

The majority of people on this planet identify with their negative conditions and situations; this is how they define themselves. Many people have the genetics of the civilizations that were invaded; many have the genetics of the invaders. Some people are aggressive, some are passive; some are even passive aggressive, and every combination you can think of. This does not mean you have to stay this way. You always have the choice of change.

Your personal Hyperspace Signature/thumbprint in Hyperspace evolves right along with your personal changes. As you assimilate your experiences, you learn how to apply that knowledge. This changes you and in turn changes your Hyperspace Signature. Continue to do your release and deprogramming work, because all of this helps you uncover the real you. Some people say they cannot do this work because they cannot visualize.

You may think you have issues visualizing, but if you can daydream, you can visualize. If you can breathe, which I am guessing you are doing right now, then you can center yourself in two seconds and you can do this work. This is part of your capacity as a spiritual being having a human experience.

The physical body is a temporary vehicle for now. You may eventually leave this vehicle to upgrade to a better vehicle. Ultimately, you can create the vehicle at will so you do not have to constantly stay in physical reality. You can morph it into pure energy so you can be who and what you are. Then, if you need to visit a physical reality you can create a body that can exist in that physical place based on your mind-pattern. Ideally your pineal gland should be your entire brain; you should not have a left and right hemisphere, or a pineal gland. You have the capacity to do and learn energetically with no need for a physical body.

Use a carpet as an analogy. Take the tip of one little thread. In the God-Mind, one molecule on the tip of that thread, in that little minute spot represents the totality of all physical realities everywhere. The rest of the carpet is God-Mind. So, how insignificant is your physical reality? All of your challenges and all of the challenges of any physical being on any physical planet in any reality is on that one little molecule on the tip of that one little thread. The rest of what you really are is everything else. When you realize this, you begin to see your life with better clarity and perspective.

Whenever you have a challenge, feel depressed or out of sorts, center yourself at the pineal in royal blue. Then, move your consciousness out of your body into the air around you. Continue to move further away into the atmosphere until you can see the Earth from a distance. Continue moving back until the Earth is a little dot; further still until you see the entire galaxy and then keep going until the galaxy is a tiny speck.

As you observe that tiny speck, think, "All of my challenges are on a speck, within a speck, within a speck within the vastness of existence". How insignificant are these issues now? Then move yourself slowly back into your body, ground, and balance in a deep brown color. Observe how much better you feel now.

Some people say they are too depressed or upset to do this visualization. I say that when you are at your worst is when you need to do this the most, even if you have to force yourself. You came here to be challenged, so live up to the challenge.

I think a lot of people would rather lift bricks than do mental work. Why? Because after the bricks are moved, the work is done. With mental work, you have to do it repeatedly; layer after layer; deeper and deeper inside. Deprogramming work is the same. You came here to fix all these layers by removing the mind-patterns that attracted this in the first place. Do you want to keep having the same experiences lifetime after lifetime? How many times have you already had these same types of experiences? Have you had enough?

People ask, "Where is hell?" Well, you are in it. Where you are right now is the epitome of hell; life does not get any worse than this. At the same time life is heaven. Everything is about frequency. You are as dead as you will ever be. When and if you choose to leave your physical body, you are going to feel exactly the same as you do now. You are not going to grow wings and sit on a cloud.

Some people think when they leave their physical bodies that they will be in a better place. Well, as long as you take your mind, you have the same experiences. If you are a bastard when you are in a body, you are a bastard when you are out of a body. When you hear of a spirit throwing things and being mean, how do you think that spirit was when it had a body? You are now the same as you will ever be.

You might be able to do more things energetically; see things you could not see when in a body; but your personality is the same until you change it. You better learn something positive here; because when you leave your physical body and think negative things, guess what is going to happen? Manifestation can be instant and this means negative manifestation as well as the positive.

So, if you think you have troubles now you better fix yourself. Physical death does not save you. Changing the venue of where you learn only intensifies the lessons. You are going to create the same experiences over and over again until you eliminate the need for these experiences. Most people like the punishment that they get because they feel they deserve it. Punishment is a great motivator.

If you sit in a comfortable chair and someone brings you food, water, and pampers you, you never want to leave the chair. But, if someone pokes you, you are going to get up and move. You are on Earth for this very reason.

Hyperspace work is valid in both physical and nonphysical realities. People ask, "What happens when I die?" What do you think is going to happen when you die? If you think you are going to see Jesus, Mary, and Joseph, that is what you are going to see. Will it really be them? No, it will be the projection of what you expect. After you realize this, then you start to learn about what is really happening "on the other side".

We all came in to this reality in the same way. But we will all leave it in a different way; some may leave peacefully, some may not. But eventually, we are going to return to the nonphysical. When you think about it, we really are in the nonphysical now.

You go to the nonphysical every time you go to sleep. Your soul personality leaves the body to experience either the astral or Hyperspace levels so that you can assimilate what you are currently learning. You sleep 1/3 of your life, so a 75 year old person sleeps for 25 years. That is a longtime to be asleep without knowing what is going on. The ultimate goal is to become so energetically knowledgeable and aware that you can actually morph your body into pure energy. That has been done by others before but it is not taught anymore.

The bottom line is do you know who you are? Do you know where you are going from here? You need to look at your genetics. You need to look at your mind-pattern. You cannot answer this question if you do not know where you have been. You cannot answer this question if you do not know where you are now.

How can you go anywhere without a direction in which to go? If you are suddenly plopped down in Bulgaria without knowing how to read Cyrillic writing, you cannot determine which direction to take or where any direction will lead you.

You have to make these decisions; you have to determine all parts of Self. In so doing, you attract others who are doing the same. This is the most important thing that you can ever do.

Now that you know the time periods and events flow of true history, mentally verify your own role and place in true history. I urge you to do DNA opening, deprogramming, Oversoul, Golden Altar Release, and Growing Up the Child Within visualizations.

Even if you have done everything I have ever taught you 1,000 times, do it 1,001. This gives you multiple layers of input information to give you direction and focus. How many lifetimes have you experienced on this planet? Possibly thousands; even tens of thousands. Atlantis existed for approximately 300,000 years. If you had a lifetime every thousand years that is 300 lifetimes only in Atlantean times. How long do you think it would take to review 300 lifetimes?

Do you need to know every single event that has ever happened to you? No, because what you did not learn, assimilate, or release you have recreated right now in your present existence. What you learn when you do your Hyperspace/Oversoul work is that all of your genetic information and simultaneous/alternate existences reflect in your current life. Once you understand this, you can merge them all together to find answers that permanently resolve your issues.

Here is a visualization I want you to do to see what power you have and to help you realize what solutions to your challenges that you have. Simultaneously place a Brown Merger Archetype through your pineal gland, Reptilian brainstem, heart chakra, above your head at the Oversoul Archetype, and above that through the Gold Aleph God-Mind Archetype. One Brown Merger through each of these areas; 5 Brown Merger Archetypes total.

Now merge all of these into your Self. Do this every single day and you will have an optimal perfect future. If we all do this individually, and collectively, then humanity will have a better future. Each and every person, individually, and collectively, is responsible for the entire future of humanity. This is the most important concept you can learn from this book.

ARTICLES BY JANET DIANE MOURGLIA-SWERDLOW

1. Unholy Trinity

As God-Mind explored Itself, It thought of Duality. As soon as there is a Thought within God-Mind, there is a Response. Everything happens in the Eternal Now. The immediate response out of God-Mind was the Christ Consciousness energy frequency. This was the first illusion of separation. Because God-Mind is All Things, It can never be separate from Itself. The Christ Consciousness energy frequency is a reflection of God-Mind Itself.

The Christ Consciousness energy then created the infinitely repeating 13x13x13 Oversoul Matrix through which all lifestreams pass, with the Angelic Hierarchy at its tip. Together, this forms a tetrahedron, the symbol of perfection within God-Mind. All of Physical Reality is a reflection of this Oversoul Matrix.

For this reason, the 13x13x13 cube became the model for programming and mind-control. This cube is seen in the Islamic Kaaba, as well as in the New Testament of the Bible where it is referred to as the "Holy Spirit". The cube is the basic architectural format of the original Temple of Solomon, as well as ancient Catholic cathedrals in Europe.

A portion of the Angelic Frequency decided that it was equal to the totality of God-Mind. This is what is called "Luciferian" energy, which means "of the light". The light became enamored with itself, and started to create a microcosm of the God-Mind. This is when the octahedron began to form around the tetrahedron. This was the start of the Unholy Trinity. Out of the Luciferian energy descended the energy frequency known as Satan.

Satan believes itself to be the equivalent of the Christ Consciousness. In turn, out of it descended the Devil energy frequency which sees itself as the equivalent of the Oversoul Matrix. So, at one end of the octahedron within the tetrahedron is the Holy Trinity known as God-Mind, Christ Consciousness, and Oversoul Matrix. At the opposite end of the octahedron is the Unholy Trinity, known as Lucifer, Satan, and the Devil. This is the balance of God-Mind Intelligence expressing in physical reality as Duality.

Both positive and negative are a part of the Duality that God-Mind is exploring. One cannot exist without the other. The Unholy Trinity represents the most negative intelligence, and the Holy Trinity represents the most positive intelligence. "Evil" is a judgment of negative intelligence; "good" is a judgment of positive intelligence. Everything in between is a composite of positive and negative, or good and evil. This is a matter of polarities and balance.

The Oversoul Matrix permeates both the Holy Trinity and the Unholy Trinity. It is this Matrix that permeates all life forms in physical reality. Because the octahedron construct (created by Lucifer) essentially came out of the tetrahedron (Angelic Hierarchy), it must be reassimilated back into God-Mind through the tetrahedron.

The illusion of "fighting" against the Angelic Hierarchy gives the Unholy Trinity polarity and existence. It must create the illusion that it is in control, because in True Actuality, it can never be in control.

God-Mind continued to explore Duality through this process of reshaping and remolding Itself. Thus continued the evolvement of Intelligent Energy as It created the illusion of Independent Intelligence within each form.

As the Independent Intelligences split and divided, the illusion of separation continued. From there, the illusion separated into the conscious mind (present moment), subconscious mind (memories/merging of conscious and superconscious minds), and superconscious mind (God-Mind connection), with all three parts forming its own reflection of the Original Trinity of Creation.

As the division and splitting continued, the illusion that this part of God-Mind was moving further away from Itself continued. This is known as the Original Descent. Lucifer, the lead "descending" Intelligence, began to believe in its conscious mind that it alone was Creating. It "forgot" the Intelligence behind it. The function of

Lucifer was to entice more illusionary "divisions" to follow it. Lucifer showed these divisions "its" creations. Lucifer said, "Look what I created!" The others thought that Lucifer had great power as they, too, "forgot" their origins.

They became mesmerized, desiring to learn how to create like Lucifer. Fascinated with its own creations, Lucifer wanted more and more creations so it could see what it could do. Many followed this original descent into physical reality.

Because God-Mind is always in balance, other Intelligent Energies had to follow to correct the imbalance. As these Intelligent Energies followed, they also divided and split, learning how to create in the same way as Lucifer. In a sense, they became like spies - absorbing Luciferian knowledge so that eventually they could "lead" these mesmerized intelligences "back" to their Source in True Actuality. As the "spies" created they became fascinated with what they, too, could manifest. Eventually, they fell deep into the illusion of separation from their Source. Unlike Lucifer, they longed to be reunited with their Source but "forgot" the way.

As Luciferian energy descended and created, it became increasingly enamored with the power that comes with creation. It learned to make its creation exponentially dense, and then continued to split itself so that it could inhabit its creations. As a response to the Luciferian method of creation, the other faction of the Angelic Hierarchy had no choice but to do the same so that it could inhabit its creations and manipulate physical reality in the same way.

As a reflection of the Unholy Trinity, the other faction began to think, "See what I created?" Considering that God-Mind is the Intelligence behind all creation, whether acknowledged or not, this continues the illusion of Duality and Separation. Because Lucifer started the descent, its function is to create the greatest separation from the God-Mind (or the appearance of) that it possibly can. Now, most intelligent beings believe the illusion that they are separate from God-Mind. They have fallen into the fascination of personal creation as opposed to God-Mind Creation.

Lucifer looks for ways to express itself through its creation. This is its play, entertainment, and ultimately self-exploration. It moves in and out of its creations - people, places, and things. It is an Intelligent Energy that creates and continues to explore the depths of Duality and Separation within the Mind of God.

Now, people do not think about how to do anything for themselves. If the body is sick, they go to a doctor to heal it. They have forgotten that all they have to do is use the power of their minds to heal it. If they want to learn about nutrition, they go to the library to read a book because they have forgotten their Source. If they want to travel, they get into a vehicle. They have forgotten that their minds can take them wherever they need to go.

They have forgotten that the body does not need to age. They go to a plastic surgeon to correct the effects of aging rather than look within. They go further and further away from God-Mind as Creator. When they build a car, they say, "Look what I created", or when they secure a wonderful business deal, they say, "Look what I created", just like Lucifer. They forget the Intelligence working through them.

Lucifer continues to look for outlets to express itself. It has tricked the other faction of God-Mind into believing that they create, rather than acknowledge that God-Mind creates through them. The devotees of Lucifer meet the needs of all before anyone even knows that he/she has a need! Go into any store needing absolutely nothing, and there will be some "thing" that catches your eye.

Suddenly, you "need" that thing! The object of your desire is created outside of you before you even realize that you have a desire for it! You come home with an armful of material possessions that keep you occupied so that you do not even have to think about thinking for yourself. Why bother, when someone else from the outside world already thinks for you?

People now place their devotion in the "things" that will take care of them as well as in the people who bring them these things. People sell their souls for "things". They beg for more "things". People put "things" ahead of all else, with the pursuit of "things" as the ultimate goal. People are lulled by "things" as they continually move further away from their own internal ability to express God-Mind creating through them.

Mesmerized like a cobra, the outer world now run by Luciferian energy simply plays a tune and the entire group consciousness follows it without question. This week they play, "Eggs are bad for you" and the collective conscious mind sways to the music. The next week, they play, "Eggs are good for you" and again, without question, the collective conscious mind blindly follows. Hypnotically, slowly, methodically, minds are dulled and numbed to their own Source until the people are led like the children of the Pied Piper into the river to drown.

"Things" are the most important part of people's lives. They easily hand their children over to the care of strangers to raise them while they pursue their "things". What would the children rather have... "things" or their parents?

Pursuit of "things"; fascination with "things" - this is what got humanity into trouble in the first place. Humanity wants to create. Humanity wants to be God rather than allow God-Mind to operate in and through it. Humanity follows the path of Lucifer who wanted to be God. Humanity wants to be God so that humanity can think that it creates instead of being the vehicle through which God creates. Humanity is wrapped up in "things"; this is its distraction and imprisonment.

Now, it is time to remember that you are simply the vessels through which God-Mind creates. Stand still, and allow this Intelligence to move through you rather than going seeking. "Be still". This does not mean to sit in silent meditation for endless hours. This means to acknowledge the inner connection from which you are not separated and have never been separated.

Lucifer always seeks vessels through which to operate. It gains an increasingly greater hold in its own insidious way. It inserts its frequency into what ordinary people judge as "good". Then the frequency is piggybacked with an "evil" frequency that walks right in through your front door. Evil is invited in without question. If you do not even know your own frequency, how can you recognize that which is within you that does not belong?

And, since you are the one who invited this guest in, you are the one who must determine how to get the guest to leave. Sometimes the guest is purposely invited in as the only way to explore it. Sometimes, you decide to eat at the same table as this guest so that you can continue your undercover work to understand it in every way possible so that you can eventually lead it "back" into the God-Mind. You cannot divest yourself, or this reality, of anything unless you know what it is.

Lucifer is simply busy exploring itself. It creates beings and "things". Its beings create "things" for you that you welcome into your life. Lucifer becomes your companion. You do not want to divest yourself of it, regardless of your words. You are too busy saying, "Look what I created! Look at the home I built! Look at the car I bought! Look at the children I made! Look at the healing energy I sent! I, I, I, I!" Are you any better than those whom you criticize?

Luciferians simply explore their Creator as they understand It. They explore the opposite end of the spectrum of God-Mind. They help God-Mind understand Itself through Duality, through Separation. You are a willing participant in their study. You allow yourself to be lead outside of yourself for answers. You send your children to classrooms to read out of books. Are the books correct? You look to the "experts" for the answers. Do you question the "experts?" Who are they?

The "studies" by "experts" ask, "Are you nervous in front of a crowd? You have anxiety disorder... take this pill", so you take the pill. And more pills and more pills until people are so drugged that they do not have a chance of having a sane conversation with themselves or their bodies. Did anyone force the pill into your mouth? No. You ask for it, you pay for it with your own money, and you put it in your mouth with your own hand. Who did this? You!

No one questions. No one is a leader. Everyone is so distracted in the process of procuring their "things" that no one has time for any self-exploration. They let others explore and then "trust", not even having a clue about whom it is that they trust.

Now, everyone works for Lucifer as Lucifer goes about creating its playthings. Now, we are the playthings of Lucifer. We work and struggle day in and day out to pay our bills and give our children a better life. But who benefits the most from our work? The top of the pyramid. They are supported by our efforts, with our labor, by our taxes. They have incomes that are unimaginable to most people. They have the finest that the world has to offer. They started creating "things" and they believe that the "things" are theirs. They believe that we are their slave creations.

They implemented the "Monarch" programming, knowing that the "monarchs" are the kings and queens from God-Mind that are now slaves to the Luciferian energy. This is their cosmic joke. They have the secret knowledge about our true heritage because we agreed to forget it. They remolded and reshaped our history because we let them. They genetically engineer us so that we can serve Lucifer, their god. They feel that they have the right to do this. They brought our mothers and fathers together to create what they feel, is genetically superior progeny. They built the bodies, knowing the type of soul-personality that the body would attract.

The Luciferians aid the idea of separation. They take you so far outside of your Self that you totally forget your connections. They take away your original food sources, symbolic of the control that they have over your mental food. They continually replace what is natural to you in this environment with what is easiest to control the group mind. You are fed "herd" food, such as beef, rather than animals that are more aggressive and independent like wild game and buffalo.

You no longer eat according to season, climate, geographical region, or the need of your body. Many, many indigenous fruits, vegetables, and vegetation are no longer even in existence. They control your eating habits, spending habits, clothing habits, social habits.

They gently lead the lambs to slaughter. And you obediently follow. No one takes anything from you. You give everything to them. All internal power and knowledge you hand over on a silver platter.

They already control your mind - now they only want to make it official instead of secret. A little chip in your brain will make you smarter. Why rely on your mind when you can rely on a chip? You have been lulled into a dull complacency. You take the short-term, they take the long-term. They plan for decades and centuries, slowly and patiently, as you are lead away from your idea of the Creator and slowly embrace theirs.

Remember that you are the vessel through which God-Mind creates. Release your need to be the Creator. Remember your True Origins. "Remember" that you are already connected. Claim your internal power. Know who and what you are. Change yourself, change your world. Take back your power. No longer allow the outside world to control you. Stop being the lamb who is led to slaughter. When you stand in your strength and power, you release the need to fear.

What is the True Story of the Original Fall From Grace? Find your own answers. You know them. They are within you. Look, feel, listen, absorb, know. The beginning of this physical reality exists in the Eternal Now.

Locked deep within your genetic code are your memories of your Original Descent into this physical reality. With your mind focused at your pineal gland, visualize the DNA archetype in a deep, dark green. Allow it to open as you stand in your center, anchored firmly in the strength of Self, Oversoul, and God-Mind. With your internal eyes open, allow the experiences that link "you" to your Original Descent flow to you.

Feel yourself in the midst of Creation Itself, moving out from God-Mind for the first time ever, swimming in creative energy, moving through the tetrahedron and into the octahedron, seeing/being archetype, feeling/being color, hearing/being tone. What is your experience as you move your consciousness back to the Eternal Now?

Who are you really and why are you here?

2. WHAT IS THE ASTRAL REALM?

These are the "End Times". The Astral Realm plays an increasingly important role as the Global Handlers try to merge the Astral into this Reality. As the time lines are being artificially compressed, your thoughts turn increasingly to the Astral Realm simply because this is where you are unwittingly being focused. And, what you focus on grows.

What exactly is the Astral Realm and why does it get so much attention?

The astral is the thin energetic band around the Earth plane that holds the collective unconsciousness as well as Earth-bound energies and entities. This energy is easy to tap into because the Astral Realm is like a bridge between the physical Earth plane and the nonphysical realm of Hyperspace.

Most paranormal experiences occur via the Astral Realm. This is why the New Age directed everyone's attention to such activities as astral projection, out-of-body experiences, and channeling. With everyone's attention in the Astral Realm, no one thought to look beyond into Hyperspace. People spent decades trying to do astral projections and learn to channel. What a great distraction for so many for so long!

The Astral Realm is where souls newly departed from their physical bodies go before journeying on into the deeper Hyperspace Realm. Many who are strongly attached to the physical have a mind-pattern which keeps them in the Astral Realm - the true state of limbo. Their mind-patterns do not allow these souls to move on nor go back into a physical body. These souls are stuck here until the mind-pattern changes.

These astral-bound souls are often Earth-bound because of their strong attachment to activities of the flesh, including food, alcohol, drugs, and sex. They hang around unsuspecting people, whispering at them to participate in these activities of their lower animal minds.

These astral-bound souls want to continue to experience the flesh even though they are not in the flesh. The closest way for them to continue these experiences is to share the body of someone still living.

These astral-bound souls do not want you to quit any addictive behaviors because then they lose their tie to the Earth plane. These types of souls are often vindictive, manipulative, and controlling. They have no regard for people now, nor did they before their passing. When the physical body is left behind, the active personality remains the same - it just no longer has a physical body.

Others in the Astral Realm include recently departed who do not yet know that they no longer have a body, or those who have a worry or concern about those people left behind. These souls may try to finish loose ends or fix something that they perceive was not corrected before their passing. These souls usually eventually find their way beyond the Astral Realm and into Hyperspace once they are at peace.

This is why the New Age credo directed people to go to the "white light" - because this will take them into the Astral Realm where their energy can be used by anyone who wants to manipulate it. People passing out of the physical body need to go to the violet or gold light as these color codes provide safe and easy passage through the astral and into Hyperspace.

The Astral Realm is where your undirected thought-forms hang out as they gather with other matching thought-forms, garnering strength and energy. These thought-forms still belong to you energetically. However, they still gain strength and energy from other matching thought-forms by intermingling. These thought-forms are still tied to you - kind of like a rubber band.

This is also how anyone who knows how to manipulate the Astral Realm can use you against yourself. All your undirected thought-forms can be manipulated and gathered into one place. If you have a weak place in your mind-pattern, and someone wants to target you, your own images and vices are propelled back at you. Energetically they hit you like a ton of bricks.

For example, you decide to give up drinking alcohol. Every time you want a drink the thought-form goes into the astral and is captured. If you think 20 times a day that you want a drink, that thought collects with the others in the astral realm.

After a few months, there are a lot of these thought-forms collected. One day you are abstaining from drink and doing really well, and the next day you are overwhelmed into drinking yourself silly. What happened? If you are a target, your own thought-forms were simply directed at the weak area in the mind-pattern. You accept the thought-form because you recognize the frequency as your own.

This same collection happens to humanity. Matching thought-forms are collected, feeding a specific aspect of the collective unconscious. When humanity least suspects, this energy is whirled back at them. People wonder what happened and why. Anyone who knows how to manipulate energies can re-direct this collection of energy back to its origin.

No one does anything "to" you. You only do it to yourself. Any thought-form can be collected, categorized and used against you. You create the weapon and you accept the weapon. Then you wonder why.

This explains the necessity of releasing to your Oversoul moment by moment, every day - so that your thought-forms do not take up residence in the Astral Realm, strengthening something that is not benevolent or for the benefit of Self or humanity.

These thought-forms can even combine to create astral entities that deem themselves deities - because they take on a life of their own. These astral entities know how to manipulate other thought-forms. To uninformed people, these deities look like gods of darkness.

If these gods of darkness do not have their combined thought-forms pulled back to the originators they can exist eternally. People who partake in Black Magick feed these gods of darkness.

Sexual Ritual feeds the Astral Realm as this is where unharnessed, expended sexual energy hangs out. This is why wanton sex is encouraged. Everyone is told to have sex because it feels good. If you are not having sex or sex does not give you pleasure, then the current mode of thinking is that you need help.

The sex act is a great energy generator. When this creative sexual energy is not directed, it goes into the Astral Realm for collection and later use. This sexual energy is gathered in a giant holding pen, then turned on like a faucet and directed by those who know how to use this energy. Sexual energy is used to create a pathway to bring the nonphysical into the physical.

Use of hallucinogenic drugs opens you up to the Astral Realm. The drugs loosen the buttons of the chakra bands so that you are not tied into the body very well. This allows astral energies to enter into you as well as influence you.

Once in you, these entities and energies are not always so easily disposed of. This is why some people have flashbacks after using drugs. They are not really having flashbacks - they are having another, new experience as they make contact once again with the astral. Drugs rip apart your chakra bands and allow you to be infused with more complicated frequencies that distract you from who and what you are. Always say no to drugs.

The frequencies of music are these days designed to open you up to the astral. The low steady beats of heavy metal and rock music open the lower chakras for easier Astral Realm entity entry as well as "looser" sexual activity. Be mindful of the music you listen to and how you feel during and after. This will provide you with the information that you need regarding what you "should" listen to. Create your own music. You have a powerful voice. Tone and you will be amazed at the information as well as correction that can happen on body, mind, and soul levels.

The beat, or "tone/frequency", is what is used to open you up to astral hooks, especially in the lower, or sexual chakra bands. In addition, sexual triggers such as ads, films, photos, and Internet sites create deep astral links that remain with continuously new ones added throughout the rest of our life. Notice how you feel and what part of your body is left open. Be sure to do your chakra band spinning and T-bar archetype balancing every day, along with your protection techniques.

Astral energies often attach when you are very young. If you have a traumatic experience, feel alone, and/or frightened, these astral energies will take the guise of friend and comforter. This usually happens when you are young enough to still see them.

You accept the energy because this is what gives you solace in your time of heartache, grief, and loneliness. Your acceptance is really an invitation. You invite the energy in, it attaches to you, and you do not realize what you are doing.

As life goes on, you are so accustomed to this energy that you do not even realize that the astral energy is not a part of you. These types of energies create havoc. Besides the physical issues previously mentioned, they stir up emotional issues.

For example, they do not want you to have stable relationships or happiness in your life, because then you might not need them anymore, casting them out. These astral energies want you isolated, alone, and frightened so that the part of you who knows them, keeps them.

Sometimes these energies are already attached to you because of simultaneous existences when you might have been involved in Black Magick or activities of the flesh. Without awareness, these entities will continue to stay with you. Once you develop awareness then you can make your decisions.

This is why it is important to find out who you are by finding out who you are not. As you discard and dismantle who you are not, you go deeper into your own core. Ridding yourself of this extraneous baggage allows you to more clearly see yourself. Once you know what to look for, your decisions and choices become clearer, even though perhaps increasingly challenging.

Be sure you have all your protection techniques in place before you go to sleep at night. Mentally program yourself to wake up if any outside frequencies try to come into you during the night. However, when you are accustomed to allowing these frequencies entry 24/7, it is a challenge to pick them out especially at night. This is why it is so important that you do your release work during the day. Release what you are not so you can determine what you are. Extremely simple, but takes some time and dedicated focus.

Visiting the Astral Realm can be enticingly exciting. Most people hunger to know what lies beyond their current existence. The Astral Realm provides part of the answer, but not all of it. People do not look beyond the astral, thinking that the astral is the answer. The astral is exciting compared to the monotony of everyday life that most people experience.

But, the astral is fraught with danger. Most people do not know how to navigate or use the astral, so the astral winds up using them. People get sucked into it because the energies there consider the people gullible. The energies act friendly and benevolent until at some point, once the energies are adequately attached, they turn, using you when you least suspect it.

Indigenous peoples knew how to navigate and use the Astral Realm. They used it in conjunction with Earth energies. They were experienced astral navigators. They passed their knowledge down from generation to generation. Sometimes they used hallucinogenic drugs to help enter the astral, but they knew what they were doing and how to do it. They prepared themselves mentally, emotionally, physically, and spiritually.

They cleansed their bodies and strengthened their mind-patterns. They became strong so that they could remain focused and balanced regardless of what they faced in the astral. Usually these people were the shamans of the tribes. The shamans had respect for its dangers as well as the knowledge that could be accessed there. This was not a hit and miss activity. Entering the astral was structured and purposeful.

There are Earth energies that support the Astral Realm and also provide easy access to the astral. Often these areas are swampy or dark areas. Many times burial and ceremonial grounds as well as churches are built on these geographic locations. The indigenous peoples knew that these grounds helped the passing of their peoples from one level to the next. These peoples used the boost of the Earth energies into the astral for their ceremonial grounds.

To stop others from easily accessing the Astral Realm, and to gain easy access for themselves, the early churches often constructed their buildings on these grounds. This is why the churches are used for ritual. Even the hymns and prayers are developed with intonations (tones) that feed the astral as well as open the worshippers to receive the astral and today, ELF bombardments.

This explains why many churches have heavy energy, keeping the buildings dark and dimly lit, preferring candles to natural light. Many old cathedrals also have extensive burial chambers underneath them, or display old relics and bones. These are all tethers into the Astral Realm. Relics hold the soul energies to the Earth Plane so they cannot move on. This is why some cultures burn the bodies upon physical death - to release the ties to the physical body so the soul can move on. By holding these "relics" and dispersing them around the globe, the souls become more Earth-bound.

There is a lot to explore in the Astral Realm. Some people do it consciously and willingly. Some explore it without understanding or caution. To enter the Astral Realm, you must be extremely strong on all levels to withstand all that it contains. If you overestimate your strength, the astral will use you faster than you can blink.

As you strengthen and fortify yourself in this Reality, then you will be able to face all Dark Forces. Those who are programmed have been through much at the hand of their programmers so that they could enter into the astral without being destroyed. Only the strong have survived. And even those programmed to withstand these Dark Forces are always at risk.

You can easily already be an unwitting pawn in this bridge between the Earth plane and Hyperspace. But, now that you are aware of Hyperspace, connect with your Oversoul and God-Mind. Allow your Oversoul to explain the specifics of the Astral Realm and any connection you have to it. You might be surprised at what you learn, so if you ask the question, be prepared for the answer, whatever it is. No one should be tapping into "Astral Power". You should only tap into Oversoul/God-Mind frequencies. Learn to anchor Self in the ultimate triad: Self, Oversoul, God-Mind.

3. Gone to the Dark Side & Proud of It

I like to tell you about my life and my struggles, because I think it is important for you to realize that I am just like you. The only difference is I have spent more time looking at my inner world. Because of this I have the opportunity to share with you what I know and what works for me.

As you know, these past few years has truly been a year of clearing for me. One of my biggest challenges was when two people I considered my absolute biggest supporters left my life. They sent a long letter explaining their decision, but there was one thing they said that to me was the most ridiculous of all.

They said that I had "gone to the dark side". I just couldn't get over this accusation. Every time I thought of them, this kept coming up in my mind. I kept "brown x'ing" out my thoughts of them, because to me it was just like not one, but two, people had died - amongst many others they took with them in the fallout.

I did my best to release them from my mind. Then I went through a period that summer when I kept running into them wherever I went. I acted like they were the strangers that I realized they had been all along - the false happiness and false support that had to be removed. But still their accusation that I had "gone to the dark side" stayed with me. Out of the multiple pages of accusations, this was one that continued to stay with me.

Well, now I know why. Because it's true. And I'm going to tell you why.

I realized while we were on our "Exploring Atlantis" cruise that I have gone to the dark side. But not in the way they intended; not in a "bad" way. But in a positive way.

On the ship I had the opportunity to observe the frequency of the Black Race. Because we were in the Southern Caribbean, a lot of the Black Race had been brought there as slaves, so this frequency is rich within this region.

One group that entertained during the day by the pool was a group of young Black men from Guyana. I was entranced by the intrinsic beauty that emanated from them. Through them, I tapped into the Pure Black Frequency.

I touched into the deep, dark secrets that the Black Race has been entrusted with. I felt the Purity and the Power inherent in this frequency. It is mysterious and goes back to the process of Creation Itself. I felt the Black Frequency in the deepest part of soul - at least as deep as I am able to access at this point in time.

I was so touched and enamored with my findings. I felt like I was floating in a pool of calm, serene water that was bottomless. I felt the Oneness of the Black Race with its Natural Environment, which is much difference than my Native American genetics allow me to feel. Yet, it is the same type of experience.

I recognized at this point that I had "gone to the dark" side because I have embraced the dark part of my Self and thus, the God-Mind. The totality of Its richness. The hidden; mysterious; purity; power. I have looked beneath what most people seek to avoid. And then dug deeper. I have embraced all aspects of my Self and love all aspects unconditionally, recognizing that all aspects have brought me to where I am today.

This reality is about conquering and enslaving whatever is not understood. People who are different are not honored for the different aspects of the God-Mind that they represent. People who are different are used for what they can be used for and then discarded like trinkets only to be replaced with the next flavor of the day.

People work to enslave and ensnare, not to understand and appreciate. I have been admonished more times than I can count because I did something nice for someone else "just because". The recipient looks at me like "what do you want from me" first before even considering appreciating the kindness.

As I have also mentioned to you, I have literally seen people "go off the deep end" after spending time with Stewart and I; they simply cannot accept others being nice to them because they cannot accept themselves. It is easier to throw stones at us than to accept a place in this world where they are deemed "ok as is".

This is replicated throughout society. Power Games abound. What can I get from you? How can I use you? Who do you know that you can connect me to? People forget that they must depend on their Oversoul and God-Mind. This is "who" they know; this is "what" can connect them; this what each person must "use" to get what he/she wants from life.

When I wrote my first book I was so thrilled. I didn't realize that the challenging part was actually selling it. One day, I was complaining to myself about how I didn't "know anyone" who could help me and my Oversoul said, "You have Me". How could I argue with that?

Yet, because we are in a human experience we want "people, places, and things" that feel more tangible in the moment. We have to learn to rely upon our Spiritual Nature to surpass the limitations of this reality. And this means merging with it into the totality of Self.

My thoughts about this even brought me to one of my favorite foods and perhaps one of yours: chocolate. It is dark yet always portrayed as slightly "forbidden". Rich and smooth are descriptions often balanced with guilty and sinful. Why? Because the Global Handlers don't want you loving the dark sides of life, much less the dark sides of your Self.

So, once again, you work to "conquer" your love of the dark instead of embrace and merge with its goodness. Are you willing to do this? What are you trying to conquer rather than merge with? Are you trying to conquer your dark side so that it isn't in charge of you? Or are you merging with the richness of its mysteries? Is this the next step in this reality, through this reality, or beyond this reality?

This is a part of the understanding of Duality. You must understand the Positive side of every situation as well as the Negative side. The dark and the light. Opposite sides of the same coin to define the coin. Once the definition is met, what next? Will embracing the dark side bring an end or a transition into something else? What do you think?

I know I hit onto something important. I will continue to study and explore this concept. And in the meantime, I for one, am glad that my journey has been recognized. Yes I HAVE gone to the Dark Side and am Proud of it. And if you are too busy trying to ensnare, enslave, and conquer your Dark Side to journey with me, then thank you for calling it quits. This path is not for the weak or faint of heart. If you are strong enough to journey along my path, I welcome you as a companion.

4. EXPLORING THE DARKNESS

Do you feel that you are struggling in more areas of your life than you think that you would ever consciously choose? Do you feel overwhelmed?

Are career, relationship, health, relocation, financial, self-identification, information, disinformation issues simultaneously pushing at you from every direction? Do you feel that you are on overload?

Welcome to the club! Everyone who is growing right now feels all of the above pressures. Everyone is struggling though a myriad of issues. No one person is dealing with one single issue.

Every person is dealing with multiple issues coming at him/her from all directions, seemingly unrelentingly. When the light at the end of the tunnel becomes clear, you start moving that direction. Then, something else falls in your way, blocking the light.

When that obstacle is removed, another, and another, keeps coming at you, faster and faster. Struggle, struggle, struggle.

Everyone is struggling, struggling, struggling, for breathing room. You may feel that there just does not seem to be any.

Do you feel pushed up against a wall, with nowhere to go, and no room to breathe? When you think that you are almost out of breath, are you pushed until you find a little more?

And then, when you absolutely know without a doubt that you are out of breath, do you get pushed again to find just one more gasp? This happens again and again until you really are ready to give it all up.

At this point, you are set free to fully breathe once more. This is happening to every growing soul-personality right now.

Consider the analogy of a butterfly inside its cocoon. When you see the butterfly struggling, you are tempted to peel the cocoon off to free the butterfly so that it can fly away.

But what happens to a butterfly when it does not have the necessary struggle to free itself from its cocoon? Its wings are weak. The butterfly soon dies. The struggle makes the butterfly strong.

Think of yourself as a butterfly, locked in your cocoon. Your struggle gives you strength. Without the struggle, you will not be strong enough for the next phase of your life.

At times you may want someone else to resolve your issues for you, wishing for less on your plate. But, like the butterfly, if someone solves these issues for you, you will not grow strong enough to move into the next phase of your life.

The Earth plane is equivalent to the butterfly's cocoon. This reality is designed to pull you down so that you have to struggle to get out of it. This struggle teaches you about who and what you are; what you can and cannot do.

The struggle is what pushes you further into your depths than you ever thought possible. The struggle forces you to examine your darkness when you finally realize that the light does not contain all of your answers.

The struggle is your path to freedom, whether you consciously recognize it or not.

The "dark forces" are only a magnification of a part of your own totality that you choose to ignore. When you deal with the darkest parts of Self, then the outer magnification is no longer necessary, fading away.

All is only a projection of your own mind-pattern, and that of society's as a whole. You can stay and play the game of the collective unconscious group mind. Or, you can claim the totality of your own soul-personality.

You can move through the group mind and out the other side into individualized consciousness. Whatever/whomever you see as your greatest adversary is your greatest teacher.

Pay attention and learn, rather than run away. Stand up and greet that force, for it is only a reflection of your deepest, truest, most inner Self. Rather than fight it, embrace it, for it is a part of your True Totality.

The Earth Plane is a side-trip that you choose to take. What do you think is the next journey for your soul-personality when it finally releases from this prison-cage of "frozen light"?

What other rules/worlds are waiting for you to explore?

Do you want to be strong enough so that you can reach them and be functional within them as well?

What kind of soul-personality are you forging through your trials by fire?

What kind of strengths are you gaining?

Are you being forced into the depths of self-discovery as far as you are allowed within this dimension?

A runner knows that he/she runs faster when there is a competitor. The faster the competitor runs, the more the runner pushes him/herself, oftentimes beyond what he/she thinks can be endured. The competitor forces the runner into his/her best.

Competition is one way of using an adversary in a positive way. You push yourself into something better because of the perceived adversary.

Everyone uses everyone else to determine where he/she is in life - who has this or that possession, career, relationship, knowledge, etc.

Is this a judgment of "good" or "bad", or simply an objective status report of possibilities and potentials? Used as a self-evaluation tool, without judgment or criticism, this can push you into new levels of Self.

There are reasons for everything. What you label "bad" and/or "negative" exists for reasons beyond your comprehension until you are strong enough to understand.

Appearances can be deceiving unless you have the inner strength to delve into the mud and muck to determine the ultimate forces at work.

Consider these two stories:

Story #1   *Two men were traveling and needed a place to stay for the night. They came to a wealthy man's beautiful home, and asked if they could stay. The man refused, so they begged and pleaded because it was late, cold, and they were hungry.*

Finally, the wealthy man relented, putting the travellers in his cold, damp, dark basement with a few scraps of food. Gratefully, they accepted.

During the night, one man awoke to find the other repairing holes in the basement wall. He was surprised to see his friend doing this repair work at this hour. Tired, he fell back to sleep.

The next night, the two men came upon a small tiny cottage belonging to a poor farmer. When asked for lodging, the farmer invited them in.

The travellers were fed the best food the farmer had. They were even given the farmer's bed while the farmer and his wife slept on the floor.

During the night, the first traveller heard a loud bang. He awoke to see that the other traveller had shot the farmer's only cow!

Distressed, he asked, "Why did you repair the holes in the nasty wealthy man's home and shoot the kindly farmer's only cow?"

His companion replied, "There was gold hidden in the wall of the wealthy man's house so I made sure he would not find it".

"Here, tonight, the Angel of Death was coming to take the farmer's wife. So, I gave the Angel of Death the cow instead".

Story #2   *Two men were walking together. One was an unscrupulous character known for cheating others. He led a scandalous life. The other man led an exemplary life, helping everyone that he knew.*

As they walked, the unscrupulous man found a $20 bill. He was so excited that he started dancing about! In the commotion, the other man's foot caught in a crack on the sidewalk causing him to fall and break his ankle. This thrilled the unscrupulous man even more!

He exclaimed laughingly to the other man, "Look at me, I found a $20 bill! Look at you! You, who do only good, got a broken ankle! The joke's on you!"

Suddenly, an Angel appeared, and said to the unscrupulous man, "You were scheduled to come into a great fortune, but because of your lifestyle, all you got was $20".

Turning to the other man, the Angel continued, "You were scheduled to be hit by a car resulting in a horrible accident, but since you have lived such an exemplary life, you only received a broken ankle".

Life is full of deceptions. These deceptions are not always what you think they are. There are many unscrupulous people who look like they are getting away with everything.

In the same way, there are many who live exemplary lives who may appear to you to not receive what they deserve. This is why it is extremely important to look within the depths of Self via the Over-soul level. Otherwise it is extremely easy to misunderstand/misjudge what is truly happening.

Most people only look at outer appearances. This means they reach outer conclusions. This in turn makes it "easy" to throw stones at those they do not understand. These people miss the deeper meanings of life experiences.

Your struggles are your "trial by fire" that strengthen and forge the totality of your soul-personality. Understanding your own darkness is the only way you can understand who and what you are as well as the reflections of the outer world.

As the undercurrents of society rise from their hiding places, coming increasingly out into the open, your personal undercurrents also rise to the surface, ripe for exploration.

Most people explore only their daily life, because this is what most affects them on an ongoing basis. Sometimes, this leads to further self-exploration such as habits, relationships, personal trends, physical issues, etc.

This can keep people busy for years. Underneath lie the undercurrents that few people dare to enter. These undercurrents are not so easily identifiable, yet they propel all of daily life.

To explore these hidden areas, you must align Self with your Oversoul and God-Mind. To do this, take a look at how far your energy field extends from your physical body. Then, pull it in close to your body, placing it in a violet bubble. Now you have boundaries of where you start and stop.

Use your breath to find your center. Breathe in from the top of your head to the base of your spine, exhaling in reverse, sending your breath all the way up into your Oversoul and God-Mind. Work with your breath until you feel centered.

Breathe in the strength of your Oversoul and God-Mind, exhaling all that no longer belongs within your being. Breathe in the strength, exhale all that you no longer need.

As you do so, feel yourself sinking deeper and deeper inside of your Self, anchored deep in strength of your Oversoul and God-Mind. Allow your consciousness to sink further inside, into depths that until now you did not even consciously know existed.

Allow yourself access to the deepest levels of Self-knowledge that you can, with the least amount of discomfort. If at any time you feel traumatized or upset, put yourself in brown for grounding and conclude the exercise.

Go as deep within yourself as you feel led to explore. If you feel strong enough, place a clear black color at your pineal gland. The positive aspects of black are depth, mystery, and the hidden.

Use this color code to explore deep within your Self. Next, surround yourself in a layer of royal blue, then a layer of violet, a layer of silver, and finally a layer of gold.

If you have a tendency toward depression or unstableness, omit the black color code at this time. Use only royal blue, violet, silver, and gold.

Before you conclude your visualization, understand that you can breathe yourself into alignment, touching into the strength of Self, Oversoul, and God-Mind at any moment necessary. Know that the alignment and strength are always there any time, day or night, 24/7.

Focusing upon this perfect alignment simply brings what already exists into your conscious mind. The true test of your abilities lie in the outer world.

It is easy to be a "perfect person" when you are alone, but how about in a busy, hectic world? You may wish that you live where it is quiet so that you can mediate more and connect even deeper within.

Yet, if you can do this in a noisy environment, you can do this anywhere. The same with a family that you feel is unsupportive; or coworkers that "push your buttons".

What can you do within an environment that is designed to pull you down?

How strong are you?

Can you walk through the darkness of the outer world stronger and better for the experience?

Or, do you allow outer circumstances to pull you down and into them?

Can you keep yourself clean no matter how deep the mud and muck?

Can you maintain and retain your personal integrity regardless of the degradation of society and its attempts suck you into its pits?

Just because "everyone does it", do you have to join in?

Do numbers of people make something correct?

Are you strong enough to be your own person regardless of how many people fight against your right of personal self-expression?

There is a reason why you chose to be here at this particular time, with the increasing undercurrents of darkness that are rising to society's surface.

This is a perfect opportunity for you to allow your personal undercurrents of darkness to do the same. In this way, you explore what is hidden within so you can make conscious choices.

Is the darkness "bad"?

Or is it simply dark?

Why does it exist within you?

Why does it exist within society?

Take all your findings up to your Oversoul and ask for explanation. You already know. Now it is time to bring that knowledge into focus.

When you understand the depths of your own being and take the time to penetrate the multi-layers/levels, you will in turn take the knowledge into your understanding of the outer world.

Self-knowledge also reflects back to you in the outer world. If you cannot clearly define your own center, how can you possibly know when others are off-center?

If you do not understand your own boundaries, how can you know when others step outside of theirs?

If you do not understand the depths of your own inner levels, how can you identify the deeper levels of others?

Do not confuse darkness with "bad". The darkness is really the hidden part of your Self. Or, more accurately, that part of Self that is not in your focus at this moment.

Everything serves a purpose. Everything is a part of, and defines, God-Mind in Its Self-exploration.

Does the exploration of undercurrents and darkness bring fear to the surface?

Anchor yourself in your center. Allow the fear to rise up in a way that you can handle. This is your opportunity to face fear and walk through it.

Whatever is hidden, whatever you avoid, develop your center and strength so that you can bring it out in the least uncomfortable way. Then, explore and release whatever arises on up to your Oversoul, giving thanks for the lessons learned and assimilated.

When society reflects these dark undercurrents, outer circumstances control you until you can find a way to turn the tables. This puts you in a reactive position.

Consciously choose to explore the dark undercurrents of Self so you are in a proactive position. A proactive position means you control the situation before it controls you.

By consciously choosing to explore your own inner darkness, you learn to know yourself on all levels. When you know yourself on this level, you know others and the projections of the outside world for what each truly is.

Understanding Self is always the key to all things. You are a microcosm of the macrocosm. When you are capable of knowing your Self on both ends of the spectrum, you no longer fear who you are, what you are, and your own potential.

You control your Personal Power under the direction of your Oversoul and God-Mind. In the Eternal Now, your experiences encompass both light and dark. Your focus determines your current life experiences. When you function at this level, you control your own experiences rather than your experiences controlling you.

Choose to create your own inner catalysts to explore your own inner darkness. This not only changes your experiences, but as a result, changes the outpicturing of the world. Choose to walk through the darkness unharmed and unaffected. This can only happen when you are brave enough to look deep within your own internal darkness.

5. The Illuminati's #1 Secret Weapon

This Secret Weapon is hidden in plain sight so obviously that nearly everyone overlooks it. This Secret Weapon adds to the daily destruction of your freedom, mental prowess, physical health, financial strength, and interpersonal relationships.

There are approximately 7.3 billion of these Secret Weapons located throughout the globe - do these numbers give you a clue?

If you guessed YOU, then you are correct. The Illuminati uses you to destroy yourself!

The Illuminati merely sets up the scenario and you walk yourself down the path.

How can this happen? How do these Beings have so much knowledge that they can control and manipulate you into your own self-destruction?

While you struggle on a daily basis, each and every weak spot that you have is exploited and exaggerated to such a degree that there are dozens of pitfalls around you - so many, that you think these pitfalls are simply ordinary parts of life. You willingly jump into these pits and holes around you, totally ignoring the safe zones.

These pits are highlighted and emphasized everywhere you look. You think you have choices and you do - this pit or that pit? You no longer even recognize the safety zones. When you see the safety zones, you run away from them because they are now foreign to your conscious mind. The safety areas now seem the most frightening; the most frightening areas now appear to be the safest.

Thus, you run to your perceived safety zone, deep within the pits that others have dug for you. You willingly jump in and laugh at anyone pointing to a real safety zone! You no longer are able to distinguish between what is artificially created and what is not.

You have lost your semblance of reality - what is real and what is not. Everything blends together. You are lost and do not realize it. You fight against yourself and your fellow humans. Your angers, fears, frustrations, morals, ethics, and even your sexuality are opened and directed every day.

You cannot even sleep in peace, as the skies are filled with equipment that bombards you with ELF to direct your dreams and "rest" periods.

Your negative mind-patterns are artificially enhanced; you willingly ingest chemicals and non-foods in your bodies; you take legal and illegal drugs to numb your feelings, you buy smaller homes and cars to represent feeling small and overwhelmed; you vote in artificial elections; you fund-raise for diseases that do not exist; you take pay cuts while CEOs make millions; your children spend long days at school being indoctrinated instead of educated ... the list goes on and on.

Every single day, you live the life that "they" create for you. Where are "you" in the process? You are HELPING them dig your own grave! The human body is designed to live forever! God-Mind is limitless! You are hooked up to your own Source - Self, Oversoul, and God-Mind - this is the greatest power that exists!

Why do you refuse to use what is already the most natural and self-inherent power available to all? Why do you gullibly look away from what you are? How can you allow yourself to set foot on the path to not only self-destruction, but worse... to self-enslavement?

Observe how you participate and then throw epitaphs at others! You are not an innocent victim! You are a willing participant in someone else's game.

You cannot blame anyone for what you do or do not have; for opportunities that never come your way; for elusive health and relationships; for disappointments in life; for mind-control and ELF. You willingly walk the path that is prepared for you.

YOU are the best secret weapon that anyone could wish for!

Now that you are in the middle of the game, or some might say toward the end, you are finally waking up to the reality of the path that you have willingly chosen. What are you going to do about it? Why do you think that you have to work harder to get out of it?

This isn't "their" fault... put responsibility where it rightfully belongs... within YOU!

Quick, before it is too late, get into your mind-pattern, make some challenging choices, because at this stage it is not going to be so easy. Remember that you always live your past. You are living the past that you set in motion many, many years ago.

Now, you have to put the brakes on and throw yourself into a skid before you can stop the game and get onto another path. While you are skidding to a stop, there is a whole lot of shaking going on as one life experience after another bump together, creating a seemingly chaotic mess.

This is a mess that you created and you have to clean up. You cannot complain about it - you created it. You have to work harder and faster than ever to manifest a new past that you will eventually live, and this needs to be done as quickly as possible.

YOU have to prepare the path that you will walk, rather than complacently sit by while someone else does it for you.

YOU have to consciously unhook from the artificially enhanced Life Source that has been created for you and consciously hook Self into your Oversoul and God-Mind.

YOU have to discern your True Path of Self.

YOU have to actually do something proactive rather than reactively wait for everything to happen for and to you!

If you want to stop being the Illuminati's #1 Secret Weapon, you are the only one who can disengage the weapon.

How fast or slow you do it is up to you... but do not complain along the way.

6. Why the Illuminati Give you a Shelf Life: 20 Reasons

1. You are a wealth of information

2. You know history

3. You know religion

4. You know geography

5. You know how to read current language

6. You can track trends

7. You learn from past mistakes

8. You can teach others

9. You see the big picture

10. You can change the big picture

11. You can teach your children and grandchildren

12. You can improve your health

13. You can be a living example

14. You can accumulate wealth

15. You can give wealth to others

16. You have an information network

17. You have like-minded friends

18. You and your friends can create global change

19. You know the Truth

20. You might tell others. . . and others might actually believe you.

7. TRANSITIONS: IS PHYSICAL DEATH NECESSARY?

You most likely assume that you will experience death of the physical body. This is what you are taught and how society indoctrinates you. In school, you are taught that humans live approximately 75 years.

This is the imprint with which most people live life. You categorize life from infant, youth, middle age, and old age, culminating in physical death.

The quest for the "fountain of youth" is unending, whether it is in eating a specific food or herb, or through oxygenation, injections, and surgery. If the mind can dream it, someone is trying to find an outer "cure" for physical death.

This imprinting is generational and strong. People live in this illusion. Most have forgotten that regardless of what happens to the physical body, the mind-pattern is the ultimate determining factor.

Is physical death as it is now known absolutely necessary?

Is it possible to transmute the physical body into something else?

Is it possible to lighten up the cellular structure?

With enough control over your own thoughts and mind-pattern, can you "shapeshift" yourself into other dimensions, realities, and/or forms?

Most people do not have the fortitude to do this, because they do not want to leave the known. They do not want to be done with their lessons and move onto something else, regardless of their words.

People want to cling to whatever they have, whether it is material possessions, thoughts, things, or relationships. They forget that they are totally evolving energy on a journey into and through God-Mind.

That is the illusion, or delusion, of physical reality.

This is also what keeps you focused in the present moment. Experiencing too many realities at once would not allow you to focus on your specific purpose at this specific time.

If you cannot deal with your life as it is, why add the burden of other lifelines?

However, as you allow your soul-personality to evolve in the natural upward spiral, your outer world reflects this evolution.

You naturally begin to explore other worlds, realities, and dimensions. And, your experiences naturally flow along this course, continuing to support the mind-pattern that you hold.

Physical death is now the accepted vehicle that allows the soul-personality to transition from one phase of life to another. Physical death of the body simply reflects a mind-pattern that needs the death of current situations.

The soul-personality is ready to go onto something else. Because the conscious mind doesn't know how to halt, the subconscious, or God-Mind connection part of your mind, takes over.

Subconsciously, you slowly start experiencing physical death. Your energy starts leaving the physical body long before the physical body ceases to exist. This is why there are apparent diseases and degeneration.

If you have emotional issues that you feel are smothering you and with which you cannot deal, then you may develop lung cancer. This simply means that the life force leaves the lungs first.

How can you stop the physical body from degenerating if the body follows the mind?

The mind-pattern must be reversed for the body to reverse its course. You may be able to put the physical deterioration on hold to try to force the mind into a new pattern.

If you are successful with the mind, then the body is given what it needs to boost the newly forming mind-pattern.

No death is really ever "sudden" even though it may appear so. When you look at a person's energy field, you can see how much "vital force", or psychic energy, exists within the body.

When a person is ready to transition out of the physical body, regardless of chronological age, the life force diminishes. The soul-personality starts the journey out of the body long before the body ceases to function. Always remember that each cell of the physical body contains its own consciousness.

The body can remain animated without much of the soul-personality left. When the soul-personality makes the final tug, pulling the rest of its life force out of the physical, then the body ceases to function.

If the person has many unresolved emotions, he/she may have sent the energy of the heart, which is the center of emotions, out of the body long ago.

This can result in anything from heart problems all the way to death when the final vestiges of life force is wrenched from the body as the soul-personality takes its flight of perceived freedom.

When any organ, or part of the body, starts to fail, it does not suddenly happen. The psychic energy, which is the energy that runs the physical structure, starts to leave with every negative thought you think. For example, if you "hate", even if you feel it is justifiable, your cells respond by life force leaving. Thus, you destroy your body. When you send out positive thoughts, you maintain and increase your psychic energy. Your body responds by building itself even stronger.

When the going gets tough, some people do consciously think of leaving through the method known as suicide. Suicide is not on the upward spiral of evolution. Suicide throws you backwards instead of forward. It is an effort to escape rather than a fortification that allows your soul-personality to move forward.

Anyone that thinks he/she is escaping his/her lessons will find that suicide only intensifies the lessons. Plus, they have to deal with the emotional distress of those left behind.

People often fear physical death, and/or its consequences, because without fear, it would be too easy to simply leave this dimension whenever life is perceived as too difficult.

Fear of the Astral as well as having to face what they have done in life is why people fear death. This is the first thing that happens upon leaving the physical body - you must review absolutely everything you have ever done or said. This experience is often called "purgatory". This is another reason why you must release to your Oversoul and God-Mind now. If you leave your physical body, what you experience will be considerably lessened.

Some people have done some really horrible things. They must re-live all of this when they leave the body to review their life and make decisions what will happen next. Sometimes it is re-lived from the point of the person who was maligned. Rough stuff. Releasing every day to your Oversoul lessens what happens if you choose to leave the physical body. Be ever vigilant in what you give out, as it will come back to you.

In the Catholic religion, the priests took on the role of the Oversoul in daily confessional. Instead of going directly to your Source, the Catholics ask you to go to a priest who communicates with your Source for you, thus removing you one more step away from who and what you are.

While in this body, using Oversoul work, you review your day, what you experienced, and what others experienced. Then, you assimilate your lessons, make adjustments, and give that knowledge and infor-mation up to your Oversoul to pass on into God-Mind. By doing this you lessen what you go through at the moment of physical death. You still review your life, but because most of your life has already been reviewed, it will not be so intense.

Whatever you give out in your life is what you experience at the moment of physical death. If you caused harm to another, you will feel that harm being done to you. If you wished anything harmful on anyone for any reason, you will experience what you wished.

The more energy you put into the negative, the more you experience it. If you put enough energy into hating something, you actually create what you think you hate.

Your next life stream will then put you into the same situation that you wished for the recipient of your ill will. You will learn about the totality of your life experience. You always receive what you give out.

Where does the soul-personality go? It goes to wherever the mind-pattern pulls it. Remember, your world is held together by your mind-pattern. If you believe in heaven and hell, that is where you go. If you believe in the "white light" that is what you experience. If you believe you will be greeted by family and friends, this is your experience. If you believe in nothingness, that becomes your next reality.

Your mind-pattern creates your experiences, regardless of the dimension, plane, or reality in which your soul-personality exists. After a period of acclimation, you may "wake up" from this experience. Or, you may be subject to your "mentors" who automatically make the decision of where you need to go next. Your participation in the creation of your lifestreams depends upon how willing you are to be responsible for your Self at that moment.

If you are flamboyant, or adventuresome in life, you may want to experience this type of physical death. What may seem painful and traumatic to others may be exactly what you need and want to experience.

Perhaps you choose a dramatic exit to be remembered. Sometimes the most quiet, shy-appearing individuals choose to make a statement in this way. What could not be said in life is said in death.

Those that leave young may have had only a few things to accomplish; then it is time to exit. Or, they have lessons to teach those they leave behind. Or, they have choices - to stay or to go. They will go where they feel they can make the best use of their life - this Physical Reality or somewhere else.

Many people are now choosing to exit the Earth plane for a variety of personal reasons. It is not anyone's place to judge these decisions, but you can evaluate and decipher what is happening and why on the Oversoul level.

All you have to do is ask your Oversoul to contact the Oversoul of the person involved. Tell your Oversoul anything that you would like him/her to know.

Ask that this message be passed on via his/her Oversoul. His/her Oversoul will relay the message without disturbing the soul-personality, and the work that he/she is currently doing.

You can also ask that any messages that he/she wishes to relay back to you be done in this way via the Oversouls. On some level, your souls are already communicating. In True Reality, there is only One Soul and no separation. There is no true disconnection from one another - only the illusion that is perpetuated in this reality.

There will come a time when physical death ceases to exist. Instead, the soul-personality journeys on in conscious awareness.

What will be your next step in the upward evolutionary spiral?

What kind of choices will you make?

How will you build your mind-pattern to determine your next phase of existence?

What is important to you?

What kind of possibilities can you dream?

If you can think it, somewhere, someplace, it already exists. Now, hold your focus there, and bring it to yourself.

Consciously create your own transitioning, wherever it may be, however you desire it to occur. As always, the choice is yours.

8. Death Program... And How To Stop It!

Death Program...

Ages 0-9 You are told the average life span of a human.. This imprints your conscious mind with a "Death Program" for (literally) the rest of your life.

Ages 10-19 This is the decade of New Beginnings. These are your teen years when you are out exploring the world, never giving much thought to the Death Program that is now running through your subconscious mind. You may have to answer a question or two about this in your science class from time to time.

Ages 20-29 This is the decade of Duality. You learn the positive and negatives of life as you enter into adulthood. The Death Program is running but you tend to block it out of your conscious mind until you approach the end of your 20s. Then you start thinking about what you have not accomplished, realizing that "the rest of your life" is not that long!

Ages 30-39 This is the decade of Perfection of earlier learning. The Death Program speeds up. It tells you that your life is most likely half-over. You worry about your health (worry creates disease) and start to notice how others are "aging" compared to you. You may help contribute to a worthy health cause - walking for cancer awareness, raising money for MS, donating blood, etc. because you realize that "someday this may be you". Women reach the end of their child-bearing years. They are now "old".

Ages 40-49   This is the decade of Physical Reality. Often your financial picture improves or the direction you need to go in life becomes clearer. In the meantime, the Death Program creates mid-life crises, saying that you are officially in middle age. You decide you better take better care of your health so you do not end up like everyone else you know. You read the health articles wherever you see them to make sure you do not have the symptoms of some dreaded disease. These articles promote fear, and fear creates dis-ease.

Ages 50-59   This is the decade of self-healing. You have now lived long enough that you consider yourself "wiser" than those with less life experience. You no longer care as much about what others think. You speak up more easily. You may have more time for yourself as you settle into your career.

You feel more confident and competent - until the AARP mailings and retirement brochures start rolling in, depicting little old bent over people with canes telling you to plan for old age and your funeral to make it easier for your loved ones upon your demise. The Death Program goes visual and you fight your inner response.

Ages 60-69   This is the decade to end the series of cycles that may be running your life. This is the opportunity to end the old - which some people manifest as the end of good health, the end of viable relationships, the end of careers, and the Death Program says you are getting closer to the end of your life - better get prepared. People reach retirement age - they are now cast aside and are officially "old".

Ages 70-79   This is the decade of Completion. According to the Death Program which is now becoming increasingly active, what you learned as a child is about to come true. You are reaching the end of the life span of the average human. You either give in or do your best to beat the odds. Most people forget that Completion means one door closing and another opening - unless it is the door to Heaven.

Ages 80-89   This is the decade of your Oversoul. Your Oversoul is your point of origin out of the Mind of God. This is the decade when you most naturally consciously connect to your power Source. Rather than stay here and utilize this powerful and natural connection, what a great time for the Death Program to kick in, telling you it is time for you to connect in another reality.

Ages 90-99   This is the decade that ends all cycles since birth. If you have not left yet, it is time for the "big heave-ho" to get out the door. Otherwise, what a wealth of information and history you contain! If you are still healthy and of sound mind, what an influence you could be to the "new crop" of worker bees arriving into this reality, now ages 0-9. The Death Program is running full speed ahead now, pushing you right through Heaven's Gate.

Ages 100 Plus   New beginnings - but the Death Program has already shown you that you do not want to live this long. You will be alone, ill, and with no one to take care of you. "They" do not want you to be a living storehouse of knowledge that can influence generations. The Death Program is designed so that you absolutely do not follow through on this path of New Beginnings - if you make it this far.

... & HOW TO STOP IT

Refuse to participate in the Death Program.

Develop your awareness that the Death Program exists for a reason. Refuse to participate and learn to reverse the process. Ancient peoples, from Biblical Times to Atlantis and Lemuria were rumored to have lived for hundreds of year - is this a possibility for you, too?

Release your experiences as they occur up to their point of origin - your Oversoul and on up into God-Mind. Carrying the experiences of your past fills you up, creates weight, changes relationships, redirects career paths, affects financial status, distorts the mind and body, and recreates the beautiful body into which you were born into something else.

If you do not empty out now so you are ready for year 100, then you need to go out of the body to do this - and the Death Program wins again.

Your mind is the most effective tool you have for building yourself up or tearing yourself down. You have the tool. You already own it. It is Free. Use it appropriately and the Death Program turns on itself. Kill the Death Program instead of it killing You.

9. Crucifixion Program & More

Every artificially created holiday is an opportunity for your Programming to be enhanced and more deeply imprinted upon your mind-pattern. That is, unless you actively deprogram so that the normal "triggers" do not activate or embed upon what already exists within you.

You already know how to Balance your Brain via Pineal Gland, keep your chakras in the proper colors and order, and keep the "Brown Merger Archetype" in place as well as stay in heavy protection.

But as you go through this now daily regimen, do you take the time to go deeper into the outside world? Do you understand the artificialness of what you see?

Are you able to see the "set-ups" that are in place to snare your subconscious mind?

First of all, you have to understand that organized religion is all about the Paranormal, except no one publicly acknowledges this. Instead, you hear about "Miracles" which someone else can do, but not you.

Paranormal simply means "beyond" normal. However, "Paranormal" is normal. The hoodwink is that you think "paranormal" is special. It is not. Paranormal is Natural and Normal. Some religions even teach that this realm belongs to the Devil.

Imprinting Message #1: Stay Away from your Normal and Natural State of Being. If you display paranormal abilities, then you have been compromised by negative entities. Or, you have a mental or physical disorder. If you hear voices, see lights and colors, disincarnate beings, or have other "para"normal experiences, then you need medication to dull the pineal gland, thus closing the gateway to other realities and dimensions.

If this fails, hospitalize you. Exorcise you. In some cases, ostracize you.

Imprinting Message #2: There is something wrong with you; you are evil. Organized religions do not allow you to have "para"normal abilities and experiences. Organized religions say that Mary, Jesus, Saints, Prophets, and even the Pope (who is said to be God's vicar on Earth) can have paranormal experiences and powers. But not you. Why?

When your attention is directed outward to "others" than you do not have time to self-explore. When you are told that "para"normal abilities are not normal, or even in some cases the "work of the devil", you certainly do not want these experiences and abilities. You do not want others to know. For these reasons, you automatically self-suppress and self-monitor.

Yet, the paranormal frequency does exist. As a microcosm of the macrocosm, it is within you. Because in the overall picture, God-Mind must always be in balance. Because the controllers know that which is suppressed must eventually be expressed. Or the suppressed frequency erupts with violent, uncontrollable forces.

Imprinting Message #3: Others can perform miracles but not you. The controllers know that there must be a safety valve to keep the suppressed in balance with the unsuppressed. So, you are given Religious icons. Mary, Jesus, Saints, Prophets. The Pope.

Religious icons provide this safety valve. They have paranormal powers. They provide paranormal experiences labeled "miracles". All that is within you is poured forth into these icons.

This takes your attention away from your Self. You become self-monitoring. You do not want these experiences because:

1. They might come from the devil.
2. You might be declared physically ill.

3. You might be declared mentally incompetent, medicated and/or hospitalized.

4. You might be considered spiritually compromised or possessed.

5. You cannot find a legitimate source of answers.

You may resort to taking medications to stop the experiences.

Because you do not know:

* Who/what it is
* How to deal with it
* How to protect yourself from it
* Where it comes from
* What to do if it happens again
* Who to talk to

You may question if your experience is real or a dream.

These experiences fall outside of what you are formally taught. The best you may be able to do is to try to take what you already know to explain what you do not know.

Imprinting/Message #4: Self-Isolate. When you find someone that you can trust, then you want to learn from that person. As you get stronger in your understandings and convictions, you may feel that you are "equal to" the teacher.

After a while, when you recognize that your teacher is simply a person with negative attributes as well as positive ones, you begin to feel superior. You lose respect for your teacher, perhaps going so far as to trash and vilify this person everywhere you go. Because your programming has kicked in; specifically Crucifixion Programming.

Crucifixion Programming has been systemically imprinted not only upon Christians but amongst all people who know the conventional Biblical Story of Jesus.

The basic story is that Jesus came to save the people. The very people who he came to save crucified him upon a cross.

Imprinting Message #5: Crucify those who come to help you... and you do. You crucify your leaders. Anyone who steps out of the pack. Anyone you perceive better than you. You bully, push around, and stomp on that person until he/she is driven into the dirt. Not above you, or beside you, but trampled into the ground to be walked upon. Get rid of the leaders, visionaries, philosophers. Anyone who would lead you beyond your current status quo.

This is the group-mind mentality activated in full force. This is why people often behave differently in groups than alone. These are weak and powerless people who only garner a feeling of power from "the pack" - like a pack of animals. So, they pick on those people who they perceive have power. This is the story of what happened to Jesus retold millions of times in millions of different scenarios. Same song, different verse.

Imprinting Message #6: Rip to shreds anyone who tries to lead the pack. The cross is a Hyperspace Symbol that has been denigrated into a symbol of slavery.

The Ancient Hebrew word "Tslav" means "cross".

In Latin, "esclavo" means "slave".

Every time Catholics make the sign of the cross on themselves, they use Hyperspace Language to imprint their mind-pattern with "slave". Every time you see a cross you are being imprinted with the sign of the slave.

Imprinting Message #7: You are a slave. Take this a step further. Jesus is often depicted nailed to the cross. Notice that with feet nailed to the bottom part of the cross and arms spread out to either side with hands nailed to the crossbar, his body takes on the Hyperspace Archetype of "Y".

What does "Y" mean in Hyperspace? "Choices".

What was Jesus supposed to do? "Save you".

What did you do to your savior: "Nail him upon the cross of slavery".

The head is a "dot" on top.

What does a "dot" mean in Hyperspace? "Consciousness".

What's on the Christ figure's head? "Crown of thorns".

What does this crown of thorns do? "Causes bleeding".

What is blood-letting? "Loss of Joy".

Imprinting Messages. . .

#8. Your choices are nailed into slavery.

#9. Crucify that which comes to save you.

#10. Always crucify your savior.

#11. You are a slave to this mentality.

#12. Put a crown of thorns on your consciousness.

#13. Your consciousness is destined to cause you loss of joy.
Take this a step deeper. The Reptilian Brain Stem in Hyperspace is a reddish-brown "Y".

Christ Consciousness is part of the Holy Trinity.

Your Christ Consciousness is nailed to and enslaved by your Reptilian Brain Stem. You therefore cannot effectively use the True "Holy Trinity" but must stay subservient to the "Unholy Trinity".

Imprinting Message #14: You crucified your savior causing your savior to leave/abandon you. You must worship your savior from afar. Nothing in this reality will help you. You must rely on other realities that you are not privy to at this time. Now do you understand how the New Age imprinted you with "Space Brothers" by hooking onto this imprinting? A program upon a program upon a program. . .

If you behave appropriately "someday" you will be rewarded. But not now when you need it.

You will never have what you want in this reality. Instead, you must wait and wait and wait until you are dead. And then maybe you will receive your reward.

Everything that will "save" you will abandon you. People abandon you, finances abandon you, self-worth abandons you. You are the reason your world is in such a terrible state. You are a bad person. You deserve this and worse.

You are now filled with deserved guilt. You find a million reasons and more to beat yourself up. No one has to do it for you.

Imprinting Message #15: You have passed the indoctrination - you can successfully self-flagellate. People who are kindhearted, generous, and loving are especially prone to Jesus Complex Programming. They give and give to others until there is nothing left for them to give. They will curl up and die while the takers simply walk over the dead body looking for the next person from whom they can extract their life force.

Some men with Jesus Complex Programming may actually grow their hair long, wear a beard, and emulate the pictures that depict Jesus. Some people may appear arrogant with an air of superiority as they perceive themselves as a savior to others.

Imprinting Message #16: False Saviors are among you. People with Jesus Complex Programming have to remember that they need their own life force to live. They cannot give so much that there is nothing left of them. They must think carefully about what they give and to whom. Oversoul communication for these people is paramount. Learning how to establish boundaries is essential. Discernment of who merely needs a hand to pull them up vs who grabs your hand to pull you down.

The holidays leading up to the Crucifixion further enhance your Programming and Imprinting if you let them.

During "Lent" you have to give up something that you love. For 40 days. "4" is about anchoring into physical reality.

Imprinting Message #17: Anchor into physical reality the mind-pattern of suffering as you give up that which you love. On "Ash Wednesday" you spread waste (ash) and confusion

(Hyperspace meaning of the color "gray") at the pineal gland (your receptor to the "para"normal).

Imprinting Message #18: Your receptor to the "para"normal is wasted and confused. Palm Sunday has your Savior riding on a Donkey - not a noble beast in today's times. On "Palm" leaves, a double entendre referring to the palms of your hands - open to slavery.

Imprinting Message #19: Anyone that tries to save you is an ass and a slave, just like you. "Maundy Thursday" is the "Last Supper" of your savior. The last time that your savior will receive Earthly sustenance.

Imprinting Message #20: Prepare for the death of any-one/thing that tries to save you. "Good Friday" is not a good day if you consider Jesus your savior. Good Friday is a day of mourn-ing, both for the death of Jesus and for the sins of the world that his death represents.

Imprinting Message #21: Label the death of anyone/thing that tries to save you "good". "Holy Saturday" is the last day of the week spent in prayer and often fasting, representing "doing without".

Imprinting Message #22: Suffer. If Jesus was put to death on Friday night and rose 3 days later, then why is the Resurrection celebrated on Sunday, 2 days later? Because 3 represents the Super-conscious Mind - your God-Mind connection.

1. Represents your Conscious Mind-connection with the outer world

2. Represents your Subconscious Mind-connection between outer and inner worlds

3. Represents your Superconscious Mind-connection to inner world of the God-Mind which "they" want to create the illusion that you do not have.

Imprinting Message #23: You are connected to the outer world but your God-Mind connection is disabled. Whether you are Christian or not is inconsequential. You react to all symbols/Archetype imprinting whether or not you consciously understand their meanings and significance.

You are subconsciously imprinted every day with similar symbols/Archetypes that you do not recognize unless you develop your conscious awareness that hooks you only and directly into your own Oversoul and God-Mind.

When Self is strongly anchored in the True Holy Trinity of the Oversoul Matrix, Christ Consciousness and God-Mind, these symbols and Archetypal messages/imprinting do not affect you like they do the masses. You see through the illusions that the controllers perpetuate for public consumption. You do not subscribe to the delusions. You know by knowing what is correct and not correct.

You must repair the cracks in the mind-pattern that allow the Unholy Trinity to encroach upon and defile your efforts. These days are your "trials by fire". You chose to be here. Utilize the learning opportunities to their fullest extent.

Use your available tools to stay strong and steadfast, clear in Oversoul and God-Mind Objective Truth. Even if thousands are deluded, and you are the Only One, stay your course. You are charting the course that someday, when ready, others will follow.

10. MY WALDENSIAN ANCESTRY

Waldensians eventually settled into what is now the Cottian Alps of Northern Italy. However, at various times throughout history, this area belonged to France or Italy and sometimes it was its own country of Savoie/Savior if you want to look at the etymology.

Mary Magdalene took refuge here as did St. Paul.

Waldensians organized themselves along the line of the New Testament, spreading seeds of thought that fueled the 16th Century Reformation. In fact, many credit the Waldensians as being the "Mother of the Protestant Reformation". Yet you have probably never even heard of them. Why not?

One Roman Catholic author, Rainier Sacho, wrote: "There is no sect so dangerous as the Leonists (another name for Waldensians because they were from the Lyons section of France) for three reasons: 1. it is the most ancient; some say it is as old as Sylvester, others say it is as old as the Apostles themselves, 2. it is very generally disseminated; there is no country where it has not gained some footing. Third, while other sects are profane and blasphemous, this retains the utmost show of piety; they live justly before men and believe nothing concerning God which is not good". Sacho admits that the Waldensians flourished at least 500 years before the time of Peter Waldo, who later was credited by the Roman Catholic Church with beginning the sect.

The early Waldensians trace their ancestry back to earliest Christianity to the Church of Vaudois. Although many people believe that the earliest sacraments of the Waldensians are missing, they contend that the Waldensians followed the earliest literal application of the teachings of Christ as contained in the gospels. They rejected Mass and

Eucharist, and believed that the true Church was the community, not the buildings. They believed that the buildings should be destroyed. They did not believe in a hierarchal church and they believed in the right of women to preach - heretic at the time.

According to Allix Churches of Piedmont: "The Reformers held that the Waldensian Church was formed around 120 AD, from which date on they passed down from father to son the teachings they received from the Apostles". The year 120 is consistent with the dispatch of the disciples of Polycarp from Smyrna and Ephesus.

To end their persecution, in 1531 the Waldensians decided to align with the Protestant doctrine which they believed "the lesser of the evils" compared to the Roman Catholic Church, their other choice. In spite of this step, from 1540 to 1690 they witnessed a wholesale destruction of their churches.

During this time period, the Duke of Savoy granted them peace in 1561. However, in 1624 Spanish troops tried to wipe them out, killing thousands of Waldensians. The Council for the Propagation of the Faith then met in Turin, resulting in all Waldensians being ordered back into the mountains of Italy. Even though they went, 15,000 troops were sent in to destroy them. This massacre shocked Europe and in 1685 the Edict of Nantes was revoked which stopped the killing.

In 1686, Louis XIV asked the Duke of Savoy to persecute the Waldensians. The Swiss offered the Waldensians exile, however another 20,000 were still killed. By this time it was thought that only about 200 Waldensians were left in the mountains. These remaining few fought so hard that 3000 imprisoned Waldensians were released and guaranteed safe passage to Switzerland. This happened in the middle of the winter.

All children under the age of twelve were separated from their parents. The children were sent throughout Europe to prevent return to their families and to be raised as Roman Catholics. Many Waldensians who left for Switzerland died on the twelve day journey through the bitter winter snow. Sound like a familiar protocol for destroying history, family and true religion?

The Waldensians fought again from 1690 to 1694 when they were granted religious liberty. But the senate in Turin, Italy forbade publication of the edict under penalty of death. By 1700, it was written that "had they been able to, the Roman Catholic Church would have killed every single Waldensian until they had exterminated them from the face of the Earth". In late 1800s, 45 families fled to Uruguay, then to New York City, Monett, Missouri, and Valdese, North Carolina.

Many other Waldensians fled throughout Europe and even into the Soviet Union and Asia to escape persecution. So is it possible that you have Waldensian frequency in your genetics?

I am a direct descendant; my paternal great-grandparents and grandparents belonged to the Waldensian Church of Monett Missouri. The Waldensians consider themselves the Original Christians because their information came directly from Mary Magdalene and the Apostles. They do not consider themselves Protestants. However, the churches outside of what is now Italy were forced to join with Protestant denominations to protect themselves from total annihilation by the Catholics. In doing so, their true history became lost to the public.

What few people realize is that Waldensians in Italy were only granted religious freedom in 1986. I spent over two years tracing my family history to prove my lineage so that I can continue my Waldensian research in the land of my ancestors. It also appears that I am related to Jacqueline Bouvier Kennedy Onassis, as the Bouviers were originally Waldensian. It is interesting that when I was 12 my orthodontist told me that I had the exact same facial structure as Jacqueline Kennedy.

I invite you to spend time tracing your ancestry so that you, too, have more doors to your own true world history and personal history. What you find may change your entire perspective on your life as well as influence your goals and the direction you take. Participating more fully in your own life reveals your own mysteries so that who and what you are takes on a much deeper, fuller, richer meaning. You deserve to know.

GLOSSARY OF TERMS

Activation: When a program is brought to full function.

Affirmation: A statement that defines a course of action, or a state of inner being; repeating words many times by thinking, speaking, or writing it to bring new avenues of action into your conscious mind.

Alien: A physical being from another planet.

Alter: Section or compartmentalized personality within a programming matrix.

Androgynous: Male and female combined without sexual distinction.

Archetype: Symbol or glyph from hyperspace or mind-patterns.

Astral Plane: The border zone between physical reality and hyperspace.

Aura: Your personal energy field.

Bisexual: Sexuality desiring both males and females.

Center: Your center is aligned along your spine, providing a safe space from which to work; you pull yourself into it by willing yourself into it.

Ceremony: Gathering to celebrate or honor an entity or Illuminati holiday.

Chakra Band: Energy center of the body and encompassing area.

Chakras: Along the human spinal column there are main nerve bundles called ganglions, which are esoterically called "chakras", a word which means "wheels" in Sanskrit. They form along the "S" curve of the spine which looks like a snake. For this reason the chakra system is referred to as "Kundalini", the Sanskrit word for snake.

Collective Conscious Mind: The body of space that contains the accumulated known knowledge of humankind.

Collective Unconscious: The body of space that contains the accumulated thoughts of humankind; these established thought patterns directly affect what you move through today.

Conscious Mind: Contains your present.

Construct: Similar to a physical object created in the programming matrix to work with the alter in a specific function.

Deprogramming: Techniques to block and/or remove mind-control/programming.

Direct Awareness: To know by experiencing the knowledge.

DNA Sequences: This refers to the DNA sequences opening up in the body which is a form of Kundalini activation. DNA codes are the instructions that tell your body what to do and be. Some instructions you are running at birth. These dictate that you will have blue eyes, two legs, two arms, etc. Others activate later in life, such as health conditions, ability to play music, sing, etc.

ELF: Extra low frequency generally related to microwaves for mind-control purposes; energy waves that influence body and mind.

Energy: A physical substance consisting of shape, weight, consistency, and color.

ET (Extraterrestrial): Borderline physical/non-physical beings not bound to our reality.

Frequency: A rate of vibration that distinguishes one flow of energy from all other flows.

God-Mind: Neutral energy; All That Is.

Group-Mind: Formed when vibrations band together.

Habit Response: An established pattern of behavior that allows you to react to any given situation without thinking, whether physical or mental. It can be positive, negative, or neutral.

Horizontal Experience: Pulls you out into similar growth.

Hyperspace: A region of consciousness that exists outside of linear space and time.

Illuminati: Member or associate of one of the 13 ruling families on Earth.

Illusion: The way you perceive things to be.

Know by Knowing: To understand through direct awareness; to understand the feeling of an experience.

Knowledge: Information.

Language of Hyperspace: The Original Language that emanates from the Mind of God consisting of color, tone, and archetype (symbol).

Love: Neutral energy that emanates from God-Mind that does not discriminate.

Lyrae: Star system in the Milky Way Galaxy that is the origin point for all humans.

Macrocosm: God-Mind; All That Is; the larger picture of everything.

Matrix, Programming: The structure in the mind that facilitates mind-control; 13x13x13 which equals 2,197 compartments.

Meditation: A process that moves you beyond words and connects you with silence, the level of feeling; the listening from which information is gathered; centered in the right-brain.

Microcosm: You; a world in miniature.

Mind-Pattern: Blueprint of a persons' thoughts.

Negative: Negative is not "bad", but merely a condition that exists; the opposite of positive, which explains another part of the same experience.

New World Order (NWO): Global government dictatorship being created by the Illuminati.

New World Religion: Global religion.

Objective Listening: Listening and evaluating without judgment or criticism.

Objective Observing: Watching and evaluating without judgment or criticism.

Oversoul: Neutral energy that comes out of God-Mind; your Oversoul is to you what your Earth parents are to your body. Your Oversoul is your point of origin out of God-Mind.

Pineal Gland: Organ at the center of the head.

Positive: Positive is not better than negative, but is merely a condition that exists; the opposite of negative, which explains another part of the same experience.

Prayer: Request that affects the results of meditation; centered in the left-brain.

Proactive Learning: Active learning; gathering knowledge before an experience occurs.

Psychic Energy: Your personal energy; it flows back and forth, and is horizontal.

Reactive Learning: Passive learning; gathering knowledge after an experience occurs.

Reality: The way things really are; it may vary considerably from your perception of the way you think things are.

Reptilian: A being with lizard-like characteristics from either the inner Earth or Draco star system; colonized Lemuria.

Shapeshifter: A person who physically changes from one species to another.

Silence: The deepest level of inner awareness; the level of feeling; you connect with your Oversoul and God-Mind within silence.

Simultaneous Existence: All lifelines occurring at the same moment in the Eternal Now.

Soul-Personality: Individual strand of an Oversoul.

Spirituality: A state of inner being.

Sub-Personality: A group of similar emotions that becomes strong enough to develop its own consciousness; a sub-persoanlity is not you, but it is a part of you.

Subconscious Mind: Contains your memories, moment by moment, lifeline by lifeline.

Superconscious Mind: Provides the direct link to your Oversoul and God-Mind.

T-Bar: Archetype emanating from the pineal gland relating to balance.

Trigger: Sensory input that opens a program.

Universal Energy: Energy that is available to everyone; using it allows you to keep your psychic energy; it flows up and down, and is vertical.

Universal Law: Rules and regulations that pervade all creation; emanates from God-Mind.

Vertical Experience: Pulls you up into new growth.

Vibration: Frequency rate of an energy.

Vibratory Imprint: Accumulated feelings of like experiences; they cause you to react to your experiences of today through your accumulated feelings of yesterday.

Visualization: Creating a mental scenario that can be manifested either mentally or physcially; centered at the pineal gland.

Wisdom: Knowledge applied.

You: Individualized neutral energy.

INDEX

10 Commandment tablets, 176
10 Commandments, 145
10 plagues, 50, 109, 145
100 billion galaxies, 3, 239
13 Illuminati families, 239
13x13x13 cube, 253
16 rays of the central sun, 40
19.5 degrees latitude, 7, 8
22 chapters, 219
22 letters, 219
28 kHz frequency, 160, 161, 163
3 global rituals, 54
39th Move, 217
3rd Reich, 197
3rd Reich, people, 194
4th Reich, 191, 192, 194–197, 230, 231, 239
4th Reich programming, 202
4th Reich, bases, 195
4th Reich, people, 194, 195
5th Reich, 230
60 million years ago, 16
7 domed areas, 14
7-headed Reptilian, 28
9 Templars, 125, 130

3, 54
22, 219
666, 171
1945, 54
1969, 54

a-Viking, 83

abduction(s), 195, 232, 237
Aborigine, origin, 21
Aborigines, language, 115
Abraham, 40
Acre, 123, 127
activities of the flesh, 262
actual reality, 218
Adair, James, 65
Adam, 17, 68
Adam and Eve, 17
Adam, meaning, 24
Adamites, 24
Adonai, 18
Adonai, meaning, 238
advanced civilizations, 159, 166
Afghani, 122
afraid, 222
Africa, 19, 152, 187, 189, 190, 211
Africa, North, 83
Africa, Queen of, 189
Agartha, 203
Aix-en-Provence, 134
Akkad, 159
Akko, 123, 127
Alaska, 155, 201, 222
Albania, 59, 122
Aldebaran base, 207
Aldebaran culture, 195
Aldebaran influences, 194
Aldebaran(s), 27, 194, 197, 203, 230
Alexander the Great, 60, 79
Alexandria, 95
alien abductions, 232

alien bases, 195
alien beings, 227, 232, 237
alien beings and humankind, 215
alien civilization(s), 27, 207, 222, 223
alien craft, 196, 221
alien energy, 207
alien features, Noah, 32
alien group(s), 68, 230, 231
alien invaders, 223
alien manipulations, 27
alien presence on Earth, 57, 222
alien technology, 113, 233
alien voices, 196
alien(s), 58, 108, 221, 222, 227, 237–239
alien, Bible Code, 58
alien, God, 33
aliens civilizations, 50
aliens, existence, 46
aliens, humanoid-type, 227
Allan Hills, Antarctica, 13
Allix Churches of Piedmont, 308
alternate dimensions, 230
alternate existences, 249
alternate reality/realities, 57, 218, 230, 244
alternate universe, 237
alternate versions of you, 238
America, Columbus, 88
America, opposite of, 40
America, salt mines, 21
American Empire, 217
American Indian cultures, 20
American Indian symbol, 212
American Midwest, Vikings, 88
American ships, 95
Americans, 1
Amminadab, 173
amplifier, 150
ancestry, 108, 128, 235, 236, 309
Andean Mountains tunnel system, 195
Andes Mountains, 2, 104

androgynous, 4, 15, 17, 72
androgynous Reptilian, 4, 15, 17
androgyny, 4, 17, 39, 41
androgyny, Reptilian, 72
Andromedans, 230
Angel of Death, 78
Angelic Frequency, 253
Angelic Hierarchy, 253–255
angers, 284
Angkor Wat, 28
Annunaki, 35, 36
Antarctic Peninsula, tunnel, 195
Antarctic programming, 202
Antarctic winter, 198
Antarctica, 10, 191–194, 201–203, 207, 230, 231
Antarctica, access, 202
Antarctica, airline, 201
Antarctica, Allan Hills, 13
Antarctica, anomalies, 197
Antarctica, base(s), 192, 195, 201
Antarctica, climate, 191
Antarctica, first exploration, 191
Antarctica, flight(s), 201, 202
Antarctica, Google, 200
Antarctica, maps, 198
Antarctica, military expedition, 194
Antarctica, Nazi, 191
Antarctica, Operation Highjump, 193
Antarctica, people, 195
Antarctica, pyramids, 157
Antarctica, radio signale, 196
Antarctica, rescue, 198
Antarctica, ship that sank, 198
Antarctica, sickness, 198
Antarctica, temperatures, 199
Antarctica, territories, 191
Antarctica, transport to, 193
Antarctica, tunnels, 195
Antarctica, underground paradise, 192
Antarctica, volcanoes, 199

Antarctica, Vril craft technology, 197
anti-Catholic, 133
anti-Catholicism, 170
Anti-Christ number, 171
anti-New World Order groups, 196
anti-Reptilian groups, 196
Apostle Peter, 216
Apostles, 99, 131, 138, 307–309
Apostles, descendants of, 131
apple, 18
aquifer, 43
Arabian Peninsula, 51
Arabic, 67, 69, 122
Arabic cultures, 211
Arabic Jews, 54
Arabic sounding names, 142
Arabs, 54, 65, 121
Aramaic, 67, 215
Ararat, Mount, 32
Arcturus, 27
Area 51, 196
Argentina, 141, 192, 196, 209, 213
Argentina's secret police, 213
Argentina, Waldensians, 141
Arizona, 22, 47
Ark, 32, 51, 53, 54
Ark of the Covenant, 51–53, 190
Armenia, 32
artifacts, alien, 192
artifacts, ancient Israel, 76
artifacts, Atlantean, 192
artifacts, Celtic, 97, 144
artifacts, Chinese, 119
artifacts, copper, 154
artifacts, Egyptian, 47, 87
artifacts, Hebrew, 54
artifacts, Javanese, 148
artifacts, Mayan, 144, 153, 154
artifacts, Michigan, 144
artifacts, Minoan, 144
artifacts, Monks Mound, 152
artifacts, Notre Dame, 46

artifacts, Ogam, 97
artifacts, Persia, 89
artifacts, Sumer, 40
artifacts, Templars, 128, 129
artifacts, Viking, 89, 144, 153, 154,
        156
artifacts, Waldensian, 141
Aryan characteristics, 192
Aryan genetics, 213
Aryan Super Race, 213
Aryan(s), 63, 192, 214
Aryan-like nation, 214
Aryan-type people, 193
Ashkenazi (Khazar) Jews, 64, 65
Ashtar/Ishtar, 77
Asia, 28, 32, 115, 122, 144, 148, 152,
        217, 309
Asia, Central, 31, 83
Asian cultures, 28
Asian genetics, 116
Asian legend, 28
Assyria, 159
asteroid belt, 11, 95
asteroids, 12, 36, 49, 50, 95, 223
astral energy/energies, 211, 264, 265
astral entities, 218, 263
astral hooks, 264
astral levels, 248
astral links, 264
astral navigators, 266
Astral Power, 267
astral projection, 261
Astral Realm entity, 264
Astral Realm, manipulate, 262
Astral Realm/astral realm, 239, 261–
        264, 266, 267
astral-bound, 261, 262
Astral/astral, 23, 24, 233, 261–264,
        266, 267, 292
Athens, 59
Atil/Itil, 63
Atl, 15

Atlans, 15, 31
Atlantean alphabet, 59
Atlantean continent, 16, 21
Atlantean culture, 31, 91
Atlantean tectonic plate, 108
Atlantean(s), 15, 16, 19, 20, 31, 59, 147, 151, 156
Atlanteans, electromagnetic pulses, 16
Atlanteans, flight, 19
Atlanteans, geomagnetic weapons, 19
Atlanteans, self-destruction, 19
Atlanteans, wars, 16
Atlantic (Ocean), 22, 31, 49, 50, 165
Atlantic civilizations, 49
Atlantic, pyramids, 165
Atlantis, 13, 15, 18, 20, 22, 23, 33, 37, 38, 43, 59, 91, 95, 103, 109, 113, 151, 194, 237, 249, 297
Atlantis culture, destroyed, 31
Atlantis, destruction, 91
Atlantis, existence, 20
Atlantis, remnant colonies, 59
Atlantis, sinking, 22
atmosphere, 6, 8, 11–14, 23, 31, 45, 163, 197, 230
atmospheric pressure, 8
Attila the Hun, 115, 116
Auckland, New Zealand, 47
August 12th, 109
aurora borealis, 8, 10
Australia, 19, 21, 28, 39, 47, 115
Australia, Queen of, 189
Australia, Western, 21
Austria, 192, 195, 211
axis of evil, 231
Aztec civilization, 112
Aztec Emperor, 111
Aztec Empire, 111
Aztecs, 111, 112
Aztlan, 153

Baalbek, Lebanon, 159
Babylon, 159
Babylonia, 95
Babylonians, 63
bad God, 134
Baffin Island, Newfoundland, 87
Baikal, Lake, 210
ballots burning, 173
ballots, Papal elections, 173
Baltic, 49
Baltic countries, 86
Baltic Sea, 49, 196
Bangladesh, 189
bank of computers, 107
Bank of England, 190
banking system, 129
Barcelona, 212
Base 211, 192, 197, 230
batteries, Baghdad, 40
Bavaria, base, 230
Bavaria, Germany, 195, 207
Bavarian region, 213
Bay of Campeche, 69
beaver, Mayan carving, 154
beavers, gigantic, 154
beavers, Mayan art, 143
Belize, 109, 157
Ben-Gurion, David, 99
Benedict XVI, Pope, 169
Berbers, 121
Berlin, 192, 203, 210, 212
Bermuda Triangle, 144
Berrien County, Michigan, 154
Bethlehem, 125
Bethulia, 175
Bible, 17, 18, 50, 51, 55, 56, 69, 99, 101, 215, 238, 253
Bible Code, 49, 55, 57, 58
Bible of today, 215
Bible, ancient Hebrew, 56
Bible, instructions, 51
Bible, Original, 215

Biblical artifact discoveries, 218
Biblical flood, 145
Bigfoot, 20
biorhythm, 24, 37, 38
Black Africa, 190
Black Death, 183
Black Frequency, 270
black hole, propulsion system, 11
Black Irish, 183
Black Jews, 53, 65
Black Magick, 263, 265
Black Plague, 138, 183
Black Pope, 130
Black Race, 35, 270
Black Sea, 59
black, aspects, 278
blond hair/blond-haired, 6, 103, 192, 195, 212, 214, 236
blood, 38, 40, 78
blood of Christ, 78
blood sacrifice, 39, 77, 78
blood, copper content, 38
blood, human, 39
blood, nourishment, 27
blood-letting, 303
blue blood, 38
Blue Blood True Blood, 31
Blue Book, 223
blue eyes/blue-eyed, 6, 103, 147, 192, 195, 212, 214, 236
Blue Mountains, Australia, 47
Blue Nile, 53
Bolivia, 2, 107, 157
Bolivia Underground Tunnels, 107
Book of Revelation, 215–219
border, energetic, 23
born in sin, 139
Bosnia, 122, 123, 159, 164, 165
Bosnia, central, 167
Bosnia-Herzegovina, 157
Bosnian pyramid complex, age, 168
Bosnian pyramid discovery, 167

Bosnian pyramids, 157
Bosnian tomb, 168
Bosnian Valley of the Pyramids, 161, 168
Bosnians, 79
Boston Harbor, 88
Bouviers, 309
brain surgery, Inca, 105
Branson, Missouri, 1
Braun, Eva, 212, 213
Brazil, 209
Bremerhaven, Germany, 193
Britain, 187, 209
British, 1, 119, 134, 183, 187, 189, 191, 239
British Antarctic Survey, 199
British Empire, 187, 190
British Empire, asset, 190
British Empire, dissolution, 187
British Empire, existence, 187
British Guiana, 190
British Kings, 190
British people, origin, 86
British Royalty, 190
British Royalty assets, 190
British Royalty, taxes, 190
British ships, 95
British, new world, 129
British, occupied countries, 187
bronze, 150
Bronze Age, 150
Buddhism, 119
Buenos Aires, Argentina, 212
Bulgaria, 123
Bulgarians, 79
Byrd, Admiral Richard E., 1, 9, 194
Byzantium, 61

Cahokia, 153, 165
Cahokia Mounds UNESCO World Heritage Site, 153, 165
Cairo, 68
California, 19, 22

California, Republic of, 189
Cambodia, 159
Cameron, Ewen, 210, 222
Canaan, 50
Canada, 155, 183, 185, 187, 189, 209, 210
Canada, dominion of, 189
Canada, northwestern, 199
Canada, Queen of, 189
Canary Islands, 159
cancer, 209
Caribbean, 89, 144, 165, 195
Carolinian, 85
Caspian Sea, 63
Cathars, 132–134, 138
cathedrals, 267
Catholic armies, 134, 137, 139, 142
Catholic cathedrals, 253
Catholic Church, 1, 46, 69–73, 85, 99, 101, 112, 121, 127, 129, 131–134, 137, 138, 141, 142, 170, 173, 175, 183, 185, 307–309
Catholic Church commission, 99
Catholic Church, undermining, 127
Catholic Church, women rights, 175
Catholic country, 122, 133
Catholic families, 133
Catholic Irish, 134
Catholic Portuguese, 75
Catholic religion, 292
Catholic territory, 133
Catholic(s), 61, 75, 76, 121, 134, 174, 183, 292, 302, 308, 309
Catholicism, 75, 88, 89, 121, 133, 134, 169, 183, 185
Catholics, Europe, 123
Caucasian(s), 37, 38, 63
Caucasus Mountains, 32, 63, 99
cave systems, 141, 191, 238
cave(s)/cavern(s), 8, 19, 21, 22, 32, 47, 70, 73, 89, 104, 107, 119,

120, 167, 191, 216, 229, 238
caverns, Antarctica, 191
Cayce, Edgar, 101
Celtic altars, 97
Celtic civilization, existence, 97
Celtic culture(s), 20, 97
Celtic Empire, 97
Celtic inscriptions, 97
Celtic Kings, 88
Celtic language, 97, 148
Celtic people, 20, 31, 97, 98
Celtic priests, 97
Celtic religion, 85
Celtic rule, 86
Celts, 31, 97
Celts, North America, 97
Central America, 28, 101, 103, 109, 111, 151–153, 195
Central Asia, 50
ceremonial area, Sistine Chapel, 171
ceremonial caverns, 153
ceremonial ground, Egyptian, 47
ceremonial grounds, 266
Ceremonial Language, indigenous, 143
ceremonial protocols, 45
ceremony, Reptilian, 40
CERN, 228
chakra band spinning, 264
chakra(s), 28, 264, 299
chamber network, 168
channel, 261
channeling, 261
Chanukah, 60
Charlemagne, 63, 85, 86, 121, 138, 142
chemicals, manipulated, 210
Cheops/The Great Pyramid, 159
Cherokee, 147
Chet, 174
Chile, 192, 196
Chilean Air Force base, 196
China, 28, 63, 116, 119, 120, 159,

164, 165
China, Christians/Jews, 99
China, Khazar Empire, 148
China, Persian/Islamic, 120
Chinese, 119, 120
Chinese dynasties, 116
Chinese dynasty, last, 119
Chinese Emperors, 159
Chinese proverb, 167
Chinese, Russia, 116
chocolate, 271
cholesterol, high, 209
Christ, 68, 69, 71, 78, 79, 99, 112,
     125, 128, 132, 133, 223, 307
Christ Consciousness, 253, 254, 303,
     306
Christ figure, 68, 69, 216, 302
Christ, blood of, 78
Christ, genetics of, 129
Christ, words of, 101
Christian cult idea, 77
Christian Jews, 75
Christian pilgrims, 125
Christian population, 75
Christian(s), 64, 77, 122, 123, 125,
     301, 306
Christian, China, 99
Christian/Jews, 79
Christianity, 46, 72, 75, 77, 79, 85,
     86, 88, 122, 138, 216, 307
Christianity, creation of, 144
Christians, Original, 79, 135, 309
Christic figure, 68
Christmas day, 92
Christmas Island, 92
Christmas, origin, 77
Clear People/beings, 3
Clement, Pope, 128
climate, manipulate, 163
code, 57
Coeur d'Alene, 22
Cold War, 222

collective conscious mind, 257
collective unconscious, 274
collective unconscious(ness), 261, 263
color, tone and archetype, 56
Colorado, 214
Colorado Springs, 164
Columbus, 88, 89, 121, 146
Columbus Day, 89
comets, 12, 95
Committee of 300, 239
commonwealth, 187, 189
Communion, 40
concentration camps, 209
concrete, 160, 163, 166–168
conductor, 150
confusion, 189, 304
conscious mind, 254, 278, 283, 290,
     295
Conscious Mind-connection, 305
Constantine, Emperor, 61
Constantinople, 61, 80, 215
control, 189, 212, 216, 222, 254, 259,
     260, 280, 281, 289
control force, 216
control system, 231, 233
control, galaxy, 24
control, people, 79
control, Reptilian, 18
controllable, 240
controllable population, 210
controllers, 300, 306
controlling souls, 262
copper, 95, 149–154
copper fittings, stone slab, 43
corn syrup, 210
Corsica, 59
cosmic north, 166, 167
Costa Rica, 109, 164
Cottian Alps, 140, 141, 307
Council for the Propagation of the
     Faith, 308
Council of Nicaea, 215

Crete, 59
Cro-Magnon, 18
Croatia, 122, 123
Croatians, 79
crocodile fat, 69
cross, 79, 302
cross of slavery, 302
Cross, Maltese/Magdalene, 127, 132, 146
cross, Templar, 127
Cross, Waldensian, 132
crucifixion, 68, 75, 78, 79, 304
Crucifixion Programming, 301
Crusades, 122–124
crystal skulls, 113
Cuba, 165, 217
cube, 253
cube, 13x13x13, 253
Cumaean Sybil, 174
Curry grid, 161
cyclops, 2, 107
Cydonia plateau, Mars, 45
Cyprus, 59
Czechoslovakia, 214

da Vinci, 176
Damu, 39
Dan, tribe of, 99
Danes, 80, 85, 86
Danish, 83
Danmark/Denmark, 99
Danube River, 99
Dark Forces/dark forces, 267, 274
Dark Side, 269
David, 174
Davidovits, Joseph, 160
de Medici, 171
de Molay, Jacques, 129
death, 78
Death Program, 295–298
Deception Island caldera, 199
deceptions, 277
deep space, 230

deep space travel, 219
Delle Rovere, 173
delta-T antenna, pyramid, 164
demonic entity/entities, 19, 99
demonic figures, 72
Denmark, 49, 85, 86, 99, 214
dental work, Inca, 105
deprogramming, 232, 236, 246, 247, 249, 299
Descent, Original, 260
destruction and creation, simultaneous, 54
Deutsche Antarktische Expedition, 192
device, 204
device, electronic communication, 51
device, interdimensional, 45
device, monitoring, 228
devices, anti-gravitational electromagnetic, 197
Devil energy frequency, 253
Devil's Triangle, 144
devil, work of the, 300
Devil/devil, 254, 299, 300
devora, 174
diabetes, 209, 210
dimension, 238
Dimona nuclear power plant, 54
dinosaur(s), 1, 2, 14–16, 72
Djes-eb, Lord, 47
DNA, 19, 39, 57, 58, 200, 236
DNA archetype, 236, 260
DNA opening, 249
DNA Origins, 3
DNA symbol, 132
DNA, amber, 200
DNA, Bible Code, 58
DNA, Christ, 223
DNA, creation, 19
DNA, Egyptian, 236
DNA, human, 39
DNA, junk, 18
DNA, Reptilian, 5, 129

dolphins, 237
Dome of the Rock, 54
double-agent Illuminati programmers, 225
Draco, 3, 5, 6, 11, 13, 14, 24, 27, 28, 31, 35, 40, 45
Dragon, 63
Drake Passage, 195
Dravidians, 63
drugs, 264, 266, 284
drunkenness, 175
Duality, 253–256, 258, 271, 295
Dublin, 86
Duke of Savoy, 139, 308
Dulce Base, 222
Dutch, 189
Dutch expedition, New World, 65
Dutch Guiana, 190
Dutch rabbi, 65
dwarf planet, 225
dwarves, 238

eagle, 111, 217
Earth, 5–8, 12–16, 19–24, 31, 32, 36, 37, 57, 58, 108, 109, 199, 200, 223, 227–229, 231–233, 237, 238
Earth domination, 216
Earth environment, 24
Earth homeland, ancient, 201
Earth plane, 261, 262, 267, 274, 275, 293
Earth, creatures, 238
Earth, crust, 238
Earth, danger, 233
Earth, energetic location, 233
Earth, energy/energies, 233, 266
Earth, in the, 238
Earth, inhabitants, 227
Earth, invasion, 227
Earth, life on, 234
Earth, location, 23, 24
Earth, meteors/asteroids, 223

Earth, natural climate, 23
Earth, oceans, 14
Earth, on the, 238
Earth, oppressors, 233
Earth, orbit, 228
Earth, paranormal events, 233
Earth, prison planet, 24
Earth, seeding, 223
Earth, surface, 22
Earth, unique position/spot, 232, 233
Earth, weather, 200
Earth, women of, 32
Earth-bound, 261, 267
Earth-bound energies and entities, 261
Earth-like planets, 239
earthquake(s), 7, 22, 91, 156, 164, 199, 201, 229, 245
East Pakistan, 189
Easter, 77, 78
Easter Island, 164
Easter story, 78
Eastern Asian genetics, 115
Eastern European genetics, 115
Eastern Rise, Pacific, 201
Eastern Roman, 61
Edict of Nantes, 308
edict, Waldensians, 309
eel, gigantic, 155
Egypt, 19, 31, 37, 38, 43, 45–47, 49, 50, 52, 59, 65, 68, 80, 86, 95, 109, 123, 131, 157, 159, 187, 203, 211, 216
Egypt, ancient mural, 151
Egypt, ancient schools, 216
Egypt/Gypsy, 79
Egyptian civilization, 43, 49
Egyptian coins, ancient, 153
Egyptian cultures, 20
Egyptian documents, ancient, 49
Egyptian hieroglyphs, 47, 148
Egyptian ship, 47
Egyptian stone reliefs and records,

151
Egyptian temples, 69
Egyptian-Reptilian religion, 46
Egyptians, 27, 35, 40, 45, 47, 53, 79, 86, 95, 108, 121, 150
Egyptians, pyramids, 43
Egyptologists, 45
El Salvador, 109, 157
electric phenomena, 160
electromagnetic anomalies, 197, 198
electromagnetic containment field, 233
electromagnetic energy, South Pole, 230
electromagnetic field(s), 161
electromagnetic phenomena, 160
electromagnetic weaponry, 203
electromagnetic weapons, 31
electromechanical phenomena, 160
electronic communication device, 51
ELF, 267, 284
elite, 164, 211
Elohim, 18, 238
elongated skulls, 108
elves, 238
End Times, 261
energy beam, pyramid, 160, 163
energy vortex, 144
England, 86, 88
England, Queen of, 128, 189
Ephesus, 308
equal genetics, 39
Erebus, Mount, 201
Ericksson, Leif, 87
Erik the Red, 87
Eritrea, 53
Eritrean Independence Movement, 53
Eskimo, 87
esoteric projects, 209
Essenes, 70
Estonia, 49
Estonian, 83
Eternal Now, 253, 260, 281

ethics, 284
Ethiopia, 51–53, 190, 211
Ethiopian (Falasha) Jews, 53
Ethiopian Emperor, 53
Ethiopian(s), 51, 53
Etruscans, 169, 170
EU, 189
Eucharist, 308
Europe, 19, 22, 32, 47, 49, 50, 61, 63–65, 73, 85, 86, 97, 98, 115, 121–123, 134, 137, 152, 217
Europe, Eastern, 63, 79, 80, 83, 97, 115, 131
Europe, Northern, 85, 91, 214
Europe, Southern, 131
Europe, southern part, 122
Europe, Western, 20, 31
European Union, 189
European(s), 65, 80, 152
Europeans, Eastern, 236
Eva Braun, 213
Eve, 17, 18
Evil, 257
evil, 254
evil frequency, 257
evil twins, 134
existence, foundation of, 138
existences, interdimensional, 231, 237
existences, simultaneous/alternate, 249
Exodus, 50
experimentations, genetic, 21
extraterrestrial references, 67
extraterrestrial(s), 68, 233, 237, 239
eye of Horus, 46
Ezekiel, prophet, 33

face on Mars, 45, 46
faeris, 238
Falasha, 53, 54, 65
family genetics, 235
Family Tree, 18
Farmington, New Mexico, 222

Farsi, 67
fault line, Michigan, 156
Fazhan, Dr. Cao, 164
fear(s), 2, 137, 204, 222, 223, 236, 245, 260, 280, 281, 284, 291, 292, 296
Ferdinand, King, 112, 121, 142
fetus, 16, 17, 27, 68
Finland, 49, 65, 86, 115, 212
Finnish, 115
fire flower, 195
fireworks, 195
Fleur-de-lis, 39
flood, Biblical, 145
fluoride, 209
forest, 131
foundation of existence, 138
France, 72, 73, 81, 123, 131, 133, 134, 187, 211
France, name origin, 81
France, South(ern), 59, 71–73, 76, 122, 131, 141, 142, 216
Francesco I, Pope, 130
Frankfurt, Germany, 81
Franks, 80, 81, 128, 134
free energy, 164
free flow of information and knowledge, 164
free society, 164
French, 1, 67, 140, 143, 187
French Alps, 134
French Guiana, 190
French people, 236
Friday October 13th, 1307, 128
Friday the 13th, 128
Friesland, 91
Frisia, 85
Frisland, 91, 97, 152
frustrations, 284

G-Men, 1
G7, 190
G8, 190

Gabriel, 68
Galactic History, 3
Galatia, 99
Gantenbrink, Robert, 43
Garden of Eden, 17
gardens, ancient, 154
gay, 176
gay art, 174
Geheimgesellschaften 2, 195
Geheimgesellschaften und ihre Macht im 20. Jahrhundert, 195
gematria, 55
Genesis, 18, 56, 238
genetic alteration, 50
genetic code, your, 260
genetic creations, 196
genetic evidence, 83
genetic experimentations, 21
genetic information, 18, 249
genetic input, 17
genetic lineage, 235
genetic manipulation(s), 20, 68, 216
genetic memory, 16
genetic origin, 20
genetic programs, 17
genetic qualities, 212
genetic sequences, mammalian, 17
genetic split, 39
genetic tests, 65
genetically manipulated, 37
genetically Reptilian, 35
genetics, 38, 39, 147, 195, 212, 235, 236, 246, 249
genetics of Christ, 129
genetics, Aryan, 213
genetics, Asian, 116
genetics, Eastern Asian/Mongol, 115
genetics, Eastern European, 115
genetics, equal, 39
genetics, family, 235
genetics, foundational, 16
genetics, Khazar, 65

genetics, mammalian, 5, 39
genetics, manipulate, 20
genetics, Mongolian, 236
genetics, Reptilian, 3, 27
genetics, Reptilian/Human, 103
genetics, secondary, 16
Geneva, Lake, 228
Geneva, Switzerland, 139, 228
Genghis Khan, 116
Georgia, 32, 97, 217
Germaine, St., 72
German advance, 207
German allies, 195
German documents, 197
German Empire, 203
German experimental craft, 210
German families, 214
German military, 207
German project, 213
German scientists, 209, 211
German U-boats, 211
German(s), 83, 85, 86, 140, 169, 187,
    189, 191, 192, 194–197, 203,
    209, 210, 212, 215, 231
German-ancestry royals, 86
German-speaking scientists, 209
German/Danish border, 85
Germanic tribes, 79, 80
Germany, 64, 81, 85, 128, 140, 169,
    192, 203, 210, 211, 213, 214
Germany, Catholics, 140
Germany, Nazi, 211
Ghandi, 239
ghosts, 233
giant ship, 33
giant skeletons, 153
giant wheel, 33
giants, 238
Gibraltar Straits, island, 95, 96, 109,
    151, 152
Gibraltar, Straits of, 49, 151
Gimmel, 174

Giza plateau, 43, 45, 157, 159
Glastonbury, 76
Global Agendas, 20
global control, 230
global cooling, 23
Global Handlers, 8, 141, 216, 261,
    271
global rituals, 54
global warming, 23, 199
gnomes, 238
Gnostic Gospels, 73
Goa, Christian Jews, 75
God, 18, 68, 75, 77, 132, 135, 137,
    175, 215, 238, 257, 307
god, 259
god Huitzilopochtli, 111
God, 3-horned, 39
god, fertility, 77
God, Mind of, 132, 256, 297
God-Mind, 4, 5, 17, 19, 40, 55, 68,
    73, 132, 219, 235, 238, 244,
    246, 253–258, 260, 267, 270,
    271, 278, 280, 281, 284, 285,
    289, 292, 297, 300, 305, 306
God-Mind Archetype, 250
God-Mind aspects, 270
God-Mind connection, 254, 290, 305
God-Mind Creation, 255
God-Mind frequencies, 267
God-Mind Intelligence, 254
Goddess of Death, 169, 170
gods of darkness, 263
Gods, two, 134
gold, 278
Gold Aleph, 250
gold cap, 45
gold fringe, 40
gold light, 262
Golden Lion, 63
good, 254
Good Friday, 305
good God, 134

Gospels, New Testament, 215
government investigations, secret, 156
government plan, 155
government story, 221
government(s), 65, 108, 166, 189, 194, 200, 209, 222, 223, 237, 241
government, American, 190, 211
government, Australian, 47
government, Bolivian, 107
government, Canadian, 189
government, Chinese, 120
government, Cuban, 165
government, German, 211
government, Greek, 217
government, internal, 241
government, New World Order, 223
government, secret projects, 229
government, technology, 196
government, US, 9, 147, 211
Grand Canyon, 47
Grand Master of the Templars, 129
Great Lakes, 22, 89, 97, 109, 143, 144, 146, 147, 153–156, 222
Great Lakes states, 214
Great Lakes triangle, 144
Great Lakes, natural vortex, 156
Greece, 31, 50, 59, 60, 71, 79, 95, 123
Greek, 60, 148, 171, 215, 236
Greek city, ancient, 61
Greek city-states, 59
Greek civilization, 217
Greek civilization, Ancient, 59
Greek colonies/colonists, 59
Greek culture, 217
Greek Empire, 79
Greek enemy, 60
Greek language, 59
Greek letter, ancient, 146
Greek Orthodox(y), 61
Greek prince, 47
Greeks, 1, 59, 60, 79, 99
green eyes/green-eyed, 6, 147

Greenland, 83, 87, 183, 185, 192, 195, 200
Greenland, Vikings, 91
Greenstar programming, 156, 223
Grey alien, 27
Guatemala, 109, 157
guilt, 88, 304
guilty, 271
Gulf of Mexico, 16, 69, 109
Gulf oil incident, 20
Gulf Stream, 20
Guyana, 190
Gypsies, 79, 80
Gypsy culture, 79

Hadron Collider, 228
Haifa, Israel, 123
Haile Selassie I, 53
Hamburg, 193
Han Chinese, 120
handlers of Humanity, 18
Harry Potter, 218
Hartmann grid, 161
Haunebu, 195, 196
Hawaii, 8, 19
heaven, 293
Hebrew, 18, 24, 27, 50, 55, 65, 67–69, 171, 173
Hebrew alphabet, 55, 219
Hebrew civilization, ancient, 49
Hebrew coins, ancient, 54, 153
Hebrew Empire, South of France, 73
Hebrew Kingdom of Mary Magdalene, 134
Hebrew language, 55, 171, 238
Hebrew language, ancient, 49
Hebrew letters, 54, 67, 148, 174
Hebrew letters, coded, 176
Hebrew prayer, Native American, 65
Hebrew race, 50
Hebrew religion, 70, 73
Hebrew religious artifacts, 54

Hebrew rock writings, North America, 54
Hebrew tribes, 99
Hebrew words, 55
Hebrew-Christian cementery, 75
Hebrew/Jewish slaves, 50
Hebrews, 49–51, 60
hell, 19, 247, 293
Helluland, 87
heretic(s), 99, 121, 133, 134, 308
hermaphrodite, 17
Hertzian technology, 163
hidden areas, 278
hidden folk, 238
Hillsdale, Michigan, 156
Hindu caste system, 28
Hindu symbol, 212
history, 1, 2, 59, 65, 95, 115, 134, 159, 216, 238, 259, 297, 308
history book, 1
history books, US, 9
history of Humanity, 18
history, conventional, 6, 143
History, Galactic, 3
history, hidden, 120
history, public, 1, 45, 59
history, recorded, 43
history, true, 1, 235, 236, 249
Hitler, 1, 191, 192, 203, 204, 207, 208, 211–214
Hitler's 3rd Reich, 203
Hitler's body, 213
Hitler's father, 208
Hitler's youth movement, 169
Hitler, skull, 213
Hmong, 116
Holey, Jan Udo, 195
Holland, 85, 121
Holofernes, 174, 175
holographic images, 218
Holy Ark, 51–53
Holy Chalice, 128

Holy Grail, 128
Holy Rite, 128
Holy Roman Empire, 61, 133
Holy Spirit, 253
Holy Trinity, 254, 303, 306
Homo sapiens, 18
Homo sapiens sapiens, 18
homosexual(ity), 175, 176
Honduras, 109, 157
hormones, human, 39, 40
Horus, 46
Horus, eye of, 46
Hospitallers, 124, 125
Hudson Bay, 143
Huitzilopochtli, 111
human appearance, 39
human baby, 39
human beings, 37, 112, 132
human beings, Atlantean, 19
human beings, pure, 6
human blood, 39
human body, 171, 284
human DNA, 39
human experience, 246, 271
human experiment, 215
human form, 39
human hormones, nourishment, 27
human hybrid, 38
human lineages, 68
human mindset, 39
human sacrifice(s), 40, 77, 78, 113, 203
human species, 18
human(s), 15, 21, 24, 37, 39, 108, 231
human-looking, 195
human-shaped bodies, 39
humanity, creation, 24
humanity, enticement, 18
humanity, handlers of, 18
humanity, history of, 18
humanity, origin, 3, 16

humanity, plan for, 216
humanity/humankind, 3, 5, 6, 15, 18, 24, 37, 50, 56, 57, 68, 73, 78, 204, 215, 219, 224, 233, 237, 239, 240, 250, 257, 263
humankind, creation, 18
humanoid, 3
humanoid experiments, 231
humanoid-type aliens, 227
Hundred Years War, 187
Hungarians, 79
Hungary, 115, 123
hybrid pictures, 46
hybrid(s), 17, 20, 21, 38, 39, 233
hybrid, new, 38, 39
hybridization, 31, 32, 38, 39, 68
Hyperspace, 55, 233, 261, 262, 267
hyperspace, 24
Hyperspace activities, 233
hyperspace archetypes/symbols, 55
Hyperspace Language, 56
Hyperspace levels, 248
Hyperspace Realm, 261
Hyperspace Signature, 246
Hyperspace/Oversoul work, 232, 234, 235, 248, 249

Ice age, 22, 165, 201
ice comet, 11–13, 31
ice comets, weapons, 11
Iceland, 47, 83, 87, 91–93, 104, 183, 185, 192, 195, 207, 238
Iceland, Viking maps, 88
Iceland, Vikings, 91
Icelandic language, 87
Icelandic people, 183
Icelandic population, 207
Icelandic sailors, 183
Icelandics, 183
icons, 300
Illinois, 165

Illuminati, 36, 40, 54, 68, 128, 155, 156, 194, 216, 218, 222, 223, 227, 229–231, 233, 234, 245, 283, 285, 287
Illuminati agenda, 217, 218
Illuminati creation, 194
Illuminati culture, 39
Illuminati families, 63
Illuminati programmers, double-agent, 225
Illuminati programming, 225
Illuminati rule, 86
Illuminati, beginning, 73
Illuminati, script, 215, 217
imaging technology, American, 57
immaculate conception, 68
implants, 229
imprinting, 304
Inca/Incas/Incan, 103–105, 108
incest, 175
Independent Intelligences, 254
India, 68, 75, 76, 79, 115, 116, 159, 165, 187, 189, 203, 204, 211, 216, 239
India, North(ern), 32, 63, 192
Indian ceremonies and beliefs, 65
Indian grave sites, 54
Indian Ocean, 159, 201
Indian tribe, 165
Indians, 79, 109, 189, 239
Indians, East Coast, 20
Indo-Australian plate, 201
Indonesia, 122, 159, 201
indulgences, 140
infinite dimensions, 237
infinite lifetimes, 219
infinite realities, 219, 238, 239
infrasound, 160
Inka, 104
inner chambers, 45
Inner Earth, 19, 28, 191, 192, 211, 238

Inner Earth civilization(s), 9, 196, 239
Inner Earth energies, 233
Inner Earth Reptilians, 32
Inner Earth, entrance, 31
Inner Earth, openings, 207
inner sun, 7, 8
Inquisition, 121
Inquisitors, 139
insectoid beings, 230
insects, 227
insulin, 210
Intelligent Energy, 254, 256
interdimensional device, 45
interdimensional energetic activities, 45
interdimensional energies, 164
interdimensional events, 23, 233
interdimensional existences, 231, 237
interdimensional factor, 238
interdimensional references, 67
interdimensional transport device, 45
interdimensional travel, 219
interdimensional vehicles, 210
interdimensional(ly), 24, 197, 233, 237
interdimensionality, 239
internal organs, Sistine Chapel paintings, 171
intersex, 17
Inuit, 183, 185
invasion, landing point, 156
invisibility, 210
invisibility cloaks, 210
ionosphere, 164, 200, 231
Iran, 60
Iraq, 36, 40, 115, 233
Iraq, Southern, 31, 37
Ireland, 31, 49, 86, 88, 97, 183
Irish, 134, 183
Irish travelers, 148
Irish, Catholic, 134
Isaac, 40

Isabella, Queen, 112, 121, 142
Isis, 46
Islam, 61, 64, 121, 122
Islamic, 121, 142
Islamic cultures, 122, 211
Islamic influence, 142
Islamic people, 122
Israel, 51–54, 64, 65, 75, 76, 99, 123, 187
Israel, ancient, 53, 54, 59, 69
Israeli air raid, 67
Israeli military police, 41
Israeli(s), 53, 54, 57, 60, 70, 216
Istanbul, 61
Italian(s), 67, 190, 236
Italy, 73, 131, 134, 141, 219, 308, 309
Italy, Northern, 131, 133, 142, 307
Italy, Southern, 59

Jacqueline Bouvier Kennedy Onassis, 309
Japan, 19, 75, 119, 165, 203, 216
Japanese, 75, 195
Japanese imperial family, 75
Japanese scientists, 200
Java, coin in Michigan, 148
Jerusalem, 51–54, 59, 67, 69, 123–125, 127, 170, 216
Jesuit Pope, 130
Jesuits, 130
Jesus, 67, 146, 173, 174, 215, 301, 302, 304, 305
Jesus as a twin, 72
Jesus Complex Programming, 304
Jesus, baby, 72, 134
Jewish, 65, 173, 208
Jewish Empire, 64
Jewish holiday, 60
Jewish mysticism, 171, 174
Jewish symbols, 174
Jewish synagogues, 65
Jews, 54, 60, 64, 65, 79, 89, 99, 122, 129, 173, 174, 208

Jews, Arabic, 54
Jews, Black, 53, 65
Jews, China, 99
Jews, Ethiopian Falasha, 53
Jews, Europe, 64
Jinns, 211
Jmmanuel, 67–73, 75–77, 79, 128, 133, 138, 146, 216
Jmmanuel's grandson, 75, 216
Jmmanuel's marriage, 132
Jmmanuel's mother, 71
Jmmanuel's son, Britain, 76
Jmmanuel, birthday, 77
Jmmanuel, descendants, 75, 146
Jmmanuel, grandson, 75
Jmmanuel, meaning, 68
Jmmanuel, tomb, 75
John Paul II, Pope, 169
Joseph, 72, 76
Joseph of Arimathea, tomb, 67
Joseph, brother of Jmmanuel, 76
Judah, 53
Judah, tribe of, 173
Judaism, 46, 53, 64, 75, 174
Judean hills, 70
Judith, 174, 175
Julius II, Pope, 173, 175
Jupiter, 6, 11, 12, 36
Jupiter, moons, 12
Jurassic Park, 200
Jurassic period, 155, 200
Jutes, 80

Kaaba, 253
Kabbalah, 171, 174
Kansas, 21
Kashmir, India, 75, 216
Katmandu, 204
Kazakhstan, 63
Keflavik, Iceland, 207
Kentucky, 189
Keweenaw Peninsula, 154
Keweenaw Peninsula, copper, 149

Khafre/Chefren, 159
Khartoum, Sudan, 53
Khazar connection, Michigan, 148
Khazar Empire, 63, 148
Khazar genetics, 65
Khazar language, original, 148
Khazar territory, 64
Khazar(s)/Khazarians, 63, 64, 73, 99, 115, 128
Khazaria, 64
Khazaria, capital, 63
Khazaria, King of, 64
Khazarian Empire, 64
Khazars, descendants, 54
Khirbet Qumran, 70
Khum, 68, 69
King Ferdinand, 112, 121, 142
King of Khazaria, 64
King of Spain, 88
King Olaf, 88
King Philip IV of France, 128
King Solomon, 52, 53
king, Reptilian, 28
kings and queens from God-Mind, 259
Knights of Malta, 127
knowledge, 1, 198, 259
Kok Thurki, 148
Kola Peninsula, 212
Korea, 75, 115, 116, 119
Korea, Christian Jews, 75
Kosovo, 122
Krakatau, 200
Kuiper Belt, 225–234
Kuwait, 31, 37

La Paz, 107
La Vatican, 169
Labrador Sea, 143
Labrador, Canada, 87
Labrador, Vikings, 88
labyrinth, underground, 162, 167, 168
Lake Baikal, 210

Lake Geneva, 228
Lake Michigan, 155
Lake Michigan Triangle, 144
Lake Michigan, sea creatures, 155
Lake Saint Clair, 143
Lake Texcoco, 111
Lake Titicaca, 107, 108
Lake Vostok, 197, 198
lakes, underground, 157
land of flat stones, 87
Land of the Rose, 83
land of vines or grapes, 88
language, 57
Language of Hyperspace, 56
Last Judgment, 176
Last Supper, 71, 216
Latin, 67, 171, 215
Lebanon, Eastern, 159
Lebensborn Project, 213, 214
Leif Ericksson, 87
Lemuria, 8, 13–15, 18–20, 28, 37, 39, 103, 108, 201, 297
Lemurian food, 15
Lemurian influence, 28
Lemurians, 15, 21, 31
Lemurians, wars, 16
Leonists, 307
limbo, 261
lineage, genetic, 235
lineage, Magdalene, 75, 134, 146, 147
lineage, Mary Magdalene, 76
Lion of Judah, 53
Lion, Reptilianized, 63
Lishon/Lison, 57
Lithuania, 116
Lithuanian, 83
Llullaillaco, Mount, 104
Loch Ness monster, 155
Long Island, 58
Lord Djes-eb, 47
Lord of the Rings, 218
lost tribe, 65

Lost Tribes (of Israel), 65, 80, 97, 99, 101
Louis XIV, 308
Louisiana, 153, 189
Lucifer/Luciferian(s), 253–259
Ludington, Wisconsin, 144
lunar landings, 54
lunar orbit, 228
Luther, Martin, 140
Luxor, Egypt, 195
Lyra, 3, 6, 31, 45
Lyra, colonies, 6
Lyraen Empire, 195
Lyraen Martians, 38
Lyraen refugees, 32
Lyraen(s), 3, 6, 24

Ma'arib, Yemen, 51
Macedonia, 59, 79, 122
Macedonian(s), 79
Magdala, 69
Magdala, meaning, 69
Magdalene Cross, 146
Magdalene Culture, 71
Magdalene lineage, 75, 134, 146, 147
Magdalene, symbol, 63
Magdalenian group, 63
magick rites, 203
magma, 7, 8, 200
magma globe, 8
magnetic north, 166
magnetic phenomena, 160
magnetic pole, 199
magnetic pole shift, 199
Magyar, 115
Maine, 87, 89, 148
Maldek, 6, 11, 12, 15, 31, 113
Maldek explosion, 12, 49
Maldek(ian) refugees, 14, 37
Maldek, destruction, 95
Maldekian colonists, 37
Malta, 71, 216
Maltese Cross, 127, 132, 146

mammalian, 15, 16, 39, 129
mammalian energy, 39
mammalian genetic sequences, 17
mammalian genetics, 5, 16, 39
mammoth fetus, 200
mammoth, cloning, 200
mammoth-like animals, 9
mammoths, 16
Mana, 50
manifest, 255
manifestation, 248
manifestation, initial, 4
manipulate, 263, 283
manipulated, 262
manipulations, genetic, 20
manipulative souls, 262
Manitoba, Canada, 143
Manitowoc, Wisconsin, 144
Maori, 47
Marduk/Nibiru, 35
Markland, 87, 88
maroon, 2
marriage of Heaven and Earth, symbolic, 54
Mars, 6, 8, 11–15, 31, 37, 38, 46, 68, 223
Mars refugees, 37
Martial Law, 40
Martian, 13, 15, 223
Martian colonists, 37
Martian refugees, 14, 31
Marvel Cave, 1
Mary, 68, 69, 71, 72, 134
Mary Magdalene, 69, 71–73, 76, 128, 132, 133, 138, 146, 216, 307, 309
Mary Magdalene lineage, 76
Mary Magdalene's kingdom, 73
Mary Magdalene, descendants, 146
Mary Magdalene, Gospel of, 132
Mary Magdalene, Hebrew Kingdom of, 134

Mary Magdalene, tablets, 144
Mary's tomb, 72
Maryland, 88
Mashia, 69
Mass, 307
Massachusetts, 87, 89, 148, 189
Mastodon, 155
mastodon bones, 154
mastodons, cloning, 200
Maundy Thursday, 305
Mauritius, 159
Maya, 109, 112
Mayan art depictions, 143
Mayan calendar, 243
Mayan civilization, 109, 143, 153
Mayan legends, 103
Mayan records, 109
Mayan(s), 103, 109, 112, 143, 153, 156
megalithic blocks, 161
megalithic terraces, 168
Meier, "Billy" Eduard Albert, 67
Meier, Billy, 195
memories, 254
memory, genetic, 16
Mengele, 209, 214
Mengele, dental charts, 209
Mengele, DNA, 209
Menilek, 52
Menkaure/Mycerinus, 159
mental abilities, 99
mental food, 259
mental institution, 24
mental work, 247
Mercury, 6
Mermaids/Merfolk, 20
Merovée, 73
Merovée family, 73
Merovingian(s), 63, 73, 85, 128
Mesoamerican city, largest, 111
Mesopotamians, 63
Messia, 69

Messiah, 54, 69
meteorites, 12
meteors, 36, 223
meteors, weapons, 11
Methodist churches, 141
Mexico, 111, 143, 154, 157, 159
Mexico City, 111, 154
Mexico, southern part, 109
Mexico, Western, 164
Michelangelo, 170, 171, 173–176
Michelangelo's models, 174
Michelangelo, gay art, 174
Michelangelo, Waldensian, 171
Michigama, 143
Michigan, 143–154, 156, 222
Michigan, base, 222
Michigan, Central, 156
Michigan, Lake, 155
Michigan, Northern, 154–156
Michigan, Upper Peninsula, 146, 148
Michoacán, 143
Mid-Atlantic Ridge, 22, 91, 92
Middle East, 59, 61, 65, 122, 123
Middle Eastern cultures, 20
Migdal, 69
Migdal-Elohim-Chai, 69
military expedition, Antarctica, 194
milk, homogenized, 210
Milky Way Galaxy, 23, 232
Mind of God, 132, 256, 297
mind-control, 2, 31, 203, 210, 222, 253
mind-control ritual, 203
mind-control, original form, 88
mind-pattern(s), 234, 239–241, 244–247, 249, 261–263, 266, 274, 285, 289, 290, 293, 294, 299, 304, 306
mind-patterns, negative, 284
mine disasters, 196
Minnesota, 214
Minoan, 147, 148

Minoan civilization, 50, 109, 145
Minoan language, 145, 147
Minoan tablet, 146
Minoan tablets, 144
miracle, the, 60
Miracles, 299
miracles, 215, 300
Miriam, 69
Miriam Magdala, 69
Miriam/Mary, 69
Missouri, 141
Missouri, Southern, 141
Monarch programming, 222, 259
Monett, Missouri, 134, 141, 309
Money Pit, 129
Mongol, 116
Mongol civilization, 116
Mongol Empire, 115
Mongol Empire, Second, 116
Mongol Empires, 115
Mongol genetics, 115
Mongol origins, 115
Mongol tribes, 115
Mongolia, 63
Mongolia, Khazar Empire, 148
Mongolian alphabet, 148
Mongolian genetics, 116, 236
Mongolian language, ancient, 148
Mongolian letters, 148
Mongolian tribes, 116
Mongolians, 116
Mongols, 64, 115, 137
Monks Mound, 153, 166
Mons volcano, 8
monster fault, 156
Montauk, 211
Montauk Day, 109
Montauk Project, 27, 58, 214
Montezuma II, 111
Moon, 14, 35, 175, 228, 229, 231
Moon base, 231
Moon, artificial, 14

Moon, bombing, 228
Moon, dark side, 197
Moon, explosions, 35
Moon, monitoring device, 228
Moon, Nazi base, 197
Moon, orbit, 14, 228
Moon, surface, 14
Moon, surface bombing, 228
Moon, travel to, 197
Moon, water, 228
moons, Jupiter, 12
moons, Neptune, 226
moons, Saturn, 12
Moorish civilization, 121
Moorish names, 142
Moors, 99, 121, 122, 135, 137, 138, 142
Moors civilization, 121
Moors, Islamic, 134, 142
Moors, migration, 121
Moors, origin, 121
Moors, religion, 121
Moors, Spain, 121, 122, 142, 183
morals, 284
Mormon religion, 101
Moroccan sounding names, 142
Morocco, 65, 95, 121
Moses, 50, 51, 78, 176
Moses, five books, 55
Moses, staff, 78
Mossad, 53
Mother of the (Protestant) Reformation, 133, 139, 307
mound builders, 153
MS Explorer, 198
Munich, 203
murder, 89
Muslim country, 122
Muslim esoteric/fundamentalist groups, 211
Muslim majority, 120, 189
Muslim populations, 122

Muslim raiders, 125
Muslim tradition, 173
Muslim(s), 61, 64, 121–124

Nag Hammadi documents, 132
Nag Hammadi, Egypt, 73
Naga, 28
Namibia, 190
Napoleon, 45, 140, 187
Napoleonic Complex, 187
Narnia, 218
NASA, 13, 35, 46, 197, 210, 228, 229, 239
NASA suncam, 36
Nashon, 173
Native American tribes, 65
Native American, Hebrew prayer, 65
Native Americans, 31, 65, 87
Nazi base, Moon, 197
Nazi base, underground, 192
Nazi death camp experiments, 209
Nazi Empire, 217
Nazi esotericism, 211
Nazi expeditions, 212
Nazi experiments, 209
Nazi Germany, 211
Nazi leaders, 211
Nazi occupation, 231
Nazi party, 211
Nazi regime, 212
Nazi research, 210
Nazi scientists, 210, 211
Nazi secret societies, 192
Nazi symbol, 212
Nazi time period, 191
Nazi uniforms, 192
Nazis, 169, 173, 191, 192, 194, 196, 209, 212, 230, 237
Neanderthal, 18
negative attributes, 301
negative entities, 299
negative intelligence, 254
negative ions, 161–163

negative mind-patterns, 284
Negative side, 271
negative thought, 291
negative(s), 254, 275, 292, 295
Negev, 54
Nepal, 119, 203, 204
Nepalese, 119
Neptune, 6, 226
Neuschwabenland, 192, 193
New Age, 261, 262, 303
New Berlin, 192
New England, 129, 214
new hybrid, 39
New Madrid fault line, 22, 108
New Mexico, 54, 221
New South Wales, Australia, 47
New Testament, 77, 99, 170, 215,
    216, 253, 307
New Testament, lost books, 215
New Testament, original, 215
New World Order, 40, 121, 194, 196,
    218, 223
New World Religion, 54, 130, 169
New York, 141
New York City, 164
New Zealand, 19, 47
New Zealand, Air, 201, 202
Newfoundland, 88
Newfoundland, Viking settlement, 88
Nibiru, 35, 36
Nibiru explosion, 230
Nibiru, destruction, 36
Nibiruans, 35, 36
Nicaragua, 109
nightmares, programming, 204
Nile (River), 43, 69
Nimrod, 39
Noah, 32, 175
non-Catholics, 99
non-Hertzian technology, 163
Nordic creation, 196
Nordics, 195

Norse, 80, 83
North Africa, 50, 65, 122
North America, 19, 22, 83, 87, 97,
    103, 108, 129, 148, 152, 153,
    155, 190, 207, 209, 210
North America, Celtic artifacts, 97
North America, Celts, 97
North America, Columbus, 88, 89
North America, Dutch expedition, 65
North America, first Europeans, 87
North America, Hebrew rock writ-
    ings, 54
North America, largest city, 153
North America, Ogam, 97
North America, Vikings, 87, 91
North American continent, 19
North American indigenous people,
    152
North American natives, 65
North American Union, 189
North Carolina, 88, 141, 147
North Pole, 1, 8, 9, 191, 198–200
Northern India, 192
Northern Star, 166
Norway, 49, 86–89, 183, 185, 192,
    207, 211, 212, 214, 230
Norway, Viking history, 83
Norwegian Vikings, 85
Norwegian(s), 83, 86, 143, 147, 191
Nostradamus prophecies, 169
Notre Dame, 46, 47
Novgorod, 83
nudity, 175
Nuremberg, 203
Nuremberg trials, 169, 209

Oak Island, 129
oak tree symbol, 173
Objective Truth, 306
octahedron, 43, 55, 56, 253, 254, 260
octahedron, pyramid, 164
Oester, 77
Ogam, 97, 148

Oklahoma, 89, 147
Olaf, King, 88
Old Norse, 83, 87, 143
Old Swedish, 143
Old Testament, 18, 32, 40, 55, 170, 171, 175, 176, 215
Olmecs, 101, 109, 112
onion-shaped domes, 61
Ontario (Canada), 143, 156, 187
Operation Highjump, 194
Oregon, 119
organs, human, 39
origin, genetic, 20
Original Christians, 79, 135, 309
Original Descent, 260
Original Descent into physical reality, 254, 255
Original Fall From Grace, 260
Original Trinity of Creation, 254
Orion Confederation, 6
Orion star system, 45
orphanages, United States, 214
Osiris, 46
Osmanagić, Dr., 157, 159, 162–165, 167
Ottoman Empire, 123
Ottoman Empire invasions, 123
Ottoman invasion, 122
Ottomans, 123
out-of-body experiences, 261
ovary, 18
Oversoul, 235, 260, 267, 271, 278–281, 284, 285, 292–294, 297, 306
Oversoul Communication, 304
Oversoul frequencies, 267
Oversoul level, 245, 246, 277, 293
Oversoul Matrix, 253, 254, 306
Oversoul permission, 245
Oversoul work, 292
Oversoul, release to, 263, 292
Oversouls, involved, 245

oxhydes, 151

Pacific, 165
Pacific areas, 119
Pacific Coast, 120
Pacific Island, 19
Pacific Ocean, 19, 165
Pacific plate, 22
Pacific, Eastern Rise, 201
Pakistan, 75, 187, 189, 216
Pakistan, East, 189
pale orange, 2, 245
Palm Sunday, 305
Panama Canal, 120
Papacy, 169
Papal elections, ballots, 173
Par-Isis, 46
Paraguay, 209
paranormal, 299
paranormal abilities, 299
paranormal experiences, 261, 300
paranormal frequency, 300
paranormal powers, 300
Paris, 46, 129
Passover, 78
Passover story, 78
Paul, St., 131, 307
Peenemunde, 196, 212, 213
Pennsylvania, 189, 214
pentagon, 46
people of the forest, 131
people, technologically advanced, 195
Persia, 59, 60, 89
Persian majority, 120
Persian pagan holiday, 77
Persian(s), 54, 60, 122
personal creation, 255
Personal Power, 281
Peru, 107, 157, 159
Peter (Apostle), 71, 216
phantom continent, 20
phantom limb, 20
phantom planes, 156

Pharaoh(s), 51, 78, 160
Philadelphia experiment, 211
Philip, 73
Philip IV, King of France, 128
Philip, Gospel of, 132
Philippines, 19, 122, 183
Phoenician(s), 148, 151
Physical Reality, 253, 293, 296
physical reality, 4, 5, 218, 233, 237, 243, 246, 254, 260, 290, 304
physical reality, manipulate, 255
pict-ograms, 47
pict-ures, 47
pictograms, 80
Picts, 47, 80
Piedmont, 133, 138
Pineal Gland, 299
pineal gland, 246, 300, 305
Pineal Gland Archetype, 243
Pioneer 10, 227
Pirámide de la Luna, 159
Pirámide del Sol, 159
pirates, 128, 130
place of the forest, 88
planetary science, 8
planetoid, 225
Plato, 95
Pleiadean star system, 28, 31
Pleiades, 28
Pluto, 225, 226
point of origin, 297
Poland, 64, 85, 86, 115, 116, 192, 214
pole shift, 199
poles, switching, 199
Polish, 83
Polycarp, disciples, 308
Pomonoc Indians, 58
Pope, 61, 101, 121, 122, 124, 137, 139, 140, 169–171, 173–175, 300
Pope Benedict XVI, 169
Pope Clement, 128

Pope Francesco I, 130
Pope John Paul II, 169
Pope Julius II, 173, 175
Pope's call, 123
Pope's fear, 174
Pope's official title, 171
Pope, first, 71
Pope, Jesuit/Black, 130
Pope, last, 130
population, controllable, 210
portal(s), 68, 168
Portugal, 95, 142
Portugal, island, 49, 95, 109, 151, 152
Portuguese, 67
positive, 254, 270, 295
positive attributes, 301
positive intelligence, 254
Positive side, 271
positive thoughts, 291
power, 1
Prague, 197
Presbyterian Church, 134
Presbyterian churches, 141
present moment, 254, 290
priests, 292
Priory of Sion, 130
prison planet, 23, 24
program, 2, 303
program yourself, 265
programmed, 267
programmed, Draco, 13
programmers, 267
programming, 203, 210, 222, 236, 253, 299, 301, 304
programming matrix, 218
programming trigger, 78
programming, Greek language, 59
programming, Greenstar, 156, 223
programming, Illuminati, 225
programming, inherited, 214
programming, Kuiper Belt, 225

programming, Monarch, 259
programming, nightmares, 204
programs, genetic, 17
Project Blue Beam, 218, 223, 230
Project Paperclip, 209, 211
Project Upuaut, 43
projects, scientific and esoteric, 209
prophet Ezekiel, 33
prostitute, 146
protection, 245, 299
protection techniques, 264, 265
Protestant doctrine, 308
Protestant Reformation, 139, 140
Protestant(s), 139, 309
psychic abilities, 99
psychic energy, 291
psychics, 6
Punta Arenas, 196
Pure Knowledge, 139
Putti, 174
pyramid complex, Bosnian, age, 168
pyramid complex, Mars, 46
pyramid discovery, Bosnian, 167
pyramid energies, three types, 163
Pyramid of Love, Bosnian, 157
Pyramid of the Dragon, Bosnian, 157
Pyramid of the Moon, Bosnian, 157
Pyramid of the Sun, Bosnian, 157, 160, 163, 166, 167
pyramid researchers, 160
pyramid(s), 43, 45, 69, 144, 153–155, 157, 159, 160, 163–168, 203
pyramid(s), Bosnian, 157, 160, 163, 164, 166–168
pyramid(s), Egypt, 43, 157, 167
pyramid(s), energy, 163
pyramid, center, 45
pyramid, concrete, 166
pyramid, covering, 45
pyramid, delta-T antenna, 164
Pyramid, Great, 43, 45, 53, 167
pyramid, octahedron, 164

pyramid, shape, 164
pyramid, top of, 163, 258
pyramidal structure, biggest, 167
pyramids, age, 159
pyramids, Atlantic, 165
pyramids, builders, 162
pyramids, Cahokian, 165
pyramids, China, 164
pyramids, Chinese, 167
pyramids, complex, 45, 162
pyramids, cover, 165
pyramids, Egyptian, 160
pyramids, Egyptian, paintings, 95
pyramids, energy machines, 163
pyramids, Europe, 167
pyramids, Giza, 167
pyramids, Keweenaw, 154
pyramids, locations, 157
pyramids, Mayan, 153
pyramids, Mexican, 167
pyramids, Mexico, 157
pyramids, oldest, 168
pyramids, original, 159, 164
pyramids, perpetual motors, 163
pyramids, Peruvian, 159
pyramids, replicas, 159
pyramids, step, 112, 153, 165
pyramids, underwater, 165
pyramids, worldwide network, 159

Qantas Airways, 201, 202
Québec, 187, 189
quartz crystal(s), 150, 161
Queen Isabella, 112, 121, 142
Queen Maud Land, 192
Queen of Africa, 189
Queen of Australia, 189
Queen of Canada, 189
Queen of England, 128, 189
Queen Sheba, 51–53
Qumran scrolls, 70

Raiders of the Lost Ark, 211

rape, 89
Rashid, Isa, 67
Ratzinger, Joseph Aloisius, 169
realities, infinite, 239
rebellion, 78
rebuilding of the 3rd Solomon's temple, 54
red hair, 147
red men, 151
Red Sea, 50
red-haired, 6, 103
reincarnation, 215
release, 236, 265, 267, 280, 292, 297
release work, 232, 246
relics, 267
religion, 88
religion, organized, 216, 299, 300
religious liberty, 309
Rennes-le-Château, 72, 134, 141
reptile, 14
reptiles, 109
Reptilian 3-horned God, 46
Reptilian agenda, 18, 39
Reptilian androgyny, 72
Reptilian aspect, 18
Reptilian beings, 3, 15
Reptilian blood, 39
Reptilian body, 17, 39
Reptilian Brain Stem, 303
Reptilian brainstem, 250
Reptilian ceremony, 40
Reptilian characteristics, 17
Reptilian connection, 41
Reptilian control, 18
Reptilian culture and religion, 28
Reptilian DNA, 5
Reptilian Empire, 28
Reptilian energies, 72
Reptilian form, 5, 39
Reptilian genetics, 3, 27
Reptilian Gods, 39
Reptilian gods, 112

Reptilian hierarchy, 13
Reptilian images, 40, 46
Reptilian king, 28
Reptilian mindset, 39
Reptilian perspective, 15
Reptilian place, 21
Reptilian references, 46
Reptilian religion, 39, 68, 69, 72
Reptilian species, 5, 28
Reptilian survivors, 19
Reptilian trigger, 78
Reptilian(s), 3–6, 15, 16, 18, 19, 27, 38, 39, 46, 103, 195, 204, 223, 227
Reptilian, androgynous, 17
Reptilian, genetically, 35
Reptilian/Human genetics, 103
Reptilianized Lion, 63
Reptilians, Inner Earth, 32
rescuers, 223
responsibility, 231, 243, 285
responsible, 293
Resurrection, 77, 305
resurrection, 75, 78
Reykjavik, 207
Rhode Island, 199
Rhodes, 189
Rhodesia, 189, 190
Rigel star system, 222
ritual sacrifice, 40, 72, 78, 203
ritual(s), 40, 54, 69, 77, 127, 211, 213, 267
ritual, sexual, 72, 263
ritualistic temples, 153
Rock Lake, Wisconsin, 153
Roma, 80
Roman coins, ancient, 153
Roman Empire, 61, 64, 70, 80, 99, 115, 216, 217
Roman rule, 86
Romani, 79, 80
Romania, 80, 123

Romanians, 79
Romans, 1
Rome, 49, 80
Rome, Ancient, 61
Roswell, 210, 221, 222
Rothschild(s), 128, 208
Rottweiler, nickname, 169
Rovere, 173
royal blue, 247, 278
Rune, 87
Rus, 83
Russia, 61, 86, 115, 116, 217
Russia, meaning, 83
Russian Orthodox Church, 61
Russian people, 116
Russian ships, 95
Russians, 212

Sacho, Rainier, 307
sacrifice, 39, 40
sacrifice ritual(s), 39, 40, 72, 78, 203
sacrifice, blood, 77
sacrifice, human, 77, 78
sacrifice, spring ritual, 77
sacrificed, 105, 112
sacrifices, human, 113
sacrifices, killing, 77
sacrificial altar, 112
Sagas, 87, 91, 104
Saint Clair, Lake, 143
Saintes-Maries-de-la-Mer, 71
Salta, Argentina, 105
San Andreas fault line, 19
Sarah, 69, 71
Sarah's tomb, 72
Sarajevo, 157
Sardinia, 59
Sasquatch, 20
Satan, 253, 254
Saturn, 6, 8, 12
Saturn, moons, 12
Saturn, rings, 12
Saturnalia, 77

Saudi Arabia, 51
Saul, 131
Saunière, Bérenger, 72
Savior, 305, 307
savior, 302–305
savior race, 223
saviors, 223
Saviors, False, 304
Savoie, 307
Saxons, 85
Saxony area, 85
Scandinavia, 86, 91, 104, 138, 183, 212
Scandinavian, 83
Scandinavian culture, 194
Schneider grid, 162
Schneider, Phil, 222
scientific projects, 209
scientists, 210
scientists, Antarctica, 198
scientists, Earth, 222
scientists, German, 209, 211
scientists, Nazi, 210, 211
scientists, Rigel star system, 222
Scorpio, 217
scorpion, 14, 217
Scota, Princess, 47
Scotland, 47, 86, 210
sea monsters, 155
seals of Solomon, 173
secret organizations, 239
secret police, Argentina, 213
Seder nights, 78
seed of thought, 307
Self, 249, 250, 259, 260, 263, 267, 271, 274, 275, 277, 278, 280, 281, 284, 285, 293, 300, 306
self-abuse, 241
self-awareness, 18
self-destruction, 283, 284
self-discovery, 275
self-enslavement, 284

self-exploration, 255, 258, 277, 280, 300
self-expression, 279
self-flagellate, 304
self-hate, 208
self-healing, 296
Self-Isolate, 301
Self-knowledge, 278, 280
self-monitoring, 300
self-punishment, 241
self-sabotage, 241
self-suppress, 300
self-worth, 304
self-worth, low, 241
Semiramis, 39
Semjase, 68
separation, 253, 255, 256, 258, 259, 294
separation, illusion, 254
Sephardic Jews, 65
Serbia, 123
Serbians, 79
serpent, 111
serpent, 115 foot, 155
sexual activity, 264
sexual differentiation, 17
sexual energy, 263, 264
sexual magick ritual, 203
sexual molestation, 175
sexual orgy feast, 77
Sexual Ritual, 263
sexual rituals, 72
sexual triggers, 264
sexuality, 284
Shaanxi, 157
Shambala, 203
shape-shifting, origin, 39
shapeshift, 289
shark teeth, 21
Sheba, Queen, 51–53
ship, giant, 33
ships, Viking, 85

Shroud of Turin, 223
Sicily, 59
Silbury Hill, 168
silver, 278
simultaneous existences, 249, 265
Simultaneous Existences Scans, 235
Sinai desert, 50
Sir Frances Bacon, 219
Sirian group, 230
Sirius, 45
Sirius A/B, 27
Sistine Chapel, 170, 171, 173, 176
Sistine Chapel, Central Panel, 171
Sistine Chapel, paintings, 170
Sistine Chapel, secret codes, 170
skeletons, giant, 153
skulls, crystal, 113
skulls, elongated, 108
slave creations, 259
slave people, 79
slave(s), 2, 78, 86, 89, 185, 240, 259, 270, 302, 303, 305
slave, word origin, 79
slavery, 78, 89, 302, 303, 305
Slavic people, 28, 79
Slavs, 79
Smithsonian Institute, 1
Smyrna, 308
snake(s), 18, 78, 88
snakes, two black, 41
Snofru's, 159
solar system, 3, 6, 11–13, 35, 95, 196, 225–227, 232, 233
Solar System, Evolution, 11
Solomon's Stables, 51, 54, 127
Solomon's Temple, 51, 54, 60, 170, 253
Solomon's Temple, 3rd, 170
Solomon, King, 52, 53
Sons of God, 32
soul energies, 267
soul-personalities, 233

soul-personality, 235, 275, 293
South Africa, 152, 189, 190, 192
South America, 28, 103, 104, 108, 134, 151, 152, 190, 197, 201, 211
South Carolina, Vikings, 88
South India, 63
South Korea, 122
South Pacific, 28, 201
South Pole, 8, 10, 191, 198, 199
Southern Rhode Island, 129
Soviet Empire, 217
Soviet occupation, 231
Soviet Union, 13, 32, 212, 217, 309
Soviets, 210
space, 7, 12, 14, 23, 35, 68, 225, 227, 228, 231, 243
space brothers, 244, 303
space exploration, 227
space news, 223
space society, 223
space temperatures, 23
space, manipulate, 163
Spain, 59, 65, 89, 133, 142, 185
Spaniards, 1, 103, 111, 112, 183, 185
Spanish, 67
Spanish American war, 183
Spanish conquistadors, 111
Spanish culture and territory, 121
Spanish Empire, 183
Spanish invasion, 153
Spanish prisons, 89
Spanish troops, 308
Sparta, 59
sphere, energy, 164
spherical stones, 164
Sphinx, 43, 45, 46
split, genetic, 39
spring ritual, 77, 78
Sri Lanka, 63
Srinagar, 75, 216
SS, 212

St. Germaine, 72
St. Joseph, Michigan, 156
St. Lawrence Seaway, 22
St. Louis, Missouri, 153
St. Paul, 131, 307
staff of Moses, 78
staged, 222
Staged Alien Invasion, 156, 218, 221–224, 230
staged crucifixion, 75, 79
staged event, 68
staged incident, 221
Staged Second Coming of Christ, 73, 218, 223
star gate(s), 36, 229, 233
Star of David, 53, 173
step-up transformer, 151
stone carving, 148
stone circle, Lake Michigan, 155
stone spheres, 164
stone tablets, 168
stone tablets, Michigan, 148
storehouse of genetic information, 18
storehouse of knowledge, 297
Straits of Gibraltar, 49, 151
strength, 236, 260, 267, 274, 275, 278, 280, 283
stroke, 209
sturgeon, gigantic, 155
subconscious, 290
subconscious mind, 254, 295, 299
Subconscious Mind-connection, 305
subduction, 19, 108
sulfur springs, Michigan, 156
Sumer, 31, 37–40, 49
Sumer, God and Goddess, 39
Sumer, King of, 39
Sumer, religion, 39
Sumeria, 31, 159
Sumerian Caucasian people, 37
Sumerian civilization, 32, 37
Sumerian culture, 38

Sumerian Cuneiform, 148
Sumerian descendants, 63, 99
Sumerian group, 63
Sumerian language, 115
Sumerian tablets, 35
Sumerian(s), 35, 37, 40, 63, 65
super-civilization, 159
superconscious mind, 254, 305
Superconscious Mind-connection, 305
superhuman, 196
superior technology, 159
suppressed, 59, 121, 132, 239, 300
suppressed frequency, 300
suppresses, 73
suppression, 139
Suriname, 190
Swastika, 197, 209, 212
Swaziland, 190
Sweden, 49, 85, 89, 214
Swedes, 147
Swedish, 83
Swiss, 140, 308
Swiss border, 73
Swiss Intelligence, 213
Switzerland, 133, 140, 195, 211
Switzerland, Catholics, 140
Switzerland, copper, 152
Switzerland, Waldensians, 308
Switzerland, Western, 228
symbolic script, Illuminati, 217
Syria, 59

T-bar archetype balancing, 264
tablet(s), 144–148
tablet, Mongolian alphabet, 148
tablet, Viking runes, 147
tablets, Michigan, 144
Taiwan, 165
Talmud Jmmanuel, 67, 68, 215, 216
Tamils, 63
Tana, Lake, 53
Tara, Ireland, 87
Tatar, 115

Tau-Ceti, 27
technologically advanced people, 195
technology, 37, 50, 51, 163, 166, 196,
    197, 218, 222, 227, 230
technology development, 210
technology, alien, 113, 233
technology, ancient, 160, 212
technology, current, 210
technology, government, 196
technology, Hertzian, 163
technology, non-Hertzian, 163
technology, Russian, 210
technology, Vril craft, 197
tectonic movements, 199
Templar Brotherhood, 128
Templar cross, 127
Templar information, 129
Templar legend, 129
Templar organizations, 129, 130
Templar references, 129
Templar style tower, 129
Templar symbols, 128
Templars, 125, 127–130, 132
Templars, Grand Master, 129
Templars, nine, 125, 130
temple, 28, 132, 170, 216
Temple Mount, 54, 127, 130
Temple of Mother Earth, 157
Temple of Solomon, 51, 54, 60, 170,
    253
Temple of Solomon, 3rd, 170
temples, 112, 120
Tennessee, 147, 214
Tenochtitlan, 111
Teotihuacán, 159
Tesla Coil, 164
Tesla, Nikola, 164, 210
tetrahedron, 55, 56, 253, 254, 260
Teutonic tribes, 77, 79
Teutonic tribes, Franks, 80
Teutonic tribes, German, 194
Texas, 214

Texas, Republic of, 189
Texcoco, Lake, 111
third species, 16, 18
Thomas, 73
Thomas, Gospel of, 132
thought(s), 19, 241, 243, 245, 253, 261, 263, 289
thought, negative, 291
thought-form(s), 262, 263
thoughts, positive, 291
Thrace, 79
Thracians, 79
Thule (society), 192
Thunderbird(s), 155
Tiahuanaco, 107
Tibet, 120, 192, 203, 207, 211, 230
Tibetan civilization, 27
Tibetan Monasteries, 120
Tibetan monk(s), 203, 212
Tibetan Priests, 120
Tibetan symbol, 212
Tibetans, 120, 212
tidal waves, 96
Tierra del Fuego, 195, 196
time and space, 23, 219, 243
time or space, 219
time travel, 58, 209, 210, 219
time, manipulate, 163
timeline(s), 237, 238, 243
Titan, moon, 8
Titicaca, Lake, 107, 108
Toltecs, 101, 109, 112
tomb, pyramid-shaped, 174
Tor of Glastonbury, 76
Torah, 147
toroid, 56
Trail of Tears, 147
trans-Neptunian object, 225
Transparent People/beings, 3
Tree of Life and Knowledge, 18
Triangle, Bermuda, 144
Triangle, Devil's, 144

triangle, Great Lakes, 144
Triangle, Lake Michigan, 144
trolls, 238
True Origins, 260
True Path of Self, 285
truth, 2, 195, 245
Tslav, 79, 302
tsunamis, 96
tube system, 31
tunnel entrance, 167
tunnel system(s), 21, 167, 195
tunnel(s), 43, 104, 157, 160–162, 167, 195, 228, 229
tunnel, artificially made, 167
tunnels, network, 167
tunnels, underground, 167
Turin, Italy, 308, 309
Turkey, 32, 59, 61, 65, 71, 99, 123, 131, 216
Turkey, Celts, 98
Turkic, 67
Turkish, 122
Turkish cultures, 123
Turku-Mongolian, 148
two, 41
two antagonistic groups, 18
two babies, 72
two civilizations, 16
two genders, 15
two Gods, 134
two prostitutes, 174
two species, 16, 18, 24
two symbols, 217
two types of Beings, 3

U-boats, 193
U-boats, German, 211
UFO crash, 221
UFO incidence, 223
UFO information, 223
UFO investigation group, 223
UFO material, 210
UFO reports, 156

UFO researcher, 156
UFO sightings, 223
UFO(s), 156, 223, 228, 231, 237
Ukraine, 83, 85, 115, 192
Ultimate Protection, 56
ultimate triad, 267
ultrasound, 160, 161
underground, 19, 162
underground areas, 12, 203
underground base(s), 192, 212, 222
underground chamber(s), 107, 161
underground city/cities, 191, 192
underground escape route, 229
underground explosions, 229
underground healing place, 161
underground labyrinth, 162, 167, 168
underground lakes, 157
underground natural radioactivity, 161
underground Nazi base, 192
underground network, 157
underground paradise for the Führer, 192
underground projects, 229
underground reservoir, 21
underground river, 161
underground stream, 43, 45
underground tunnel system, 204
underground tunnel(s), 161, 167, 168
underground tunnels, Bolivia, 107
underground war(s), 196, 222
underground water flows, 161
underground waters, 165
underwater cities, 165
Unholy Trinity, 253–255, 303, 306
United Kingdom, 97, 98
United Nations, 191
United States, 116, 119, 141, 187, 189, 203, 207, 209, 210, 222
Universal Law, 40, 78, 236, 245
Upper Peninsula, 145, 154, 156
Uranus, 6, 11, 199
Uranus, rings, 12

Uruguay, 141
Uruguay, Waldensians, 141
US, 187, 209, 210
US flag, gold fringe, 40
US Navy, 22
US Postal Service, 190

Valdenses, 131
Valdese, North Carolina, 134, 141
Valley of the Kings, 160
Valley of the Pyramids, Bosnian, 161, 168
valley with pyramids, 157
van Helsing, Jan, 195
Vasilyev, Dmitry, 63
Vatican, 73, 130, 141, 170, 171, 173, 190
Vaticana, 169, 170
Vaudois, 131
Vaudois, Church of, 307
Vaudois, meaning, 131
Venus, 13, 14
Venus, creatures, 14
Venus, seven domed areas, 13
Venusian atmosphere, 13
Vermont, 189
vessel(s), 211, 257, 260
Vicarivs Filii Dei, 171
victimization mentality, 239
Viking chieftains, 87
Viking cities, old, 86
Viking civilization, 115
Viking culture, 83
Viking Empire, 85
Viking group(s), 104
Viking groups(s), 83
Viking heritage, 83
Viking history, 83, 87
Viking language, 83, 87
Viking legends, 88
Viking lodge, 156
Viking long ship replicas, 85
Viking long ships, 85

Viking maps, 88
Viking records, 91
Viking rule, 86
Viking Sagas, 87
Viking seafarers, 119
Viking settlement(s), 87, 88
Viking settlers, 83
Viking ships, 85
Viking strongholds, 83
Viking times, coins, 148
Viking tribes, 86
Viking uprisings, 85
Viking(s), 83, 86–89, 91, 92, 103, 104,
        109, 115, 119, 138, 147, 148,
        150, 156, 183
Viking, meaning, 83
Vikings, North America, 87
Vikings, Norwegian, 85
Vikings, Polish, 83
Vikings, Swedish, 86
vindictive souls, 262
vine, intoxicating, 169
Vinland, 87, 88
violet, 245, 278
violet bubble, 278
violet light, 262
Virginia, 88, 189
Virginia, Central and Northern, 229
virtual reality/realities, 218
Visoko, 157, 167
vital force, 291
volcanic, 8, 91
volcanic activity, 8, 45, 92, 200, 207
volcanic chambers, 207
volcanic eruption(s), 8, 96, 199
volcanic island, 8
volcanic stones, 109
volcano, 8, 93, 104, 200
volcano, largest, 8
volcano, Minoan, 145
volcanoes, 7, 156, 199, 200
volcanoes, largest, 7

volcanoes, old, 156
volcanoes, undersea, 199
Von Braun, Wernher, 210
vortex, 168
vortex, energy, 144
vortex, Great Lakes, 144
vortex, natural, 156
Vostok, Lake, 197, 198
Voyager 1/2, 227
Voynich Manuscript, 219
Vril, 197
Vril craft, 197, 203, 210
Vril craft technology, 197
Vril craft, fleet, 230

Wald, 131
Waldensian Apostolic refugees, 134
Waldensian beliefs, 131, 132, 175
Waldensian Church, 308
Waldensian churches, 141
Waldensian churches, affiliation, 141
Waldensian Cross, 132
Waldensian documents, 141
Waldensian frequency, 309
Waldensian history, 141
Waldensian population, largest, 141
Waldensian refugees, 139
Waldensian symbol, 132
Waldensian territory, 131
Waldensian way of life, 138
Waldensian(s), 131, 133, 134, 137–
        142, 171, 307–309
Waldensians, Apostolic, 134
Waldensians, Argentina, 141
Waldensians, early, 307
Waldensians, exterminations, 137
Waldensians, Monett, Missouri, 309
Waldensians, New York City, 309
Waldensians, original, 141
Waldensians, sacraments, 307
Waldensians, Switzerland, 308
Waldensians, Uruguay, 141, 309
Waldensians, Valdese, 141, 309

Waldensians, verbal history, 131
Waldo, Peter, 131, 307
Wales, 86
wars in space, 35
wars, Atlantis and Lemuria, 16, 18
wars, Draco and Lyraen, 6
wars, underground, 196
Washington D.C., 76, 229
water planet, 108
weapon(s), 2, 36, 45, 163, 197, 203,
       223, 263
Weapon, Secret, 283
weapons, electromagnetic pulse, 16
Wends, 83
Werewolves, 20
West Virginia, 229
Western US, 28
whale bones, 154
wheel, giant, 33
white light, 262
White Nile, 53
Windsor control, 190
Wisconsin, 144, 154, 222
Wisconsin, Southern, 153
woolly mammoth skeletons, 95
world domination, 203, 217, 218
World War I/WWI, 123
World War II/WWII, 65, 169, 173,
       187, 189, 190, 193, 197, 209–
       212, 214

Xinjiang, 120
Xizàng province, 120

yellow arm bands, Jews, 173
yellow circle, 173
Yellow Dragon King, 28
Yom Kippur, 69
Yonaguni, 165
York, 86
Yucatan, 68, 153
Yucatan, trench, 16

Zimbabwe, 190
Zyklon-B gas, 169